MARKET POWER AND THE LAW

A report of the Committee of
Experts on restrictive business practices

ORGANISATION FOR ECONOMIC CO-OPERATION AND DEVELOPMENT

The Organisation for Economic Co-operation and Development was set up under a Convention signed in Paris on 14th December 1960 by the Member countries of the Organisation for European Economic Co-operation and by Canada and the United States. This Convention provides that the OECD shall promote policies designed:

— *to achieve the highest sustainable economic growth and employment and a rising standard of living in Member countries, while maintaining financial stability, and thus to contribute to the world economy;*
— *to contribute to sound economic expansion in Member as well as non-member countries in the process of economic development;*
— *to contribute to the expansion of world trade on a multilateral, non-discriminatory basis in accordance with international obligations.*

The legal personality possessed by the Organisation for European Economic Co-operation continues in the OECD which came into being on 30th September 1961.

The members of OECD are Austria, Belgium, Canada, Denmark, Finland, France, the Federal Republic of Germany, Greece, Iceland, Ireland, Italy, Japan, Luxembourg, the Netherlands, Norway, Portugal, Spain, Sweden, Switzerland, Turkey, the United Kingdom and the United States.

FOREWORD

This report, which was prepared by the OECD Committee of Experts on Restrictive Business Practices, deals with the legal attitudes towards the control of market power and the techniques employed in OECD Member countries and the European Communities. In addition some information is included on the relevant EFTA provisions and experience. The report generally reflects the position as of May 1969.

The Committee considered that publication of this report appeared opportune in view of the particular concern of most Member countries with the control of market power under their restrictive business practices laws and the growing importance in recent years of larger enterprises and economic concentration.

The Committee was aware that a study of the control of market power under the legislations on restrictive business practices covers but one aspect of a complex problem. It has nevertheless attempted, in the Introduction and in the Summary and Conclusions, to draw the attention of the reader to the other, particularly the economic, aspects of business power and its control.

CONTENTS

Part Two

CRITERIA FOR TAKING ACTION AGAINST THE DETRIMENTAL EFFECTS OF MARKET POWER

Part Three

MEASURES AND PROCEDURES TO CONTROL MARKET POWER

Part Four

SUMMARY AND CONCLUSIONS

Annexes

LIST OF ABBREVIATIONS USED IN THE TEXT

Activity Report — *Bericht des Bundeskartellamtes über seine Tätigkeit im Jahre [...] sowie über Lage und Entwicklung auf seinem Aufgabengebiet,* Drucksache des Deutschen Bundestages (Federal German Cartel Office report on its activities for the year [...] as well as developments within its field of competence.)

Annual Report — Report of the Director of Investigation and Research, Combines Investigation Act.

ATF — Arrêts du Tribunal fédéral (Decisions of the Federal Swiss Court).

AWD — *Aussenwirtschaftsdienst des Betriebs-Beraters* (Foreign Economic Service of the review "Betriebs-Berater").

BGH — Bundesgerichtshof (Federal German Supreme Court).

BGHZ — Entscheidungen des Bundesgerichtshofs in Zivilsachen — Amtliche Sammlung (Official record of the Federal German Supreme Court's decisions in civil cases).

BKartA — Bundeskartellamt (Federal Cartel Office).

C.C.C. — Canadian Criminal Cases.

C.R. — Criminal Reports, Toronto.

D.C. — District Court.

D.C.N.D. — District Court, Northern District of ...

D.C.S.D. — District Court, Southern District of ...

D.L.R. — Dominion Law Reports, Toronto.

F. — Federal Reporter.

F. Supp. — Federal Supplement.

Glossary — *Glossary of Terms Relating to Restrictive Business Practices,* published by the Organisation for Economic Co-operation and Development.

GRUR — Gewerblicher Reelesschutz und Urheberrecht (German legal periodical).

Guide — *Guide to Legislation on Restrictive Business Practices,* published by the Organisation for Economic Co-operation and Development.

11

HMSO	Her Majesty's Stationery Office, London.
N.S.	*Nederlandse Staatscourant.*
O.R.	Ontario Reports.
Pa. L.R.	*Pennsylvania Law Review.*
R.G.Z.	Entscheidungen des Reichsgerichts in Zivilsachen — Amtliche Sammlung (Official record of decisions of the German Imperial Court in civil cases).
R.T.P.C.	Reports of the Canadian Restrictive Trade Practices Commission.
Sup.Ct.	Supreme Court.
Trade Cases	Collection of court decisions on trade regulation published by Commerce Clearing House.
Trade Regulation Reports	Reports on trade regulation published by Commerce Clearing House.
U.S.	United States; United States Supreme Court Reports (Official).
WuW/E	*Wirtschaft und Wettbewerb,* Entscheidungssammlung (Decision section of the German periodical "Wirtschaft und Wettbewerb).
WWR	Western Weekly Reports.

INTRODUCTION

1.   The control of monopoly power is one of the oldest problems of competition policy. Long before the enactment of modern restrictive business practices legislation which has established the contemporary legal basis to deal with the monopoly problem within the larger context of general competition policy, legislators and courts especially in England and later in the United States had already attempted to control monopoly power. A famous example is the British Statute of Monopolies of 1624 according to which, "all Monopolies and all Commissions, Grants, Licences, Characters and Letters Patent heretofore made or granted or hereafter to be made or granted to any Person or Persons, Bodies Politic or Corporate whatsoever, of, or for the sole Buying, Selling, Making, Working or Using any Thing within this Realm ... or of any other Monopolies, or of Power, Liberty or Faculty ... are altogether contrary to the Laws of this Realm, and so are and shall be utterly void and of none effect and in no wise to be put into use or execution".[1]

2.   While the Common Law Countries (Canada, United Kingdom and United States) still use the concepts of monopoly or monopolization which have been incorporated into current restrictive business practices law, many of the other Member States which have adopted restrictive business practices laws introduced the concept of "market dominating enterprises" or "dominant position". Even before the Second World War this term was used in Norwegian and Danish law and since then it was adopted in 1951 in the ECSC (article 66, para. 7 of the ECSC Treaty), in 1956 in the Netherlands (section 1 of the Economic Competition Act), in 1958 in the EEC (article 86 of the EEC Treaty) and in Germany (section 22 of the Act Against Restraints of Competition), in 1959 in Austria (section 36(d) of the Cartel Act 1959), and in the EFTA (article 15 of the Stockholm Convention), in 1963 in France (article 59 bis as amended by the Act No. 623-628 of 2nd July 1963), and in 1964 in Spain (section 2 of the Act Against Restraints of Competition) and in Switzerland (section 3 of the Cartel Act). Similar concepts were introduced in

---

1.   21 Jac. 1, c.3. There were, however, broad statutory exceptions limiting the effect of the principle. For further details on early legislation and common law on monopolies in England see Wilberforce, Campbell and Ellis, *Restrictive Trade Practices and Monopolies*, 1966, paras. 104-156. As to early American law see Thorelli, *The Federal Antitrust Policy, Organisation of an American Tradition*, 1955, pp. 36-50.

1955 in Denmark ("substantial influence on price, production, distribution, or transport conditions", section 6 of the Monopolies and Restrictive Practices Control Act) and in 1960 in Belgium ("Economic power", article 1 of the Act on Protection against the Abuse of Economic Power). The growing importance of the control of economic power in recent years is underlined by the fact that some legislations have recently strengthened this control by supplementing the existing control machinery (the United Kingdom in 1965 by the Monopolies and Mergers Act and Germany in 1966 by an amendment to section 22 of the principal Act). This importance is also illustrated by the much more rigorous enforcement in the United States, since 1962, of section 7 of the Clayton Act, amended by the Celler-Kefauver Act of 1950, against horizontal, vertical and conglomerate mergers[1] after the Supreme Court in Brown Shoe Co. v. United States[2] had set the guideposts for the application of this provision.

3.　It cannot be determined whether this growing concern of many Member countries with market power and market domination is due to an increase in the number of powerful or dominant enterprises or in economic concentration, or is merely the result of a better recognition of the problems created by the existence of such enterprises. The answer to this question would require statistical data for all Member States which are either not available[3] or do not reflect the market power or concentration of enterprises in specific markets.[4] This study will therefore not attempt to give an account of the actual extent of market power and concentration in the Member States nor deal extensively with the causes and overall effects of larger enterprises resulting from normal business expansion or mergers[5] with other enterprises.

4.　The reasons which may inspire enterprises to expand their size (turnover, assets, employees) are manifold. In some industries, to make production technically possible, a certain minimum size of plant is required. The same applies to other business decisions such as the use of modern equipment (e.g. computers). However, more important than such decisions are the economic advantages of expanding the size of plants to the optimum where costs per unit are at the lowest possible level. The optimum size of a plant can in many cases only be attained by large-scale production. In addition to these single-

1.　For definitions of these terms see Glossary of Terms Relating to Restrictive Business Practices, A-6, D-1, D-2 and D-3.

2.　370 U.S. 294, 1962 Trade Cases para 70,366.

3.　Statistical data on concentration are available for Germany (Report on the result of an enquiry into economic concentration, 1964 (Bundestag Printing Matter IV/2320), the Netherlands (Enige gegevens over de concentratietendens in het bedrijfsleven, Parliamentary Document 1965-1966, 8038), in Sweden (Koncentrationsutredningen III-V S.O.U. 1968: 5-7, 1968) and the United States ("Economic Concentration", Hearings before the Subcommittee on Antitrust and Monopoly 1964-1968 Parts I-VII; Bureau of Census, Concentration Ratios in Manufacturing Industry 1962, Parts I-II).

4.　This will be explained in detail in Part I when the market concept is analysed.

5.　The term merger, unless stated otherwise in this study, is used in a broad sense including acquisition of assets.

plant economies, cost savings or higher efficiency may be achieved by uniting several plants within a single enterprises (multi-plant economies), e.g., by centralized administration, research and other activities.

5. The problem of the size and efficiency of enterprises has been frequently studied in recent years, especially in the United States, [1] and – in connection with the expansion of international trade and competition – also in Europe. [2] The considerations in Europe centre on the question how the size of enterprises can be adapted to the dimensions of the Common Market or the EFTA and to withstanding competition from their, in many cases, larger American competitors. A number of studies recently undertaken in the United States turned on the question whether, on the basis of actual business results, large enterprises are, in fact, more efficient. These studies have questioned the theory of Professor Schumpeter, [3] that large firms are generally more efficient especially with respect to technological progress, research and innovation. [4] There is no doubt that the advantages of a large size for the enterprise itself are not limited to possibly higher efficiency in production, research, innovation etc. as compared with smaller enterprises, but may also lie in better financial resources and stronger market power. It is at this last point that the problem of public control of monopoly and of market power in order to maintain competition, the subject of the present study, arises.

6. Several approaches to this problem in restrictive business legislation are possible and, as will be seen in the further course of this study, are in fact found in the laws of Member States. Depending upon the evaluation of the effects of economic power on competition there may either be a "structural" or a "conduct" approach or a combination of both. Under the first approach the formation of "unreasonable" or "undue" market power by mergers or otherwise is restricted and such power already in existence is dissolved with a view to preventing, *a priori,* the emergence of the expected adverse consequences of market power. One reason for this "structural" approach may be the opinion that the adverse effects of market power cannot be effectively controlled as long as the position of power itself continues to exist. Under the second approach the formation and existence of market power as such is left unaffected, but business practices of powerful enterprises insofar as they have detri-

---

1. See, e.g. the hearings on Economic Concentration referred to in footnote (3) to para. 3.; Caves, *American Industry, Structure, Conduct, Performance,* (1964); Scherer, Firm-Size and Patented Inventions (1965) *American Economic Review* 1097; Comanor, Research and Technical Change in the Pharmaceutical Industry (1965) *Review of Economic and Statistics* 190; Adams and Dirlam, Big Steel, Invention and Innovation, 80 *Quarterly Journal of Economics* 167 (1966).

2. See, e.g., Memorandum of the EEC Commission on Concentration in the Common Market of 1st December, 1965, Doc. SEC 3500; Swan and McLachlan, *Concentration or Competition; A European Dilemma?* Chatham House and P.E.P., European Series No. 1, 1967;

3. Schumpeter, *Capitalism, Socialism and Democracy,* 2nd ed. 1943, pp. 79 ff.

4. See especially the article by Adams and Dirlam, *supra.*

mental effects are subject to governmental control. The main consideration behind this "conduct" approach seems to be that interference with structural changes could prevent the achievement of improved efficiency resulting from such changes, a consideration which may especially apply to small countries. Interference may also be thought unnecessary because the possibly detrimental effects of market power can be sufficiently held in check by a system of market behaviour control. Finally, the combined approach is made where neither of the two foregoing approaches is by itself considered to be a sufficient safeguard for the maintenance of effective competition. The underlying considerations for this approach may be that, on the one hand, structural measures may not always be technically feasible or economically reasonable, especially where normal business growth of enterprises is involved, while, on the other hand, conduct control cannot always deal effectively with the adverse effects of market power, especially where powerful positions formed by mergers would exclude competition entirely.

7.   This study analyses the three approaches insofar as they are incorporated in the restrictive business practices laws of OECD Member countries, the EEC and ECSC. The analysis covers the provisions in these laws dealing with mergers, monopolization and with practices of powerful enterprises. Special attention is given to the practical application of these laws and the interpretation by the courts and enforcement authorities of their mostly broad legal terms.

8.   The analysis in this study is made from a comparative law viewpoint. Therefore, the material is arranged and studied by subject rather than by country. This approach has the great advantage that problems such as market definition, determination of economic power, and assessment of the detrimental effects on such power can be analysed in the larger context of all laws where the particular problem is dealt with. The synoptical presentation of the individual issues not only facilitates comparisons between the various laws studied, but also helps to reveal the essential features of the laws dealing with market power.

9.   The study is divided into three main parts: Part I deals with the determination of market power. It is shown how the two elements implied in this term: the (relevant) market and the concept of power on, or domination of, this market, are determined under the various laws. The influence of foreign product alternatives (imports) will be considered in this context. Part II examines the criteria for taking action against the formation of market power by merger and monopolization and against specific acts of business conduct of existing powerful enterprises. This examination turns on such criteria as "substantially to lessen competition", "monopolizing", "abuse", "violation of the public interest", "unreasonable prices and business conditions", etc. Finally, Part III describes the measures which may be and have in fact been taken under the various laws, after detrimental effects of mergers, monopolization, or of specific business conduct have been found to exist. This covers the procedural means of governmental intervention and the sanctions available to public authorities and private persons. A brief account is given of other

ways of influencing the existence and use of market power, which are outside restrictive business practices laws.

10. The study thus goes far beyond the scope of the concept of market domination as incorporated in the laws of several Member countries and of the EEC and ECSC. It covers essentially all provisions of restrictive business practices laws where the formation or possession of market power is a relevant factor. All legislations with the exception of Ireland and Sweden have specific provisions on the control of market power and even in these two countries market power is an important factor taken into consideration by the authorities. The terms "market power" and "powerful enterprise" as used in this study should be understood as designating that degree of market power which a particular law considers significant. The use of the term "market dominating enterprise" in the study does not necessarily imply that particular legislations dealt with in the study do in fact use this concept or apply the same or similar criteria to assess the effects of dominant enterprises as the legislations with special provisions on market dominating enterprises.

11. As was said earlier, this study is essentially a legal analysis. It does not give an account of the actual extent of market power and economic concentration in OECD Member countries and in the European Communities. Even if it were possible for the Committee to conduct the necessary empirical research, it will become apparent from the analysis of the concepts of market power and market domination, that lists of powerful or market dominating enterprises cannot normally be given.

12. The study also does not analyse the reasons why certain enterprises have gained or maintain market power or market dominating positions. There are many reasons for this, reaching from "natural" conditions ("natural" monopolies), legal restrictions of market access (e.g., patents, import restrictions), financial power and technical superiority (know how) to restrictive business arrangements (e.g., cartels resulting in "collective" monopolies). Again, extended empirical research would be necessary to show what the precise reasons were for the achievement or maintenance of market power in specific cases. Such research would have exceeded the means of the Committee and the scope of a legal study. Nevertheless, Part III, Chapter II states some of the factors which are relevant in this context.

13. The authors of the study are aware that an analysis of the laws dealing with market power does not indicate to what extent such power is, from a factual point of view, a matter of serious concern to the Member countries of OECD and to the European Communities. They also realize that these laws do not entirely reflect the attitude of individual countries and communities towards the problem of market power. For market power in particular countries may be effectively coped with by general restrictive business legislation or by the means described briefly in Part III, Chapter II. Finally, it is recognized that market power is but one aspect of economic power in general and that the important question must be left for further studies whether the concept of market power is still adequate to cover

17

all the manifestations of business power and their effects on competition. [1]

14. A study like the present one, made within an international organisation such as OECD, can, for obvious reasons, not attempt to give a critical appraisal of the *pros* and *cons* of the various national and community approaches. Nor did the Committee think it appropriate to make recommendations for future policy in the form of a model law on market power or to suggest measures that should be taken by particular countries or of joint action within OECD. By stating and analysing the legal issues of the various laws dealing with market power and by recording the practical experience made with the application of these laws the study may nevertheless serve three useful purposes: it may help the national and community legislators to recognize more clearly the various legal issues to be considered when dealing with market power; it may facilitate the interpretation and practical application of the laws on market power by courts and administrative authorities; and it may prepare the ground for later policy considerations of OECD in this field by providing the legal background material.

1. See Corwin D. Edwards; The Changing Dimensions of Business Power, in: *Das Unternehmen in der Rechtsordnung, Festgabe für Heinrich Kronstein,* 1968, pp. 237-260. This article is summarized in the concluding part of the present study.

Part One

THE CONCEPT OF MARKET POWER: CRITERIA FOR ITS DETERMINATION

Chapter I

GENERAL APPROACH AND BACKGROUND

15. In Part I the various aspects of the concept of market power taking the form of "market domination" or of corresponding concepts will be analysed. The term "market dominating position" is defined in the OECD Glossary of Terms relating to Restrictive Business Practices as "the position occupied either (*a*) by a single enterprise or (*b*) by a group of enterprises between which no effective competition exists, which does not encounter effective competition in a market."[1] Market domination within the meaning of this definition thus depends on two factors:

i) the identification of the relevant market or line of commerce.

ii) the determination whether an enterprise or group of enterprises is exposed to effective competition in this market.

16. The identification of the relevant market embraces essentially two elements: (*a*) the identification of what may be termed the product market, i.e. the goods or services which are in such a close competitive relation with one another that they may be considered as essentially satisfying the same need or, as is sometimes said, as being "functionally interchangeable"; (*b*) the identification of the geographical market, i.e. the territory in which the relationship described under (*a*) is effective.

17. Since there are normally several products or services available to satisfy a particular demand, which are not physically identical, the problem of defining the product market leads in most cases to the question to what extent substitute products have to be taken into account. Economists have proposed several abstract "tests" to determine whether substitute goods or services are functionally interchangeable[2] of which the cross-elasticity concept[3] appears to be the most frequently referred to. The analysis in Part I of the cases under the various legislations dealing in some way or other with market power will in particular have to show how this problem of substitution has been approached from a practical point of view.

1. *Glossary*, A-2, p. 12-13.
2. See Bain, *Industrial Organisation*, 3rd ed. 1964, pp. 210-237.
3. See Triffin, *Monopolistic Competition and General Equilibrium Theory*, 1940, pp. 137-141.

18. The question of defining the geographical market was formerly mainly one of possible sub-division of national markets, especially in large countries such as the United States, into separate regional and local markets. This question comes up where not all national suppliers, for physical, economic, or other reasons, are offering their products or services in all parts of the country. Location of suppliers, transportation facilities and freight cost, and consumer habits are some of the factors to be considered in this context.

19. The definition of the geographical market comprises, however, also a foreign trade aspect which has always been of particular importance in small countries and becomes increasingly important as foreign trade barriers are removed and economic integration within economic communities, free trade areas and otherwise progresses. It is clear that foreign product alternatives will have to be taken into account to an ever greater extent, the more foreign trade barriers are dismantled. This development may affect the question of market domination in two respects: it may alter the definition of the relevant geographical market by extending the relevant territory to include several countries, for example the countries of the European Communities or the countries of the European Free Trade Association, or it may affect the competitive situation in national markets by adding new competitive product alternatives and may thereby end or weaken dominant positions of national enterprises. The foreign trade aspect will be taken into account in the further analysis in this study.

20. Once the relevant market has been defined both from a product and geographical point of view, the concept of market domination as defined above further requires the determination whether the enterprise or enterprises in question have, or — in the case of an intended merger — would have, a dominant position in this market by not being exposed to effective competition. This normally involves an evaluation of the particular competitive situation in the market concerned. The evaluation is less difficult in legislations which lay down formal criteria such as a certain market share. If an enterprise or a group of enterprises reaches this share, it is automatically deemed to have a dominant or monopolistic position, regardless of the degree of competition still prevailing in the market. This purely formal approach, however, is the exceptional case. Only Austria, the United Kingdom and Norway apply such a formal criterion. In other countries, the decision can normally be made only on the basis of a detailed examination and appraisal of all aspects of structure, conduct, and performance in the particular market in question. Moreover, it is necessary to determine whether competition, if found to exist, is sufficiently strong as to be considered effective. Again, as is the case when taking into account the existence of substitute products, economists have developed "tests", one of which, and perhaps the most frequently discussed, is the concept of workable competition.[1] The

---

1. This concept was first developed by John M. Clark, Toward a Concept of Workable Competition, *American Economic Review* 241 (1940), reprinted in: *Readings in the Social Control of Industry* (1949), pp. 452-475. See further Clark, *Competition as a Dynamic Process* (1961); Stocking, *Workable Competition and Antitrust Policy* (1961); Sosnick, A Critique of Concepts of Workable Competition, 72, *The Quarterly Journal of Economics* 380 (1958).

following analysis of cases which have arisen under the various legislations will show more clearly how these tests, if at all, have been applied in practice and along what lines a solution to the difficult question of determining the degree of competition which makes competition "effective" or "workable" has been attempted.

21. As was already mentioned earlier, the problem of market power will be studied from the following two aspects: (a) the formation of powerful enterprises by merger and monopolization; (b) the conduct of existing dominant enterprises. In both types of cases the question of defining the relevant market and evaluating the degree of competition prevailing in this market are equally important. There is, however, a difference in the legal treatment of both types of practices as far as the evaluation of their effects on competition and the measures taken are concerned, questions which will be analysed in Parts II and III. In view of this difference it is advisable, for the purpose of this study, to distinguish between mergers, monopolization and practices of market dominating enterprises. With this sub-division, the following two chapters of Part I will deal separately with the definition of the relevant market and with the determination of market power.

Chapter II

DEFINITION OF THE RELEVANT MARKET

A. MERGERS

22. The legislations with special provisions on mergers are those of the United States, United Kingdom, Canada, Japan, the ECSC, Germany and Spain – the latter two limited to a mere registration procedure. In most of these legislations the problem of defining the relevant market in merger cases has been the subject of court or administrative decisions.

23. In the *United States,* mergers are prohibited by section 7 of the Clayton Act as amended by the Celler-Kefauver Act of 1950, "where in *any line of commerce in any section of the country* the effect of such acquisition may be substantially to lessen competition or to tend to create a monopoly". The text of the law thus requires the relevant line of commerce (product market) and the relevant section of the country (geographic market) to be defined. Both types of market definition have been at issue in numerous court proceedings of which only a few can be dealt with.

24. The first Supreme Court opinion interpreting the amended section 7 of the Clayton Act came in the appeal of *United States* v. *Brown Shoe Co.,* in 1962.[1] This case laid down broad rules regarding the relevant market in merger cases. As to the delineation of the product market in section 7 Clayton Act cases the court said generally:

"The outer boundaries of a product market are determined by the reasonable interchangeability of use or the cross-elasticity of demand between the product itself and substitutes for it. However within this broad market, well-defined submarkets may exist, which, in themselves, constitute product markets for anti-trust purposes. United States v. E.I. Du Pont de Nemours and Co., 353 U.S. 586, 593-595. The boundaries of such a submarket may be determined by examining such practical *indicia* as industry or public recognition of the submarket as a separate

---

1. Brown Shoe Co. v. United States, 370 U.S. 294, 1962 Trade Cases para. 70, 366.

economic entity, the product's peculiar characteristics and uses, unique production facilities, distinct customers, distinct prices, sensitivity to price changes, and specialized vendors. Because section 7 of the Clayton Act prohibits any merger which may substantially lessen competition " in any line of commerce ", it is necessary to examine the effects of a merger in each such economically significant submarket to determine if there is a reasonable probability that the merger will substantially lessen competition. If such a probability is found to exist, the merger is proscribed. " [1]

25. The rules for defining the geographic market were stated by the Court as follows:

"The criteria to be used in determining the appropriate geographic market are essentially similar to those used to determine the relevant product market, see S. Rep. No. 1775, 81st Cong., 2nd Sess. 5-6; United States v. E.I. Du Pont de Nemours and Co., 353 U.S. 586, 593. Moreover, just as a product submarket may have section 7 significance as the proper "line of commerce", so may a geographical submarket be considered the appropriate "section of the country". Erie Sand and Gravel Co. v. Federal Trade Comm'n, 291 F. 2d 279, 283 (C.A. 3d Cir); United States v. Bethlehem Steel Corp., 168 F. Supp. 576, 595-603 (D.C.S.D.N.Y.). Congress prescribed a pragmatic, factual approach to the definition of the relevant market and not a formal, legalistic one. The geographic market selected must, therefore, both "correspond to the commercial realities" of the industry and be economically significant. Thus, although the geographic market in some instances may encompass the entire Nation, under other circumstances it may be as small as a single metropolitan area. United States v. Columbia Pictures Corp., 189 F. Supp. 153, 193-194 (D.C.S.D.N.Y.); United States v. Maryland and Virginia Milk Producers Assn., 167 F. Supp. 799 (D.C.D.C. 1958), affirmed, 362 U.S. 458. The fact that two merging firms have competed directly on the horizontal level in but a fraction of geographic markets in which either has operated, does not, in itself, place their merger outside of the country, and if anticompetitive effects of a merger are probable in "any" significant market, the merger – at least to that extent – is proscribed". [2]

26. Applying these rules the Court came to the conclusion that the merger between Brown Shoe Co., a manufacturer and retailer of shoes, and G.R. Kinney Co., a shoe-store chain, involved three different lines of commerce: men's, women's and children's shoes. The Court reasoned:

"These product lines are recognized by the public; each line is manufactured in separate plants; each has characteristics peculiar to itself rendering it generally noncompetitive with the

1. *Ibid.* p. 76,492 (footnotes in the original text omitted).
2. *Ibid.,* p. 76,497 (footnotes in the original text omitted).

others; and each is, of course, directed toward a distinct class of customers ". [1]

27. The Court rejected the company's argument that a further subdivision should be made between medium-price and low-price shoes as it would be:

"unrealistic to accept Brown's contention that, for example, men's shoes selling below $8.99 are in a different product market from those selling above $9.00. This is not to say, however, that "price/quality" differences, where they exist, are unimportant in analysing a merger; they may be of importance in determining the likely effect of a merger. *But the boundaries of the relevant market must be drawn with sufficient breadth to include the competing products of each of the merging companies and to recognize competition where in fact, competition exists.* Thus we agree with the District Court that in this case a further division of product lines based on "price/quality" differences would be "unrealistic"." [2]

28. Finally, the Court also rejected Brown's contention that children's shoes should have been further divided according to sex and age into "infants' and babies'" shoes, "misses' and children's" shoes, and "youths' and boys'" shoes as separate lines of commerce. In the Court's view such a further distinction would have been "impractical" and "unwarranted".

29. As to the geographic market the parties had agreed in this case that the relevant geographic market was the entire national territory as far as the vertical aspect of the merger (acquisition of retail outlets by a manufacturer) was concerned.

30. Dispute had, however, arisen as to the relevant geographic market on the retail level (merger of retail outlets of both companies). The Court confirmed the lower court's market definition which had found that every city with a population exceeding 10,000 and its immediate contiguous surrounding territory constituted a different geographic market for the retailing of each of the three types of shoes defined as different product lines. [3]

31. Separate product submarkets were distinguished in the following cases: industrial and household steel wool; [4] heavy duty detergents, i.e. detergents used primarily for home laundry purposes, as distinguished from other detergents; [5] paper insulated power cables

1. *Ibid.*, p. 67,493.
2. *Ibid.*, p. 67,493 (Emphasis added).
3. The District Court limited its findings to cities having a population of at least 10,000 persons, since Kinney operated only in such areas.
4. F.T.C. v. Brillo Mg. Co., 3 CCH-Trade Regulation Reporter, paras. 16,543 and 16,746 (F.T.C.-cease and desist order 1963); F.T.C. v. General Foods Corp., 3 CCH-Trade Regulation Reporter, paras. 16,612, 17,161, 17,465 (F.T.C.-cease and desist order 1966).
5. United States v. Lever Bros., 193 F. Supp. 254, 1963 Trade Cases para. 70,770. A further subdivision was made between low sudsing detergents and high sudsing detergents.

and other power cables;[1] metal curtain wall and aluminium curtain wall.[2] On the other hand, prefabricated metal buildings were not considered as constituting a separate line of commerce, the court considering that there was intense competition and a high degree of interchangeability among different building materials and buildings themselves having the same end use, that the alleged peculiar characteristics such as speed of erection and expandability were common to numerous forms of building construction, that prefabricated metal buildings had no particular end use and required no special product methods or facilities, that no special methods of sale were used or special groups of customers sold to, and that there was no difference in cost from other buildings having the same end uses.[3]

32. In subsequent cases, the Court has indicated that the product interchangeability test will not be used as a basis for expanding submarkets in horizontal cases. In *United States v. Aluminum Company of America*[4] the Court held that aluminum wire and cables rather than all wire and cables (including aluminum and copper wire and cables) were the relevant line of commerce.

33. The Court conceded that there was competition between insulated aluminum conductor and its copper counterpart and that there was therefore a broad product market for both types of conductor, but thought that this market should be further subdivided, because of the decisive advantages (mostly pricewise) of aluminium conductor over copper conductor in the field of overhead transmission lines and of the superior quality of insulated copper conductor in most other applications.[5]

34. The broad market concept in *Brown Shoe* has been used primarily by the Court in subsequent cases to define market boundaries "with sufficient breadth to include the competing products of each of the merging companies and to recognize competition where, in fact, competition exists" (370 U.S. at 326). In the case *United States v. Continental Can Co.*[6] again the issue was presented whether two substitute products constituted a single market or separate product markets. In this case the Supreme Court held that glass and metal containers have different characteristics which may disqualify one or the other for this or that particular use, that the machinery necessary to pack in glass is different from that employed when cans are used,

    1.   United States v. Kennecott Copper Corp., 231 F. Supp. 95, 1964 Trade Cases, para. 71,18:.
    2.   United States v. Aluminium Co. of America and Cupples Product Corp., 233 F. Supp. 718, 1964 Trade Cases, para. 71,243.
    3.   United States v. National Steel Corp., 251 F. Supp. 693, 1965 Trade Cases, para. 71,375 (D.C.S.D. Texas 1965).
    4.   377 U.S. 271, 1964 Trade Cases, para. 71,116 (merger between Alcoa, an aluminium manufacturer, and Rome Cables Corporation mainly a producer of copper wire and cables).
    5.   1964 Trade Cases, para. 71,116 at p. 79,408. Three of the participating eight judges dissented and thought the District Court had correctly considered both aluminium and copper wire and cable as one market.
    6.   378 U.S. 441, 1964 Trade Cases, para. 71,146 (merger between Continental Can Co. and Hazel-Atlas Co., a manufacturer of glass containers).

that a particular user of cans or glass may pack in only one or the other container and does not shift back and forth from day to day as price and other factors might make desirable, and that the competition between metal and glass containers is different from the competition between the can companies themselves or between the products of the different glass companies. It thought, however, that there was sufficient direct competition between glass and metal containers in the packaging of some products such as baby food, soft drinks, beer, food and others so as to show

> "a rather general confrontation between glass and metal containers and competition between them for the same end uses which is insistent, continuous, effective and industrywise very substantial ... Thus, though the interchangeability of use may not be so complete and the cross-elasticity of demand not so immediate as in the case of most intra-industry mergers, there is over the long run, the kind of customer response to innovation and other competitive stimuli that brings the competition between these two industries within section 7's competition-preserving proscriptions ... ". [1]

35. The same approach to market definition is reflected in the Merger Guidelines of the Department of Justice, which define a market as "any grouping of sales... in which each of the firms whose sales are included enjoy some advantage in competing with those firms whose sales are not included. The advantage need not be great, for so long as it is significant it defines an area of effective competition among the included sellers in which the competition of the excluded sellers, is, *ex hypothesi,* less effective". [2] This does not ignore the fact that less substitutable products may exist, or that competitors outside the market may still exercise a restraining influence on competitors within the market — but it does mean that these competitors and products should not be included within the market unless they are equally interchangeable in terms of price, quality, and use for a relevant group of purchasers. Thus the law is focusing on the needs of particular purchasers whose competitive choices may be foreclosed. While some decisions may appear to suggest that other elements are involved in determining relevant markets, as a whole the cases involving market definition try to achieve a reasonable economic determination of the market context in which the merger is to be evaluated. Also, the cases discussed above, to which numerous others could be added, show that the determination of the relevant product market in the Clayton Act, section 7 cases, involves consideration of a great number of factors including the product's peculiar characteristics and uses, unique production facilities, distinct customers, distinct prices, sensitivity to price changes and specialized vendors. This variety of factors necessarily means that results are not always clearly predictable. Nevertheless, in many other cases, the parties were able to agree on the definition of the relevant product market without litigating the issue. This indicates that the relevant

1.   1964 Trade Cases, para. 71,146 at p. 79,523.
2.   Merger Guidelines No. 3 of May 30th, 1968.

product market (as well as the relevant geographic market discussed below), defined in terms of the needs of particular buyers and sellers, has identifiable meaning to contending parties. It is only the difficult cases which are litigated.

36. As can be expected in such a large national market, the question of separate regional and local markets comes up quite frequently in the United States. Following the Brown Shoe case the Supreme Court in *United States v. Philadelphia National Bank* [1] decided that the four-county Philadelphia metropolitan area was a relevant geographical market for commercial banking. The Court considered that in banking, as in most service industries, convenience of location was essential to effective competition, as individuals and corporations typically confer the bulk of their patronage on banks in their local community and find it impractical to conduct their banking business at a distance. Recognizing that nevertheless, large borrowers and depositors may find it practical to do their banking business outside their home community, while very small customers may be even confined to their immediate neighbourhood, the Court concluded:

> "But that in banking the relevant geographical market is a func-
> tion of each separate customer's economic scale means simply
> *that a workable compromise must be found*: some fair inter-
> mediate delineation which avoids the indefensible extremes of
> drawing the market either so expansively as to make the effect
> of the merger seem insignificant, because only the very largest
> bank customers are taken into account in defining the market, or
> so narrowly as to place appellees in different markets, because
> only their smallest customers are considered". [2]

37. Thus while in the case of commercial banking the geographical market is largely determined by the nature of the product or service itself — the same applies to products which cannot be easily trans-ported at great distances such as milk, [3] or ready-mixed concrete, [4] or which require high transportation costs such as heavy steel products, [5] sand suitable for ready-mixed concrete [6] or portland cement [7] — the situation becomes more difficult where the effective business area of enterprises is mainly determined not by physical and technical reasons but by the market strategy of the enterprises involved. This was the case, for example, in *Crown Zellerbach Corp.*

1. 374 U.S. 321, 1963 Trade Cases, para. 70,912.
2. 1963 Trade Cases, para. 70,812, p. 78,267 (emphasis added).
3. F.T.C. v. Foremost Dairies, 3 CCH–Trade Regulation Reporter, para. 15,877 (1966).
4. F.T.C. v. National Portland Cement Co. *et al.*, 3 CCH-Trade Regulation Reporter, para. 17,186.
5. United States v. Bethlehem Steel Co., 168 F. Supp. 576, 1958 Trade Cases, para. 69,189. In this case 5 different regional markets were held to exist.
6. Erie Sand and Gravel Co. v. Federal Trade Commission, 291 F.2d 279, 1961 Trade Cases, para. 70,028.
7. F.T.C. v. Permanent Cement Co. and Glacier Sand and Gravel Co., 3 CCH-Trade Regulation Reporter, para. 16,885 (1964).

v. Federal Trade Commission. [1] In this case, the court determined the relevant geographical market as the three-state Pacific coast area in which 70% of the acquiring company's sales were made. Partly concluding from this case, the Federal Trade Commission in 1964 stated the determination of the geographical market in the following general terms:

"Determination of the relevant geographic market ("section of the country") in a horizontal merger case is a two-step procedure. First it is necessary to delimit "the area of competitive overlap" (Philadelphia Bank, at 357) between the parties to the merger... Second it is necessary to ascertain the area "to which the purchasers (located in the area of competitive overlap) can practicably turn for supplies – for those are the purchasers who will lose a source of supply as a result of the merger." [2]

38. Two cases involving mergers of breweries decided in 1966 illustrate geographical market determinations. In *United States v. Jos. Schlitz Brewing Co.* [3] the District Court rejected the contention that the entire United States was the relevant section of the country. The Court said:

"However, Schlitz seems to overlook the fact that only three brewers – Schlitz, Miller and Anheuser-Busch – actually compete on a national basis. The competitive "mix" of suppliers in the beer industry in any area or section of the country is composed of the three national brewers and a group of local and regional brewers. The evidence in this case shows that freight rates and population density and growth are among the most important factors relied upon by local and regional brewers in determining their geographic markets. Freight rates for shipping beer across the Continental Divide strongly support the conclusion that the Eight Western States area is a relevant section of the country; the population density and growth of California strongly supports the conclusion that it is a relevant section of the country. Furthermore both of the acquired American breweries made at least 90% of their sales in California or in the Eight Western States area". [4]

39. In *United States v. Pabst Brewing Co.* [5] the majority of the Supreme Court facilitated the antitrust authorities' burden of proving the existence of separate regional and local markets:

"The Government may introduce evidence which shows that as a result of a merger competition may be substantially lessened

1. 296 F.2d 800, 1961 Trade Cases, para. 70,038. The relevant product markets were census coarse paper and manufactured paper bags.

2. F.T.C. v. Permanent Cement Co. and Glacier Sand and Gravel Co., 3 CCH-Trade Regulation Reporter, para. 16,885 (1964) at p. 21,921 (footnotes in the quoted text omitted).

3. 253 F. Supp. 129, 1966 Trade Cases, para. 71,125 (D.C.N.D. Cal. 1966).

4. 1966 Trade Cases, para. 71,725 at p. 82,257.

5. 384 U.S. 546, 1966 Trade Cases, para. 71,790.

31

throughout the country, or on the other hand it may prove that competition may be substantially lessened only in one or more sections of the country. In either event a violation of section 7 would be proved. Certainly the figure of the Government to prove by an army of expert witnesses what constitutes a relevant "economic" or "geographic" market is not an adequate ground on which to dismiss a section 7 case. Compare United States v. Continental Can Co., 378 U.S. 441, 458. Congress did not seem to be troubled about the exact spot where competition might be lessened; it simply intended to outlaw mergers which threatened competition in any or all parts of the country. Proof of the section of the country where the anti-competitive effect exists is entirely subsidiary to the crucial question in this and every section 7 case which is whether a merger may substantially lessen competition anywhere in the United States".[1]

40. The following conclusion may be drawn. In defining geographic markets, like product markets, the United States Supreme Court has tended to emphasize the needs of particular classes of customers, thus the focus is primarily on economic barriers which may tend to create localized markets – including transportation costs, lack of distribution facilities, customer convenience or established customer preference. This may be illustrated by taking the *Philadelphia National Bank* case as an example. The Court pointed out that customer mobility was a function of size; for the very largest customers, the Philadelphia banks did compete directly with the large banks in New York and other financial centres. On the other hand, the Court noted that small and medium-size customers were confined for banking services to banks located in Philadelphia. Therefore, since there was foreclosure of competitive alternatives for local Philadelphia customers, the Supreme Court treated the four-county Philadelphia area as the relevant market to test the merger. The Court did not say that the Philadelphia bank did not face competition from outside the market, but it did say that the banks outside the market were not meaningful competitive alternatives for certain significant classes of banking customers in Philadelphia.

41. In *Canada,* the provision on mergers (section 2(e) Combines Investigation Act) refers to competition "in a trade or industry", "among the sources of supplies of a trade or industry" and "among the outlets for sales in a trade or industry". In the four cases where

---

1. 1966 Trade Cases, para. 71,790 at p. 82,660. In a concurring opinion, Justices Harlan and Stewart criticised this treatment of the relevant area problem as an emasculation of the statutory phrase "in any section of the country". They defined the relevant geographic market in a merger case as
   " ... an area in which the parties to the merger or acquisition compete, and around which there exist economic barriers that significantly impede the entry of new competitors ... ".
concluding that the state of Wisconsin was the relevant area, because the regional breweries, which provided about 90% of the beer sold in Wisconsin, had the benefit of consumers' recognition which was found to be a barrier against the entry of any outside brewery (*ibid.* at p. 82,664).

a merger was attacked by the Government and in the informally settled cases reported by the Director of Investigation and Research there was apparently not much controversy about the determination of the particular "trade or industry" in question or the relevant geographic market. In *R. v. Canadian Breweries Ltd.*,[1] involving a merger in the beer-brewing industry, the product market was held to be beer and the geographic market to be Canada as a whole and each of the Provinces. Finding that there was no monopolistic control of beer in any of these areas the Court rejected the Government's action. In *R. v. British Columbia Sugar Refining Co. Ltd.*, refined sugar was considered as the product market and the entire national territory as the relevant geographic market. Again the Court found no anti-competitive effects and rejected the action of the Government extra.

42. In *Germany,* the statutory criterion of a 20 % market share in section 23(1) No. 1 of the Act against Restraints of Competition necessarily requires a definition of the relevant product and geographic market. The only formal decision taken with respect to a merger deals with the question of submarkets for particular classes of automobiles.[3] In this case the Federal Cartel Office distinguished cars from other motor vehicles and further found three submarkets for cars: small, medium-sized, and large cars. The main reasons for this division were stated in the decision as follows:

> "The question is whether competition exists for a specific type of goods. Only such products which in supply and demand are interchangeable as to utilization purpose and satisfaction of consumer needs can be in competition with each other and can be "a specific type of goods" within the meaning of the Act against Restraints of Competition".

The delineation and determination of the market depends, therefore, on the functional interchangeability of the products supplied and demanded in the market. Insofar as goods, taking into consideration the above-stated criteria, are not interchangeable, they cannot be in in competition with each other, do not belong to the same particular market and cannot be deemed to be "a specific type of goods" within the meaning of the Act.

43. If this general definition of the market is taken as the basis for an examination of the automobile market, with due regard to economic analysis, it appears that there is not just one general market for all motor vehicles but that a distinction must be made between several special markets for automobiles. Cars, trucks, buses, special motor vehicles of various kinds differ substantially as to utilization purpose and satisfaction of consumer needs; these different groups are not interchangeable. The same applies to the different categories of cars. The consumer's demand for automobiles is not just the desire for transportation in a vehicle – no matter what size, purchasing price

---

1. (1960), 33 C.R. 1, *Guide,* Canada, Section 3.1, No. 2.

2. (1960), W.W.R. 577, *Guide,* Canada, Section 3.1., No. 3.

3. Decision of 11th August, 1961 WuW/E BKartA 425; *Guide,* Germany Section 3.0, Case No. 23.

or maintenance costs. The industry produces cars ranging in price from about DM 2,500 – to DM 25,000, – and more. These are all automobiles, but they are so different from each other that a general substitution between them is impossible. The trend has rather been towards the development of special markets – related in kind but differentiated in product. The differentiation is determined by motor capacity, purchasing price, cost of maintenance, fittings and accessories. Other factors are the comfort offered and the prestige value of the car. Thus standardized attitudes develop which result in particular types of market conduct of seller and buyer and which lead to the formation of special markets.

44. Thus, the car market has developed into special markets for for small, medium-sized and big cars. This grouping is a result of i.a. the income, needs and tastes of the consumer, the manufacturers' marketing policy, and technical factors. The industry takes account of these special markets and adjusts its production programmes accordingly. The delineation is usually made on the basis of the vehicle's engine capacity, but other data, such as purchasing price, mileage and engine power are also employed as features of distinction. There is no sharp line of division between these special markets; borderline areas exist. Vehicles coming into these borderline areas cannot be definitely assigned to one or the other market. This does not negate, however, the fundamental distinctions of the special markets described above. [1]

45. In the *United Kingdom,* the question of market determination may arise under two circumstances: (a) the Board of Trade when deciding whether to refer a merger to the Monopolies Commission has to check whether the merger involves at least one-third "as respects the supply of goods or services of any description" ... "in the United Kingdom or any substantial part thereof..." (section 6(1)b Monopolies and Mergers Act 1965); (b) the Monopolies Commission in its investigation whether the merger operates or may be expected to operate against the public interest may have to determine the relevant market in order to evaluate the effects of the merger on competition.

46. While it is not possible to see from the references of the Board of Trade, which are published without stating the detailed motives for the references, what considerations have led the Board to define the relevant products within the meaning of section 6(1)b, [2] the reports of the Monopolies Commission give some indication of product market considerations. Thus, in the *Fisheries case,* the Commission came to the following conclusion:

"We considered first the strength of the combined company immediately following the merger. Their fleet could be expected, on the basis of recent levels of fish supplies, to provide less than one-fifth of the total supply of fish in the United Kingdom market (excluding canned fish). If the market for fish could

1. WuW/E BKartA 427-428 (footnotes in the original text omitted).
2. See e.g. reference of the merger Guest, Keen and Nettlefolds Ltd. and Birfield Ltd., 1967, London, HMSO, Cmnd. 3186, p. 46.

properly be regarded as a single whole, in which all fish was freely and fully in competition regardless of variety, quality or source, such shares would not appear sufficient to enable the combined company to exercise undue influence on the market, even though it would be substantially larger than any other single share. However, from the evidence we have received we are satisfied that, although the market in one port is sensitive to supplies coming into other ports, the market as a whole does fall into distinct sections by reference to types of fish and class of customers and, while there is some interchange and price influence among them, there is not full and free competition. The distinctions are not clear cut; for instance, some high quality fish from near and middle waters may replace distant water fish if the latter becomes relatively dearer. But the extent of substitution is limited both by quantities available and by the fact that different outlets need different kinds of fish. We consider that the bulk of distant water cod serves a market which can be clearly distinguished from that served by, for example, high quality flat fish landed from inshore vessels and similar fish imports as quick-frozen fillets. There is no doubt a normal pattern of price differentials between the various qualities and varieties of fish and there may be a limit to which this can be be distorted but competition from fish at one end of the scale would not be sufficient to prevent variations in prices at the other end. We therefore thought it both right and necessary to consider the position in relation to cod separately ". [1]

47. The Commission in this case also considered the geographic market situation and concluded that

" at least in the Humber ports (Hull and Grimsby) if not in the fishing industry as a whole" the combined company would be in a strong position to impose their views on other companies ". [2]

48. In the case *Guest, Keen* and *Nettlefolds Ltd./Birfield Ltd.* " component parts of transmission systems of mechanically propelled land vehicles, in particular, propeller shafts" and " drop forgings" were named as relevant products in the reference of the Board of Trade. In its conclusion the Commission distinguished between propeller shafts where the merging companies were the only manufacturers and motor components in general. Since the Commission found that " the merger does not bring about any very significant additional concentration of productive capacity under single ownership in relation to particular motor components ", [3] no detailed considerations were made as to whether there are special markets for particular components.

49. In the case *United Drapery Stores Ltd./Montague Burton Ltd.* the Commission made the following remarks on the relevant market issue:

1.   Ross Group Ltd. and Associated Fisheries Ltd., A report on the proposed merger, 1966, London, HMSO, Cmnd. 42, paras. 116-118.

2.   *Ibid.*

3.   *Op. cit.,* at para. 147.

"There are various possible ways of defining the relevant 'market'; one might for instance consider the market for all-men's wear or that for men's outer wear only. However, we consider that the market for complete men's suits (two or three piece) can properly be regarded as a separate market and we regard this as the relevant market in considering the effects of the merger. Moreover within the market for men's suits we think it right to pay particular attention to the cheaper ranges, that is the market for suits selling to the public at prices up to £20".[1]

50. In the *ECSC* several merger cases have presented market determination problems. In the SIDMAR decision of 25th April 1962[2] the High Authority regarded "flat products, especially hot wide strip and cold sheet" as the relevant product market. As to the geographic market the High Authority said:

"It has to be ascertained whether in view of the modern mass production competitive influences on other large producers in neighbouring areas of the Common Market are necessarily to be expected. The evaluation of the relevant market shares would therefore have to include in the future all producers exposed to such competitive influences, even if the examination of earlier cases should show that between these areas only a small exchange of goods has taken place. Undoubtedly this potential competition has to be increasingly taken into account. In an oligopoly of this kind it must for example be considered whether in the case of a price reduction the other enterprises in a similar position have to take this reduction into account if they do not wish to risk losses of market shares. This means in regard to the flat products here in question that in the entire northern industrial triangle of the Common Market... all producers have to be considered as belonging to the same relevant market".[3]

51. In the SACILLOR-decision of 22nd July 1964[4] the High Authority again dealt with the question of the relevant market. The considerations on the geographic market are summarized as follows: "In order to evaluate the effects of the joint venture the High Authority has examined the selling market of the participating groups. It turned out that the 'relevant market' of these groups is geographically the entire Common Market excluding Italy".[5] As to the product market, the High Authority found that broad-flanged beams were competing with the other type of beams, and that there was therefore a single product market for both types of beams.

52. In *Japan*, the question of market determination is raised in merger cases by the fact that the law (section 15, para. 1) requires that the merger must not substantially restrain competition "in any

---

1. 1967, London, HMSO, Cmnd. 3397, at para. 130.
2. *Guide,* ECSC, Section 3, Case No. 10.
3. 11th Activity Report of the ECSC (1962-1963), No. 350.
4. *Guide,* ECSC, Section 3, Case 15.
5. 13th Activity Report of the ECSC, (1964-1965), No. 207.

particular field of trade". No sufficient case material is however available to see in detail how this term has been interpreted in practice. [1]

53. In *Spain,* mergers involving 30% or more of "the national market in a given product or service" are subject to registration (section 21(7) of the Act against Restraints of Competition). In a merger involving two big manufacturers of man-made fibres, La Seda and Perlofil S.A., the Service for the Protection of Competition had occasion to interpret the concept of a product market. Although the Service recognized that the fibres made by the two firms were not identical or homogeneous, it considered that they were undoubtedly good substitutes for each other. The firms were therefore required to register their merger agreement. It would therefore seem that the Spanish authorities tend to interpret the concept of a product or service market rather broadly in that not only a specific variety of product but also other varieties are taken into consideration, which are in general competition on the market in the sense that the latter satisfy the same needs of consumers or users.

B. MONOPOLIZATION

54. The legislations with provisions against monopolization are those of the United States, Canada and Japan.

55. In the *United States* section 2 of the Sherman Act prohibits "to monopolize any part of the trade or commerce among the several States or with foreign nations". The application of this provision therefore requires the determination of the relevant "part of the trade or commerce" (product market) and the relevant geographical part of interstate or foreign trade. The cases decided by the courts show that the courts have interpreted these definitions on the same lines as in merger cases. [2]

56. The determination of the relevant product market was the main issue in the Cellophane case, *United States v. E.I. Du Pont de Nemours and Co.* [3] The defendant, charged with illegal monopolization,

1. In Toho Co. Ltd. v. Fair Trade Commission, (Guide, Japan, 3.1, No. 1,) the Tokyo High Court found that a certain area in the city of Tokyo (Ginza area) constituted a "particular field of trade" for the exhibition of films in cinemas in this area which were engaged in the business of exhibiting films to a particular class of people namely persons wishing to see films in this area, and the Ginza area cinemas shared the same potential audience.

2. Cf., e.g., U.S. v. Grinnell Corp., 384 U.S. 563, 1966 Trade Cases, para. 71,789.

3. 351 U.S. 377, 1956 Trade Cases, para. 68,369. This monopolization case was decided before the 1950 Amendments to Section 7 of the Clayton Act. The Court in *Brown Shoe* cited the *du Pont* case as stating the general rule of reasonable interchangeability of use and cross-elasticity of demand between the

produced almost 75% of all cellophane sold in the United States. Other flexible packaging materials were greaseproof paper, glassine, waxed paper, aluminum foil and Pliofilm. These materials differed from cellophane and from one another in at least some of the following characteristics: heat sealability, printability, transparency, strength, permeability to moisture and gases and resistance to grease and oils. The question whether Du Pont had violated section 2 of the Sherman Act therefore largely depended on whether cellophane had to be considered as a separate product market or whether the other flexible packaging materials were such close substitutes as to form a unified product market for these materials.

57. Phrasing the issue as being one of determination "whether competition from other wrappings prevented Du Pont from possessing monopoly power in violation of section 2",[1] the court adopted the following test for the consideration of substitutes:

"In considering what is the relevant market for determining the control of price and competition no more definite rule can be declared than that commodities reasonably interchangeable by consumers for the same purpose make up that "part of the trade or commerce", monopolization of which may be illegal".[2]

58. The court admitted that "cellophane combined the desirable elements of transparency, strength and cheapness more definitely than any of the others" and continued that

"...despite cellophane's advantages it has to meet competition from other materials in every one of its uses. ...The Government makes no challenge to (the finding) that cellophane furnishes less than 7% of wrapping for bakery products, 25% for candy, 32% for snacks, 35% for meats and poultry, 27% for crackers and biscuits, 47% for fresh produce, and 34% for frozen foods. Seventy five to eighty per cent of cigarettes are wrapped in cellophane ... Thus, cellophane shares the packaging market with others. The over-all result is that cellophane accounts for 17.9% of flexible wrapping materials ... Moreover a very considerable degree of functional interchangeability exists between these products ... It will be noted ... that except as to permeability to gases, cellophane has no qualities that are not possessed by a number of other materials".[3]

59. As an example of cellophane's interchangeability with other wrapping materials the court pointed to several changes in the share of cellophane used for purposes of meat wrapping. Discussing the cross-elasticity of demand between the various wrapping materials the court found "great sensitivity of customers in the flexible packaging markets to price and quality changes" and concluded,

product itself and substitutes for it. As noted, this test was discussed as to mergers in *Brown Shoe;* however, the Court indicated that this would not preclude a simultaenous finding of one or more subsidiary lines of commerce.

1. 1956 Trade Cases, para. 68,369 at p. 71,592.
2. *Ibid.* at p. 71,593.
3. *Ibid.* at p. 71,594.

"that cellophane's interchangeability with other materials mentioned suffices to make it a part of this flexible packaging materials market".[1] Finding no monopoly power of Du Pont on this larger market on which cellophane had only a share of 17.9%, the Court held that the Government's action had to be dismissed.

60. The case *United States v. Grinnell Corp.*[2] involved the determination of the product market with respect to a service. The defendant controlled three companies which offered the service of protecting property by central stations to which electrical signals from hazard-detecting devices installed on the protected premises are automatically transmitted. One of the companies provided both burglary and fire protection service, the second provided burglary protection service alone, and the third provided only fire protection service.

61. The court held that property protection services using a central station system and being accredited by the insurance underwriters constituted a separate product market, a market on which the three companies controlled by the defendant had a share of over 87%. The court rejected the argument of the defendant that, in measuring the market share, the services of the affiliated companies could not be lumped together since they served different needs (burglary protection, fire protection or both) and were, therefore, not interchangeable and said on the other property protection services:

"There are, to be sure, substitutes for the accredited central station service. But none of them appears to operate on the same level as the central station service so as to meet the interchangeability test of the Du Pont case. Non-automatic and automatic local alarm systems appear on this record to have marked differences, not the low degree of differentiation required of substitute services as well as substitute articles. Watchman service is far more costly and less reliable. Systems that set off an audible alarm at the site of a fire or burglary are cheaper but often less reliable ... Proprietary systems that a customer purchases and operates are available; but they can be used only by a very large business or by government and are not realistic alternatives for most concerns. There are also protective services connected directly to a municipal police or fire department. But most cities with an accredited central station do not permit direct, connected service for private business. These alternative services and devices differ, ... in utility, efficiency, reliability, responsiveness and continuity ... For many customers only central station protection will do".[3]

62. The court further excluded non-accredited central stations from the relevant market because customers considered their services as inferior as compared with accredited stations and received smaller reductions in their insurance premiums. The Supreme Court in *Grinnell* in defining the relevant market relied on the merger cases,

1. *Ibid.* at p. 71,595.
2. 384, U.S. 563, 1966 Trade Cases para. 71,789.
3. *Ibid.* at p. 649/50.

particularly *United States v. Philadelphia National Bank* (discussed in the Merger Section), stating that "We see no reason to differentiate between the 'line' of commerce in the context of the Clayton Act and 'part' of commerce for purpose of the Sherman Act". The court held that accredited central alarm stations offered a "unique cluster of services" which were in effect "a single basic service – the protection of property through use of a central service station..." It ruled that the mere existence of different services did not in itself detract from a single market concept.

63. In defining the relevant *geographical* market the court held the market to be nationwide. The court conceded that the activities of individual stations were in a sense local in that they usually served only an area which was within a radius of 25 miles, but said that the business of providing such service was operated on a national level, because of national planning, inspection, certification and rate making by national insurers, national schedules of prices, though the rates were varied to meet local conditions and dealings with multistate businesses on the basis of nationwide contracts. [1]

64. The relevant market in the *Cellophane* case can best be understood as a decision that cellophane had no unique group of buyers for whom there was no equally good alternatives. The relevant product market in *Grinnell* followed the analysis used in the *Philadelphia National Bank* where the Court included various bank services, which were not substitutes, in the product market. So also in *Grinnel* the Court combined the services which it recognized were not interchangeable because "central station companies recognize that to compete effectively they must offer all or nearly all types of services". [2] The Court then excluded the alternatives for each of the distinct types of services on the ground that none of them "appears to operate on the same level as the central station services so as to meet the interchangeability test of the *Du Pont* case". [3] Thus, as in merger cases, the ultimate determining factor in defining relevant market is whether buyers have meaningful competitive alternatives.

65. In *Canada,* the provision on monopoly (section 2(f) of the Combines Investigation Act) refers to "a situation where one or more persons either substantially or completely control throughout Canada or any area thereof the class or species of business in which they are engaged...".

66. In *Eddy Match Company Ltd. et al. v. The Queen* [4] the question was discussed whether the manufacture of wooden matches was a

---

1. Three dissenting judges criticized the definition of the product market as well as of the geographical market as having been "tailored precisely to fit defendant's business". They argued that the question of whether the defendant had gained monopoly power should have been tested in economically defined areas, where a potential buyer would look for potential suppliers of the service. Therefore, the locally available alternatives of customers seeking protection of their property should have been taken into account. *Ibid.* at p. 82,654.

2. *Ibid.* at p. 572.

3. *Ibid.* at p. 573.

4. 1953, 109 C.C.C. 1.

"class or species of business" or whether the other devices for producing fire, such as paper matches and mechanical lighters had to be taken into account. The court said:

> "It is true that the manufacture of lighting devices whatever be the type or kind, can be regarded as a general class of business which would include wooden matches. But it seems strange to suggest that within the general class there can not be as many types of businesses as there are species of devices... Since this commodity can be distinguished from the other devices, such as mechanical lighters and the like, it must be said that the manufacture of wooden matches is a class or species of business...".

67. The position that competing industries are not necessarily part of the relevant market was also taken by the Restrictive Practices Commission in its report on "*Monopoly in Distribution of Propane – British Columbia*".[1] Discussing the question whether propane gas constituted a market of its own or was only part of the fuel market including also natural gas, oil coal, wood and electricity the Commission said:

> "Every type of fuel can, in a general way, be said to be in competition with every other fuel. The most advantageous market for propane exists in areas where natural gas is not available as a fuel. Its most usual competition in this market is electricity. But the fact that there exists an interindustry competition between propane and electricity does not make them the "same class or species of business". They can certainly be distinguished from each other without difficulty. Nor is it a valid argument to say that since there is sufficient possibility of substituting electricity for propane, the price of electricity always sets a limit on the price of propane. There are very few products that can be priced (even by a monopolist) without consideration being given to the potential competition of other suitable products. The consumer is entitled to have the price of propane determined by reasonable competition in the sale of propane itself and not only by the price ceiling set by some other fuel".[2]

68. In *Japan*, though section 3 of the Antimonopoly Act prohibits generally "private monopolization", it is clear that the finding of such monopolization can only be made with respect to particular products or services and particular territories. In the *Soy Sauce case*[3] the defendant was the leading soy sauce producer of the country, accounting for 14.0 % of the national supply. The Commission, in determining the product market, differentiated between the three recognized quality grades: "supreme", "superior", and 'best", apparently regarding the soy sauce of the grade "supreme" as a separate submarket. The relevant geographical market was defined as the city of Tokyo. There the defendant sold more than half of the "supreme" type and 36.7 % of all soy sauce.

---

1.   R.T.P.C. No. 32 (1965).
2.   *Id.* at 65.
3.   FTC Decision Reports (FTC, 27th December 1955) 108.

C. CONDUCT OF MARKET DOMINATING ENTERPRISES

69. Under this heading cases arising under those provisions of the laws of OECD Members which deal with the conduct of dominant enterprises will be discussed. In most of the countries which have enacted such provisions, the definition of the relevant market has not yet been the subject of court or administrative decisions. There are, however, a number of cases in some countries which illustrate the problem of market definition under a system of conduct control.

70. In *Denmark,* the issue of the relevant market arose, i.e., in the *Omega* and *Tissot Watches Case.*[1] In this case the Monopolies Control Authority had ordered a wholesale firm dealing in watches to register as a dominant enterprise under section 6(2) of the Monopolies Control Act.[2] The firm was the sole importer and wholesale dealer of "Omega". The firm was the sole importer and wholesale dealer of "Omega" and "Tissot" watches and carried several other but cheaper makes, which were sold under various brand names. The firm's market share was about 15%. Although many different makes were on the market, the Authority found that the firm in question held a dominant position in that it carried an appreciable part of the eight makes which were the only watches of any competitive consequence in this case. The Monopolies Appeal Tribunal however did not find sufficient reason to order registration, attaching special importance to the fact that the firm's share of total watch imports did not exceed 15% and amounted to only from 5 to 6% in respect of brand name watches proper.

71. In *Switzerland,* the same question of how to define the relevant market in cases of well-known branded articles came before the Federal Court in 1965.[3] In this case a wholesaler of liquors sued the exclusive distributor for Switzerland of "Black and White" whisky and "Martell" cognac for damages because he was refused further deliveries. Dealing with the question whether the exclusive distributor's line constituted a "market in certain goods or services" within the meaning of section 3 of the Swiss Cartel Act the court found that

> "the market for certain goods ... cannot solely consist of the trade in the products of a certain enterprise as long as the consumer has the possibility to choose between these products and other identical or similar ones, i.e. between goods or services which, according to the reasonable judgment of the buyer, are interchangeable because they are destined for the same end use and have the same qualities. A supplier or distributor

1. *Bulletin of the Monopolies Control Authority 1960,* p. 113.

2. Section 6(2) reads: Individual enterprises or combinations which exert or may exert a substantial influence on price, production, distribution, or transport conditions, throughout the country or in local market areas, shall be subject to notification if the Monopolies Control Authority so demands. Restrictive practices of such enterprises or combinations shall likewise be subject to notification when demanded by the Monopolies Control Authority.

3. Judgment of 22nd December 1965, ATF 91 II 489, *Publications de la Commission Suisse des Cartels,* 1966 pp. 217–220, No. 8.

of one of these commodities which are subject to effective competition from analogous products, does not dominate "the market for certain goods or services"...[1]

72. After citing German literature and the Du Pont decision of the United States Supreme Court and rejecting the approach of the Court of the European Communities in the Grunding/Consten case, the court concluded:

"Far from claiming ... that the defendant ... dominates the market for whisky and that of cognac (and even that would perhaps be a too narrow definition of "the market for certain goods" in the meaning of section 3 of the Swiss Cartel Act) the plaintiff has stated ... that the exclusive right conferred to [defendant] solely concerned the whiskies of the "Black and White" label and the cognacs of the "Martell" label, and that the sales agents of the other brands which are offered in the market do supply him with their lines. It is a well-known fact that there are many brands of whiskies and of cognac at competitive prices and qualities in the market ... Consequently the defendant ... does not dominate the market for these goods".[2]

73. In *Germany,* two recent cases have raised the question whether enterprises were market dominating in that they were not exposed to substantial competition "in a certain type of goods or commercial services" (section 22, para. 1). In the *Meto case*[3] the Federal Cartel Office held that manual price labelling machines of the type supplied by the firm Meto constituted a particular "type of goods". Regarding functional interchangeability of goods as the criterion to define the relevant product market, the Office reasoned that other labelling devices could not be taken into account because they did not offer equal product alternatives to the buyers. While stationery machines were much higher in price and could therefore only be afforded by large buyers, small price-tag printing machines did not offer the same advantages because the price-tags still had to be glued to the merchandise after printing, two stages which the Meto machines could do in one. Further stamping devices were also not considered as functionally interchangeable since they could only be

---

1. Judgment of 22nd December 1965, ATF 91 II 489, *Publications de la Commission Suisse des Cartels,* 1966 p. 219.

2. *Ibid.* at p. 220.

3. Decision of 2nd October 1967, WuW/E BKartA 1189. The Berlin Court of Appeals, which has since confirmed the decision of the Federal Cartel Office, said on the relevant market issue: "In defining the market for which the position of the appellant has to be assessed (relevant market) all equal products of other producers had to be taken into account. All products that are so closely related as to their qualities, the use for which they are determined, and their price, that the sensible consumer will compare them as satisfying a *specific* need and regard them as interchangeable, are equal for the market". The Court came to the conclusion that the average user desiring to attach price-tags bearing differing data to small or average quantities of merchandise would not consider stamping devices employing no tags nor various groups of stationery machines costing from DM 500 to DM 50.000, if there are available for that use handy labelling devices costing from DM 150 to DM 400. Judgment of 18th February 1969, Kart V 34/67.

used on smooth and unbreakable packages and because the stamped-on price could not easily be removed. This difference was also reflected by the substantially lower price of stamping devices as compared with Meto machines.

74. In the *Sporting Goods Fair* case [1] the Federal Cartel Office held that the organiser of the international sporting goods fair in Wiesbaden, a profit corporation, was a market dominating enterprise. After outlining the general criteria for defining the relevant market in accordance with the above-mentioned decision in the Meto case, the Office stated that the Wiesbaden fair was the only fair in the Federal Republic of Germany for winter sports goods. It found that the exhibition possibilities at the Wiesbaden fair were not interchangeable with other means of soliciting orders, because only the fair provided an opportunity for complete information regarding all market factors and a meeting-place for the concentrated supply and demand. Evidence of this lack of interchangeability with other means of soliciting orders was found in the fact that all enterprises selling sporting goods took pains to be represented at the Wiesbaden fair. [2]

75. In the *United Kingdom,* the issue of the relevant market in conduct cases comes up in connection with the question whether or not "at least one-third of all goods or services of any description which are supplied in the United Kingdom or any substantial part thereof are supplied by or to any one person...", [3] in which case the Board of Trade may refer the matter to the Monopolies Commission for investigation and report. The references of the Board of Trade which are published without stating the detailed motives for the reference, have, for example, defined the following "relevant markets": the supply of sand and gravel suitable for use for building or civil engineering purposes in Central Scotland, [4] oxygen, dissolved acetylene and propane [5] cigarettes and tobacco and cigarettes and tobacco machinery, [6] wallpaper, [7] petrol to retailers in the United Kingdom, [8] electrical wiring harnesses for motor vehicles, [9] colour films and the application of any process to colour film. [10]

1. Decision of 31st May 1968, BM – 76/67.
2. This part of the decision was affirmed by the Berlin Court of Appeals (Judgment of 22nd July 1968, WuW/E OLG 907) and by the Supreme Court.
3. Section 3(1)(a) of the Monopolies and Restrictive Practices (Inquiry and Control) Act 1948 and Section 2 of the Monopolies and Mergers Act 1965.
4. Report on the Supply of Sand and Gravel in Central Scotland, 1966, London, HMSO Cmnd. 222, at p. 1.
5. Report on the Supply of Certain Industrial and Medical Cases, 1956, London, HMSO Cmnd. 13, at p. 109.
6. Report on the Supply of Cigarettes and Tobacco and of Cigarette and Tobacco Machinery, 1961, London, HMSO Cmnd. 218 at p. 217.
7. Report on the Supply of Wallpaper, 1964, London, HMSO Cmnd. 59, at p. 57.
8. Petrol; A Report on the Supply of Petrol to retailers in the United Kingdom, 1965, London, HMSO Cmnd. 264, at p. 162.
9. Electrical Wiring Harnesses for Motor Vehicles, 1966, London, HMSO Cmnd. 72, at p. 16.
10. Colour Film, A Report on the Supply and Processing of Colour Film, 1966 London, HMSO Cmnd. 1, at p. 121.

76. Since the references of the Board of Trade do not state the reasons for the definition of such "markets", no further details as to the criteria on the basis of which these definitions were made can be given.

77. Although there are no cases, section 36(d) of the *Austrian* Cartel Act should be mentioned finally, because it has completely formalized the question of market definition. Under this provision an enterprise is market dominating, "if its share of the supply on the domestic market of any goods – or group of goods – which appear in the customs tariff as a single item – or as a separate sub-item – and which are not a by-product of the enterprise, exceeds, according to the criteria customarily applied in the sector concerned when estimating production, the rate of 30% or – if the domestic market is supplied by more than three enterprises – the rate of 50%". Since the only legal consequence for enterprises coming under this provision is notification, the legislator apparently intended to simplify its application as much as possible. Consequently if measures against dominant enterprises were to be taken, the dominated "market" would have to be defined in terms other than that of the customs tariff.

D. CONCLUSION

78. Although the great majority of the cases analysed above have arisen under American antitrust law, some general conclusions with respect to the problem of defining the relevant market in cases of market dominance and market power seem nevertheless possible.

79. The finding of such power depends to a large extent on how the relevant market is defined. A narrow market definition – in the extreme case limited to the product or service of a particular supplier (e.g., to a particular branded article) – will in most cases result in a finding of market power or lack of sufficient competition. On the other hand, broad market definitions, taking into account not only products and services of the same type but also actual and even potential substitutes, will make it in many cases unlikely that a particular supplier has dominant market power. This already makes it clear that the definition of the relevant market and the finding of market power in terms of lack of effective competition cannot be regarded as entirely separate issues, but must be seen in relation to each other. The conclusion made earlier with respect to section 7 of the Clayton Act that both issues overlap and that the question of market determination may even become subsidiary to the question of effective competition may therefore be considered as bringing out an aspect which applies to the problem of market power in general. This will become more apparent after the analysis of the problem of effective competition in the following chapter.

80. The cases have made it clear the *the* relevant market in the sense of being the only possible result of an application of objective

criteria does in reality not exist. The various "tests" or formulae that are applied by the courts and administrations such as "functional interchangeability", "cross-elasticity of demand", "peculiar characteristics or uses", are merely several aspects of a policy decision which has to take into account many other aspects and the essence of which is to determine which of several possible market definitions is most appropriate in the individual case in the light of the statutory purpose of the law to be applied. It is therefore not possible to draw up a list of relevant markets which could be applied in all future cases arising under a particular law, nor to regard the results obtained in a particular case in one country as an indication of how the market should be defined in cases arising in other countries. If it is nevertheless useful to compare cases that have arisen in different countries, it is to show the type of considerations on which the decision was based and the various aspects which have been taken into account. For this reason, the fact that most of the cases analysed above came up under the particular situation of the American antitrust law (section 7 Clayton Act and section 2 Sherman Act) does not prevent them from illustrating some important aspects of market definition in general, aspects which frequently will also have to be considered in other countries whatever the statutory purpose of the law and the particular market situation may be.

81. It has been shown above by comparing cases under section 7 of the Clayton Act and section 2 of the Sherman Act that the definition of the relevant market is closely connected with the statutory purpose of the particular law to be applied and thus requires a teleological, pragmatic decision. This becomes also apparent from section 36(d) of the Austrian Cartel Act which was not intended as a measure of control of market power and therefore simplified the definition of the relevant product market by the use of customs tariff positions as relevant "markets". It is clear that the possible extent of such simplification is limited where the purpose of the law is to deal with actual market power. However, some simplification in defining markets will always be necessary to make the law operational. Thus, the markets defined for the purposes of administration of restrictive business practice legislation may differ from the results of purely economic analysis, a factor which may explain to some extent the controversies about some of the market definitions in the cases discussed above.

82. In none of the cases studied, even though foreign product alternatives (imports) were available, has the relevant geographic market been extended beyond the area in which the respective law applies and no other cases with a contrary ruling could be ascertained. Even in those countries which belong to the European Economic Community and, generally, in small countries with a relatively high share of foreign trade in national product, the relevant geographic market has not been defined to include other countries or the Common Market as a whole in cases decided under national law. The cases decided under the ECSC Treaty where all or a part of the entire common coal and steel market was considered to be the relevant geographic market is no refutation of this For the Treaty applies to the entire area of

the coal and steel community. The High Authority and the Court of Justice have not extended the relevant geographic market beyond this area.

83. Generally, the availability of foreign product alternatives through foreign trade (imports) has not led to an extension of the definition of the relevant geographic market beyond the territory in which the respective law applies. This has not even been done in those countries which belong to a larger common market, such as the EEC, or to a free trade area, such as the EFTA, although foreign product alternatives have often become of particular importance in such areas due to the substantial reduction and abolition of trade barriers.

84. This limitation of relevant geographic markets to the territory of the respective country or community whose law is applied is not a necessary consequence of the public international law principle of the territoriality of laws nor does it necessarily follow from the legal texts. It is true that in most laws, e.g. in the Netherlands (section 1: "... on a market for goods or services in the Netherlands), in the United States (section 7, Clayton Act: " ... any section of the country"), and in the EEC (article 86; " ... in the Common Market or any substantial part thereof") the relevant geographic market is expressly limited to the area of applicability of the respective law. But in other laws, e.g. in Germany (section 22), Spain (section 2), and Switzerland (section 3), the legal texts refer only to "the market" in general so that it would be possible to define relevant geographic markets which extend beyond national territory. Such an extension would not be in violation of the principle of territoriality just mentioned, as long as the measures taken are restricted to national territory.

85. There is, however, no need for an extension of relevant geographic markets beyond national and community boundaries. Since foreign product alternatives can be taken into account, the definition of the relevant geographic market does not predetermine the question whether market power within a given area actually exists, or may result from a merger.

86. The limitation of the geographic market makes sense to the extent that foreign product alternatives are taken into account which is – as will be shown later – generally the case. It also makes sense when in some cases, e.g., in *United States* v. *Jos. Schlitz Brewing Co.,*[1] the national market is sub-divided, due to the special circumstances in the particular case, into regional and local markets. This observation again confirms the close interrelation between the issues of market definition and determination of market power.

1.   253 F. Supp. 129, 1956 Trade Cases, para. 71,125 (D.C.N.D. Cal.1966).

DETERMINATION OF MARKET POWER
UNDER THE "CONDUCT" LAWS

87. As has been shown in Chapter II, the definition of the relevant market and the existence of economic power on the relevant market (in the form of market dominance or otherwise) are in practice overlapping issues which may even become identical when the relevant market is defined as "area of effective competition". However, for the purpose of the present study, both issues are considered separately. The issue of the relevant market having been analysed in Chapter II, Chapter III will now show how market power is to be determined under the different laws. As was already said in the introduction, this determination can be made on the basis of formal criteria (market share) or of substantive criteria which require an appraisal of the entire competitive situation on the market such as "substantial" or "effective" competition, "normal play" of competition, or "normal operation of the market". The following analysis will therefore distinguish between laws applying formal criteria and laws applying substantive criteria.

88. While under a system of conduct control the finding of market power is merely a prerequisite to intervention against particular adverse effects (e.g., abuses), such power under a system of merger control is or may be in itself undesirable or illegal. In the case of mergers, the issue of determination of market power is therefore largely identical with that of the undesirability of their effects. For this reason, as regards mergers and monopolization, both issues will be analysed together in Part II which deals with the adverse effects of market power.

A.   DETERMINATION OF MARKET POWER BY FORMAL CRITERIA

89. Formal criteria to determine market power with a view to controlling the conduct of dominant enterprises are applied in the United Kingdom, in Norway and, for registration purposes only, in Austria.

90. In the *United Kingdom,* under section 3(1)(a) of the Monopolies and Restrictive Practices (Inquiry and Control) Act 1948, market power within the meaning of this law exists if a single enterprise or a group of enterprises which prevent or restrict competition with respect to the product concerned between them have a market share of at least 33 1/3%. In practice, as is illustrated by the reports of the Monopolies Commission, the determination of this market share in individual cases has not presented great difficulties. Apparently, only in one case so far has the Monopolies Commission found that the enterprise or group of enterprises investigated had a market share of less than 33 1/3%.[1]

91. In *Norway,* under section 34, No. 1 of the Act on Control of Prices, Profits and Restraints of Competition, an enterprise which has a share of 25% or more in the national production or distribution of a commodity or service has to register as a dominant enterprise and therefore becomes subject to the supervision of the Price Directorate under section 32. Apparently, as in the United Kingdom, the administration of this provision has not presented practical difficulties. Since the Price Directorate may, in addition to the enterprises coming under section 34, No. 1, request notification as dominant enterprises of other enterprises whose activities are "of such importance for one or more trades within the realm that special supervision is considered by the Directorate to be necessary", all cases of undesirable market power may be brought under the control of the Price Directorate.

92. *Austria* applies a formal criterion to determine whether an enterprise is considered to be market dominating. This criterion is more than 30% of the supply of a product on the domestic market or more than 50% if the domestic market is supplied by more than 3 enterprises.

B. DETERMINATION OF MARKET POWER
BY SUBSTANTIVE CRITERIA

93. Substantive criteria to determine market power with a view to controlling the conduct of dominant enterprises are applied in: Belgium, Denmark, France, Germany, the Netherlands, Spain, Switzerland, ECSC and EEC. The respective laws may be divided into the following two groups:

    i) laws which use the terms "market dominating position" or "market dominating (dominant) enterprise" (France, Germany, the Netherlands, Spain, Switzerland, ECSC, EEC);

    ii) laws which apply other criteria (Belgium and Denmark).

---

1. The Monopolies Commission: Men's Haircutting Services, A Report on a Reference Concerning the Supply of Haircutting Services for Men, HMSO, London 1968.

94. In *France,* a dominant position as defined by section 59 bis(4) of the Price Ordinance No. 45–1483 is constituted "by a monopoly or by the manifest concentration of economic power" of an enterprise or a group of enterprises. In the only case where the issue was raised, *Fédération Nationale des Cinémas Français contre Radiodiffusion Française,* [1] the Commercial Court in Paris held that the French Radio Corporation had no dominant position in buying or renting films because of the existence of numerous cinema owners equally buying or renting films.

95. In *Germany,* market domination is defined in terms of absence of substantial competition. Under section 22(1) of the Act Against Restraints of Competition a single enterprise is market dominating if it has "no competitor or is not exposed to any substantial competition in a certain type of goods or commercial services". Further, under section 22(2), two or more enterprises are market dominating "insofar as, in regard to a certain type of goods or commercial services, no substantial competition exists in fact between them in general or in specific markets, and they jointly meet the requirements of subsection (1)". While the first case essentially covers monopolies and partial monopolies [2] the second refers to market dominating oligopolies. In this case the question whether substantial competition exists has to be examined twice: first between the members of the group (oligopolists) and second between the group and outsiders.

96. The two cases mentioned earlier, Meto [3] and Sporting Goods Fair, [4] were "monopoly" cases under subsection 2. In the *Meto case* the Federal Cartel Office found that two other producers of manual labelling machines had a market share which was so insignificant that no substantial competition could be assumed even if these enterprises were regarded as competitors (of the respondent). [5] In the *Sporting Goods Fair case* the respondent was the only supplier.

1. Judgment of 8th March 1965, (1965) Revue trim. droit eur. 286.

2. A partial monopolist is defined in the Glossary contained in 1 Antitrust Law and Economics Review 129-142 (1967) as follows:

"A market situation in which all sellers except one have an insignificant individual share of the market's total sales and hence behave as perfect competitors, while that one large firm, being aware of its ability to influence the marketwide price by varying its individual output, selects its price and output accordingly. In principle, this large firm selects a price, lets its atomistic competitors sell all they can at that price, and then takes the "rest" for itself. The price it selects automatically determines both how much its small competitors will be able to sell and thus how much it gets for itself. (Given the inability of the small competitive firms to influence the marketwide price, they can only expand their volume up to the point where their rising per-unit costs collide with that price ceiling). By lowering the price, it can force them to restrict their production; by raising the price, it can let them expand. Its own large share generally rests on a cost advantage of some sort *vis-à-vis* these numerous smaller firms".

3. Decision of 2nd October 1967, WuW/E BKartA 1189. Affirmed by Berlin Court of Appeals Judgment of 18th February 1969, Kart V 34/67.

4. Decision of 31st May 1968.

5. Doubts whether these enterprises were competitors arose because they were linked with the respondent by licence agreements and certain marketing arrangements. The Berlin Court of Appeals found that Meto had a market share of 89%.

97. An oligopoly situation was presented in the *Petrol Price case*.[1] In this case the Federal Cartel Office opened proceedings under section 22 against 4 large oil companies (Esso, Shell, BP, and DEA, a subsidiary of Texaco) after it had been found that these companies had raised the retail prices of petrol on five occasions after the Suez crisis of June 1967, each time by 1 Pfennig, and retained the higher prices even after the transportation situation which the companies claimed to have necessitated the higher prices had considerably improved. The market shares of the 4 companies in petrol distribution were roughly: Esso 17%, Shell 14%, BP 11% and DEA 10%. In addition, ARAL, a company distributing petrol of a number of independent refineries, had roughly 25%. The rest was held by several smaller "brand" companies (e.g., AGIP) and by a larger number of independent distributors.

98. It was clear that since none of the 4 companies had individually a market share of more than 20%, market dominance could only be found on the basis of section 22(2). The finding of no substantial competition between these companies was based on the following considerations: in view of the high transparency of the market and the homogeneity of the product there was a particularly strong tendency to parallel conduct, the result being parallel price movements in the past and identical prices at present in the same area. In addition, the scarcity of supply reduced the intensity of competition. Further, quality competition could not be considered as significant in view of the fact that the companies exchanged large quantities of petrol among themselves and thus proved that there were no significant quality differences. Finally sales promotion (advertising) did not necessarily constitute competition as it can also be applied by a monopolist, whereas competition is characterized by the intention to increase sales at the expense of other sellers. Whether competition could be regarded as substantial depended on whether it performed its steering function. This was not the case because under conditions of substantial competition prices could not have been maintained at the high level after the cost situation of at least some suppliers had considerably improved.

99. As to competition between the group and outsiders the Federal Cartel Office found that ARAL, being merely a sales company, was no active competitor in relation to the 4 fully integrated members of the group but always followed their market policy. It was more likely therefore to consider ARAL as a member of the group but this question was left undecided for the time being. The smaller independent distributors, though they had increased their market shares over the years and were partly undercutting the prices of the large companies, did not provide substantial competition on the market as a whole. The large companies had always maintained higher prices for their brands and, as a result of their brand image, could continue to do so. Their policy after the Suez crisis had again shown that they could raise their prices without having to take into account the reactions of the small outsiders.

1.   BKA Activity Report 1967, pp. 41-42.

100. Obviously, one of the most difficult problems in this case was proving that there was no substantial competition between the members of the group. It is interesting to note that in addition to considerations of traditional market analysis (tendency to parallel behaviour, quasi-identity of quality and service, etc.) one, and perhaps the decisive, reason for this finding was that the practice which was under attack – the maintenance of higher prices after transportation costs, given as justification for these prices, had gone down – could only have been carried out under circumstances of no substantial competition on the market. Essentially, in this case, the existence of dominant market power was deduced from the lack of substantial competition on the market.

101. As the case was closed following a reduction of prices by the members of the group before a decision was rendered, it is uncertain whether the position taken by the Federal Cartel Office would have been confirmed by the courts.

102. In the *Netherlands,* a dominant position is defined in section 1 of the Economic Competition Act as "a *de facto* or legal relationship in trade or industry involving a predominant influence on a market for goods or services in the Netherlands". In the *Lijmar case*[1] it was held that about thirty manufacturers of cigars who had refused to supply a particular wholesaler under pressure from other wholesalers had a dominant position on the market for cigars in view of the fact that other sources of supply were not available. This case is somewhat similar to the German Petrol Price Case; it would clearly come under a definition as contained in section 22(2) of the German law.

103. In the *ECSC,* a market dominating position of enterprises is defined as one "which protects them from effective competition in a substantial part of the common market". In the case of the *Rheinische Braunkohlenbrikett-Verkaufs GmbH,*[2] the High Authority considered a group of sellers of brown coal as market dominating in view of the fact that this group was practically the only supplier in the common market. The smaller independent suppliers were unable to conduct an autonomous market policy.

104. In *Denmark,* although the law does not expressly speak of market dominance, essentially the same concept is used as in the laws discussed so far. The criterion of market power in the sense of the Monopolies and Restrictive Practices Control Act is that individual enterprises or combinations "exert or may exert a substantial influence on price, production, distribution or transport conditions, throughout the country or in local market areas". Such an influence was held by the Monopolies Control Authority to exist in a case involving two suppliers of electrical household equipment,[3] although the market share of each supplier did not exceed 20%. The Author-

---

1. (1961) N.S. 151.

2. *Official Journal* 1960 p. 1,089.

3. *Bulletin of the Monopolies Control Authority* 1957, p. 26; *Guide,* Denmark, Section 3, Case No. 3.

ity was, however, of the opinion that the trademarks used by these suppliers and their advertising distinguished their products from those of others to such a degree that these products were considered by the consumers as special articles. This finding includes elements of both the relevant product market and the determination of economic power in terms of substantial influence on price etc. on this market. It shows again what has already been observed earlier how closely related and in fact overlapping the two issues are.

105. In the other legislations the problem of determining market power in cases of the present type has not yet been dealt with in administrative or court decisions. *Spain* uses essentially the same definition as is contained in section 22 of the German law (section 2, para. 2). The case of the *Carbonell y Cia S.A.*[1] where it was found that the only processor of olices in a certain rural area had a dominant position was apparently a clear-cut case of a buying monopoly.

106. In *Switzerland,* the concept of market domination used in section 3 of the Cartel Act is not further defined. According to this provision (*a*) single enterprises, (*b*) enterprises which tacitly concert their conduct, (*c*) enterprises linked to one another by financial interests or by any other means, are regarded as organisations similar to a cartel when they dominate the market in certain goods or services or when they exert a determining influence upon it. There are no decisions that further elaborate this provision. However, the Swiss Cartel Commission has applied section 3 in two special inquiries under section 20.[2] In its report on the *Sanitary Industry*[3] the Commission found that the only two Swiss manufacturers of sanitary appliances – in spite of some competition from imports[4] – exerted a dominating influence on the market for ceramic sanitary appliances.[5] The Commission found that the price discussions between the two manufacturers either amounted to a cartel agreement under section 2 of the Cartel Act or were at least the basis of a tacitly concerted conduct of a "similar organisation" under section 3(b), since both enterprises had quoted identical prices.[6] Another restraint practised by a group of enterprises exerting a determining influence upon the market under section 3(b) was found in the "conscious co-operation" between the two manufacturers and the wholesalers organisation SGVSB to sell only to wholesalers approved by the latter organisation.[7]

1. Judgment of 11th November 1967 of the Court for the Protection of Competition.

2. Cf. Part III, para. 389.

3. Rapport sur la concurrence dans l'industrie sanitaire (Competitive conditions in the trade in sanitary appliances); *Publications de la Commission Suisse des Cartels,* fascicule 3, 1968, pp. 159-224.

4. *Ibid.* at p. 217.

5. *Ibid.* at p. 195.

6. *Ibid.* at p. 179.

7. *Ibid.* at p. 195.

107. The report of the Commission on its enquiry into the *Gasoline and Fuel Oil Market*[1] is the first case to illustrate that section 3(b) of the Swiss Cartel Act includes the typical oligopoly situation. The Commission found that the wholesale business in the gasoline and fuel oil market had the structure of a partial oligopoly and that the Swiss subsidiaries of the international oil firms BP, Esso and Shell with a combined market share of about 50% formed a closed oligopoly whereas the addition of 11 fully or partially integrated wholesalers and of the AVIA group resulted in a wider partial oligopoly with a share of about 80% of the market.[2]

108. The Commission explained that there are four types of possible conduct of an oligopoly:

a) unrestricted competition,

b) agreement to limit insider competition,

c) refraining from insider competition without the use of an agreement. This amounts to a tacit co-ordination of conduct which may also be called concerted action,

d) the oligopoly may use its market power by concertedly fighting existing or potential outsiders.[3]

The Commission observed that while a conduct described under (b) qualified the oligopolists as members of a cartel, the types of conduct listed under (c) and (d) qualify the oligopoly as "similar organisation" under section 3(b), if it has the necessary market influence.

109. Based on the findings that the oligopolists in the gasoline and fuel oil market did not engage in price competition aimed at larger market shares but competed only in "less dangerous" fields such as gifts and lotteries,[4] the Commission concluded that the partially and fully integrated wholesalers were subject to the provisions of the Cartel Act under section 3(b).[5]

110. The conclusions of the Swiss Cartel Commission invite a comparison with section 22 of the German Cartel Act. It seems to be easier for the Swiss authorities to conclude that an oligopoly is subject

---

1.   Rapport sur la concurrence sur le marché des carburants et combustibles (Competitive conditions in the market for liquid fuels); *Publications de la Commission Suisse des Cartesl,* fascicule 1/2 1968, pp. 17-109.

2.   *Ibid.* at p. 90.

3.   *Ibid.* at p. 70, 71.

4.   *Ibid.* at p. 89, 90, 92.

5.   "The oligopoly found in the wholesale stage of the gasoline and fuel oil market has the tendency – in certain sectors of competition (especially with regard to prices) – towards a parallel conduct which is not based on contracts, joint decisions or legally not enforceable agreements. It, therefore, consists of enterprises that dominate or significantly influence the market for certain goods or services and tacily co-ordinate at least part of their conduct (Section 3(b) of the Cartel Act). The partial oligopoly in the wholesale stage of the gasoline and fuel oil market is therefore subject to the provisions of the Cartel Act". *Ibid.* p. 100.

There was also an exchange of information – including prices – that according to the Commission "contributed to the parallel conduct of the oligopolists" (p. 92), but this aspect of the case was apparently not decisive.

to supervision than it is under German law, because the Swiss authorities concern themselves with criteria of parallel conduct which is the typical behaviour of oligopolists. In all probability, the Swiss authorities would only accept the argument advanced in the German petrol case that parallel pricing does not exclude the possibility of effective competition between oligopolists, if independent wholesalers existed whose competition had the effect of preventing parallel behaviour from resulting in an excessive price level.

111. In the *EEC,* the term "dominant position" as used in article 86 is not defined, but it appears to be generally accepted that the finding of such a dominant position has to be made in terms of lack of substantial competition along the lines just exposed.[1] Finally, in *Belgium* where the concept of "economic power" is used, defined as "power possessed by a natural person or body corporate acting alone or by a group of such persons or bodies corporate acting in concert to exert, within the territory of the Kingdom, through industrial, commercial, agricultural or financial activities, a dominating influence over supplies of merchandise or capital market or over the price or quality of specific merchandise or services", no further clarification by actual cases has been given. Again, as in the case of Switzerland, it is important to note that a group of enterprises can only be regarded as having a dominant position if there is an understanding between its members.

C. CONCLUSION

112. Market power under the "conduct" laws discussed in sections A and B of this chapter is determined essentially by two different methods. Three countries, Austria, Norway, and the United Kingdom use a formal criterion, a certain share in the supply of the product or service concerned, while the others require an assessment of the actual market position of the enterprise or enterprises concerned, an assessment which is made on the basis of such criteria as lack of substantial or effective competition, or substantial or dominant influence on the market as such or on particular market factors such as price, production etc. It is obvious that criteria of this kind must present much greater difficulties of administration than the formal criterion of a certain supply share, a fact which is clearly reflected in the foregoing analysis. Although there are still relatively few cases, especially as regards the "substantive" laws, and though these cases have to be seen in connection with the particular factual circumstances and the general context of the law under which they were tried, it appears nevertheless possible to draw at least some tentative conclusions.

1. Deringer, *WuW/EWG-Wettbewerbsrecht, EWG-Vertrag* Art. 86 Anm. 22; Braun, Gleiss, Hirsch, *Droit des ententes de la Communauté Economique Européenne,* Bruxelles/Paris, 1967, at pp. 173/174; van Gerven, *Principes du Droit des Ententes de la Communauté Economique Européenne,* Bruxelles, Emile Bruylant, 1966, at p. 91.

113. With a few exceptions the cases involved, in economic terms, monopolies, i.e. single enterprises or groups of enterprises acting in concert (collective monopolies).[1] The typical oligopoly situation where several enterprises not acting in concert (i.e. on an express or tacit understanding to exclude or otherwise restrain competition between one another) are regarded as a market dominating group because there is in fact, as a result of oligopolistic market conditions, no competition between them (only conscious parallelism in market behaviour), has presented itself apparently only in one case, the German Petrol Prices case. The Dutch Cigars case comes close to this, but since the suppliers there acted under pressure from wholesalers and perhaps a tacit understanding, this case was seemingly in reality an example of a collective monopoly in the form of a quasi-cartel. Another clear case of a collective monopoly is the ECSC case Rheinische Braunkohlebrikett-Verkaufs GmbH where the producers had formed a common selling agency. Examples of individual monopolies are found in the two German cases Meto and Sporting Goods Fair and seemingly also in the Danish Electrical Household Equipment case because there each of the two enterprises was considered as having individually a substantial influence within the meaning of section 6(2).

114. It seems therefore that all laws discussed can deal with "monopolies", i.e. powerful single enterprises or groups of enterprises acting in concert. The same cannot be said, however, with respect to oligopolistic behaviour. In most laws the question whether typical oligopoly situations, in which the individual oligopolists have adopted a policy of parallel business behaviour not resulting from an agreement or concerted action, are covered by the legal concepts of market power, is not dealt with in the law itself nor has it been decided by case law. Only in Germany, Spain, and in the United Kingdom is it expressly stated in the law that several enterprises between which no competition in fact exists and which meet the same requirements as a single dominating enterprise are considered, as a group, to be market dominating or to constitute a monopoly in the legal sense. On the other hand, some laws, such as Belgian and Swiss law, expressly require "concert" or "tacit understanding" between the members of the group. That this does not necessarily exclude the application of market power law to the typical oligopoly situation just described, is illustrated by the Gasoline and Fuel Oil Report of the Swiss Cartels Commission. The practical difficulties in applying the "substantive" laws to oligopolies have particularly been shown in the German petrol prices case, whereas in the United Kingdom, where the formal criterion of 33 1/3% market share is applied, less difficulty in this respect arises because in some cases oligopolists may reach the market share of 33 1/3% and thus become monopolists in the sense of the law.[2]

1. This would of course include "partial" monopolies in the sense defined in the footnote to para. 95.
2. This was the case, for example, with respect to petrol where BP/Shell Mex had a market share in petrol distribution of 45%.

115. There are great practical difficulties in determining market power on the basis of substantive criteria. This is especially so in oligopoly situations where findings have to be made as to whether effective or substantial competition exists and as to whether the same degree of competition exists between the oligopolists as a group and outsiders. This raises the question whether the formal criterion of a certain market share is not the preferable solution from a practical point of view. The reasons against such a solution are that market power in fact does not solely depend on the market share of the enterprise or enterprises involved and that it is impossible to fix objectively a certain market share which would cover all cases of probable market power. On the other hand, to make the law operational certain simplifications may become necessary. Therefore, although recognizing that the criterion of a fixed market share may bring within the law enterprises which have in reality no dominant market power or where the presence of such power may be doubtful and exclude others which may be in fact market dominating, such a criterion may still be preferable from a practical point of view as a workable compromise of public policy. This approach is facilitated by the fact that the finding of dominating market power within the meaning of the law does not automatically impose legal sanctions on the enterprises concerned, but only if, in addition, particular adverse effects (e.g. abuses) are found. The ultimate aim of the law is to cope effectively with such adverse effects, so that intervention against such effects could be justified even if the presence of actual market power in the particular case has not been clearly established by an extensive analysis of the competitive situation on the market. Such an analysis may sometimes be practically impossible or delay the taking of action to an extent that its effectiveness is endangered. Enterprises which do not reach the market share fixed by the law as a criterion for market power but which nevertheless are powerful, could possibly still be brought, if necessary, within the supervision of powerful enterprises. Norway gives the Price Directorate the power to require registration as dominant positions of enterprises which do not come under the formal criterion of a 25 % market share but which are nevertheless of such importance for their market that special supervision is necessary. In this connection it is interesting to note that the cases which arose so far under the "substantive" laws do not reveal a tendency to formalize the determination of market power by establishing certain "critical" market shares as was done for example in the United States in the enforcement of section 2 of the Sherman Act and, recently, of section 7 of the Clayton Act. [1]

116. The second way to facilitate the difficult proof of market power required under the "substantive" laws is to conclude the existence of market power if certain abusive practices are found. This conclusion appears to be justified where experience has shown that such abuses

---

1. Cf. e.g., United States v. Aluminum Co. of America, 148 F.2 d 416,424, where it was said that 90 % of supply "is enough to constitute a monopoly; it is doubtful whether 60 or 64 would be enough; and certainly 33 % is not". As to mergers the recent Merger Guidelines of the Department of Justice constitute an attempt to formalize the administration of the "substantial competition" clause of section 7 of the Clayton Act.

can only be practised by enterprises in possession of market power. As an example of such a conclusion the German petrol prices case was already mentioned. Similarly, in the Meto case the Federal Cartel Office argued that the tie-in clauses under attack could not be practised under conditions of effective competition. It is generally known that sometimes things can only be discovered and proved by their effects. Whether this can be done with respect to market power depends on whether it can be generally said that there are certain practices which could not be applied unless the enterprises concerned had dominant market power. It will have to be seen in the further course of this study, after the effects of market power have been analysed in detail, whether such practices can be identified. To the extent that such a relationship could be established, a separate finding of market power in cases of adverse effects – a separation which is required by the laws just analysed and reflected by the plan of this study – would in reality be no longer necessary. Some confirmation of this may be seen in the fact that two countries, Ireland and Sweden, do not require proof of the existence of market power as a precondition for taking action against adverse effects of the conduct of enterprises. It is not known exactly why these two countries, in contrast to most of the others, decided in favour of a general abuse supervision which is not expressly limited to practices of dominant enterprises, but one of the reasons may have been the idea that under conditions of effective competition no abusive practices can be applied and that, therefore, the existence of such practices *ipso facto* indicates that competition is not effective or, in other words, that market power exists.

117. As was indicated in the concluding remarks on the issue of market definition, foreign product alternatives (imports) are taken into account when the determination of market power is made. No case has been found where such alternatives, when they were at least of some significance, were expressly disregarded. The taking into account of imports may be particularly seen from several reports of the British Monopolies Commission [1] and from the Danish Omega and Tisso Watches case.[2] On the other hand, it may be concluded from the cases studied that, although imports are generally taken into account, market power may still exist, even in small countries with a relatively high share of foreign trade in the national product. It can therefore not be generally said that with the increasing opening of markets the issue of market power has lost its importance on the national level. Whether the removal of public trade barriers will reduce existing positions of market power in particular countries will essentially depend on whether increased imports in fact take place and present equivalent product alternatives to national buyers. For various reasons (e.g., difficulties of transportation, or private market allocation arrangements), this may not always be the case. Since the

1. See, e.g., Report on the Supply and Processing of Colour Film, 1966, London, HMSO Cmnd. 1, at para. 232; Report on the Supply of Man-Made Cellulosic Fibres, 1968, London, HMSO Cmnd. 130, at para. 147 and Tables 3 A and 3 B of Appendix 3.

2. Bulletin of the Monopolies Control Authority 1960, p. 113.

share of foreign trade in national product is normally higher in smaller countries than in larger ones, foreign product alternatives will usually be more significant for the determination of market power in smaller countries than in larger ones.

118. The purpose of Part I was to show how market power is determined under the various laws. It has been seen that the definition of the relevant market and the finding of market power, though logically being separate issues, are in fact closely correlated and, at least to some extent, overlapping. It also appears from the cases that criteria of absolute size have never been applied in order to determine the existence of market dominance or of market power in general. In fact, small enterprises can have dominant market power because they are the only sellers or buyers in their market or, if not monopolists, are not exposed to effective competition from outsiders. Nor does the existence of dominant market power depend on the size of the national territory. Although there may be a great number of suppliers on a national territory, including importers, dominant positions in local areas may still exist. For various reasons (e.g., transportation costs, consumer habits) no other important product alternatives may be available there. Thus the problem of market power is universal, and is not linked to a particular size of enterprise or national territory, just as the concept of the market itself. Part II will confirm this when market power in relation to mergers and monopolization is examined.

Part Two

CRITERIA FOR TAKING ACTION AGAINST THE DETRIMENTAL EFFECTS OF MARKET POWER

INTRODUCTION

119. Part II of this report will analyse the substantive law criteria for taking action against detrimental effects of market power under the restrictive business practice laws of OECD Members, the EEC and ECSC. For the sake of clarity, a distinction must be made in analysing this question between those laws which provide for action against the formation or existence of market power through mergers and monopolization ("structural" laws) and others which deal merely with specific undesirable consequences of market power without interfering with its existence ("conduct" laws). Under the "structural" laws, the existence or expected formation of market power is normally the undesirable effect against which action should be taken, at least to the extent to which this effect viewed in connection with other consequences is considered to run counter to the public interest. This is the reason why the question of market power under the "structural" laws is dealt with in this Part. Under the "conduct" laws, the detrimental effects to be considered are those of specific acts of business conduct of powerful enterprises. As the question of market power is merely a prerequisite for intervention against these effects, the problem of market power was discussed separately in Part I. Chapter I will analyse the criteria for intervention under the merger and monopolization provisions, while the criteria applicable under "conduct" laws are discussed in Chapter II.

Chapter I

CRITERIA UNDER THE "STRUCTURAL" LAWS

A. MERGERS

120. The effects of mergers on competition differ according to whether a horizontal, vertical or conglomerate relationship is involved. [1]

121. In the case of *horizontal mergers* the number of actual or potential competitors in a market is reduced. Depending on the general situation on the market, this reduction may have an adverse effect on competition. The words "may have" mean that it cannot generally be said that a reduction of the number of competitors must also reduce competition in a particular market. However, a reduction in the number of potential competitors takes place in cases of product extension mergers (an enterprise planning to extend its production into a related product field acquires another producer of this product instead of expanding internally, e.g. by constructing a new plant) [2] and in cases of market extension mergers (where an enterprise enters another geographic market by merging with an enterprise there instead of by internal expansion). [3]

122. The possible effects of *vertical mergers* (mergers between enterprises at different levels of production e.g. a producer of a finished product merges with a dominant supplier of a raw material) are:

> i) *on the producer's market,* the foreclosure of or discrimination against competitors (by keeping supplies of this material for himself or by charging competitors substantially higher prices competitors may be hampered and competition adversly affected); [4]

1. For definitions of the terms horizontal, vertical and conglomerate see *Glossary,* D 1-3.

2. An example is the case F.T.C. v. The Procter and Gamble Co. (see para. 156).

3. See, e.g., United States v. El Paso Natural Gas Co., 376 U.S. 651, 1964 Trade Cases para. 71,073.

4. This effect was e.g. considered in the British merger case Pressed Steel/ B.M.C. (see paras. 179-80).

ii) *on the market of the raw materials supplier,* the foreclosure of other suppliers from sales to the merging producer.[1] This foreclosure may put other competitors at a competitive disadvantage and discourage potential suppliers from entering the market.

123. The effects of *conglomerate mergers* on competition are much more difficult to define. Two possible types of such effects seem, however, to be clearly ascertainable:

i) by acquiring leading firms in other markets instead of entering the market through internal expansion (with or without prior acquisition of a small firm), potential competition in the form of a threat of entry of new competitors, which may be a significant limitation on the exercise of market power by the leading firms, may be reduced or excluded. This is essentially the situation in a horizontal product extension merger;

ii) by acquiring firms which are actual or potential suppliers to its customers (sellers), an enterprise may force reciprocal dealing arrangements on these customers and thereby exclude other suppliers from business with these customers. For example, if firm A buying a finished product from firms B and C acquires firm D which supplies a by-product used by B and C, A through D can refuse to continue its purchases from B and C unless they buy exclusively or preferentially from D, thus giving D a competitive advantage over its competitors unrelated to the merits of its product.[2]

124. For the application of the "structural" laws, insofar as they deal with mergers, to particular cases it has to be determined whether effects of these various kinds of mergers are likely to result or, in the case of an already consummated merger, have in fact resulted in market power and whether they are of such a degree as to come under the statutory criterion for intervention (e.g., where competition would be or is substantially lessened by the merger). If this is the case, it may suffice to consider the merger as undesirable and legally prohibited. Such a *per se* anti-market-power approach is essentially that of the United States. The other approach is to weigh the actual or expected adverse effects on competition with possible beneficial effects, especially economies. A distinction may be made between economies realized in a particular plant after a merger (single-plant economies) and economies realized by the consolidation of several plants (multi-plant economies). The first type can only be achieved if the plants are changed, e.g. one plant is closed down and the other is expanded. In this case cost savings may be obtained by economies of scale, a condition which is frequently, but not always, given. In the case of multi-plant economies, e.g. cost savings by centralizing administration and research in several plants, these economies may be

---

1.   See, e.g. United States v. E.I. du Pont de Nemours and Co., 353 U.S. 586, 1957 Trade Cases para. 68,723, (para. 144).

2.   See, e.g. F.T.C. v. Consolidated Foods (paras. 153-154).

accompanied by additional costs, e.g. higher co-ordination expenses, losses because of insufficient supervision etc. Only if the cost savings are higher than possible additional diseconomies, multi-plant economies can be said to have been achieved. Where such economies or other beneficial effects are accepted as justification for mergers, it may well be that a merger is regarded as legal in spite of the fact that its probable effect on competition is substantial and despite siggnificant market power or a market dominating position. To what extent such a balancing of effects is made under the merger laws outside the United States will be shown in the further course of this chapter.

125. The following analysis will first deal with the law of the United States where the great majority of cases have arisen so far. Thereafter the merger laws of Japan, Canada, and the ECSC will be discussed in that order.

126. In the *United States* mergers are prohibited by section 7 of the Clayton Act as amended by the Cellar-Kefauver Act of 1950 "where in any line of commerce in any section of the country *the effect of such acquisition may be substantially to lessen competition or to tend to create a monopoly*" (emphasis added). This prohibition has been applied in a large number of cases of horizontal mergers, but also to vertical and conglomerate mergers and to joint ventures. The following analysis will show how the substantially-to-lessen-competition clause of section 7 has been interpreted by the courts and is enforced by the administration.

a) *Horizontal Mergers*

127. Two important features can be identified in the courts' application of section 7 of the Clayton Act to horizontal mergers: (*i*) firstly, section 7 is construed as a prophylactic device to counteract the anticompetitive effects of mergers before they have actually arisen. In *United States v. Brown Shoe Co.* the Supreme Court said:

> "It is apparent that a keystone in the erection of a barrier to what Congress saw was the rising tide of economic concentration, was its provision of authority for arresting mergers at a time when the trend to a lessening of competition in a line of commerce was still in its incipiency. Congress saw the process of concentration in American business as a dynamic force; it sought to assure the Federal Trade Commission and the courts the power to brake this force at its outset and before it gathered momentum".[1]

(*ii*) secondly, beginning with the case *United States v. Philadelphia Bank,*[2] the Supreme Court has developed a test of presumptive illegality based on market shares and concentration ratios,[3] a test which has become the essential criterion to determine whether a merger is likely substantially to lessen competition.

---

1. 370 U.S. 294, 1962 Trade Cases para. 70,366 at p. 76,489.
2. 374 U.S. 321, 1963 Trade Cases para. 70,812.
3. I.e. the percentage of production or sales accounted for by some relatively small number of firms, generally the four largest or the eight largest.

128. In the *Brown Shoe case* the Supreme Court still proceeded with an elaborate economic enquiry before holding the merger illegal but laid already the groundwork for the market share analysis in the later cases. The enquiry in this case was based on the following general considerations:

"While providing no definite quantitative or qualitative tests by which enforcement agencies could gauge the effects of a given merger to determine whether it may 'substantially' lessen competition or tend toward monopoly, Congress indicated plainly that a merger had to be functionally viewed, in the context of its particular industry. That is, whether the consolidation was to take place in an industry that was fragmented rather than concentrated, that had seen a recent trend toward domination by a few leaders or had remained fairly consistent in its distribution of market shares among the participating companies, that had experienced easy access to markets by suppliers and easy access to suppliers by buyers or had witnessed foreclosure of business, that had witnessed the ready entry of new competition or the erection of barriers to prospective entrants, all were aspects, varying in importance with the merger under consideration, which would properly be taken into account".[1]

129. As to the horizontal aspect of the case the Court gave special attention to the fact that the combined share of Brown and Kinney sales of women's shoes exceeded 20% in 32 separate cities, that in 31 cities their share of children's shoe sales exceeded 20%, that in some cities the shares were much higher and that in 118 separate cities the share in the sale of one of the relevant lines of commerce exceeded 5%. Explaining the relevancy of market shares for the application of section 7 the Court said:

"The market share which companies may control by merging is one of the most important factors to be considered when determining the probable effects of the combination on effective competition in the relevant market. In an industry as fragmented as shoe retailing, the control of substantial shares of the trade in a city may have important effects on competition. If a merger achieving 5% control were now approved, we might be required to approve future merger efforts by Brown's competitors seeking similar market shares. The oligopoly Congress sought to avoid would then be furthered and it would be difficult to dissolve the combinations previously approved. Furthermore, in this fragmented industry, even if the combination controls but a small share of a particular market, the fact that this share is held by a large national chain can adversely affect competition".[2]

130. The Court also considered the general trend to more concentration in shoe retailing as an additional reason for its conclusion that the merger could be reasonably expected to substantially lessen competition.

1. 1962 Trade Cases para. 70,366 at pp. 76,490-491.
2. 1962 Trade Cases para. 70,366 at p. 76,500.

131. In *United States v. Philadelphia National Bank*, [1] involving a merger between the second and third largest banks in the relevant market, the Supreme Court first enunciated its test of presumptive illegality based on market shares and concentration ratios, explaining that:

> "this intense congressional concern with the trend toward concentration warrants dispensing, in certain cases, with elaborate proof of market structure, market behaviour or probable anti-competitive effects. Specifically, we think that a merger which produces a firm controlling an undue percentage share of the relevant market, and results in a significant increase in the concentration of firms in that market, is so inherently likely to lessen competition substantially that it must be enjoined in the absence of evidence clearly showing that the merger is not likely to have such anti-competitive effects". [2]

132. The Court justified this modification to the requirement of a precise economic analysis in each particular case on grounds of the practical needs of enforcement and pointed out that the question whether the effect of the merger "may be substantially to lessen competition" in the relevant market

> "requires not merely an appraisal of the immediate impact of the merger upon competition, but a prediction of its impact upon competitive conditions in the future: this is what is meant when it is said that the amended section 7 was intended to arrest anti-competitive tendencies in their 'incipiency'. See *Brown Shoe Co., supra* at 317, 322. Such a prediction is sound only if it is based upon a firm understanding of the structure of the relevant market; yet the relevant market data are complex and elusive... And unless businessmen can assess the legal consequences of a merger with some confidence, sound business planning is retarded... So also, we must be alert to the danger of subverting congressional intent by permitting a too broad economic investigation... And so in any case in which it is possible, without doing violence to the congressional objective in section 7, to simplify the test of illegality, the courts ought to do so in the interest of sound and practical judicial administration". [3]

133. Finally, the Court made it clear that the adverse effects of a merger on competition cannot be outweighed by beneficial economic effects of some other kind.

> "We are clear ... that a merger the effect of which 'may be substantially to lessen competition' is not saved because, on some ultimate reckoning of social or economic debits and credits, it may be deemed beneficial. A value choice of such magnitude is beyond the ordinary limits of judicial competence, and in any event has been made for us already by Congress

1. 374 U.S. 321, 1963 Trade Cases para. 70,812.
2. 1963 Trade Cases para. 70,812 at p. 78,268.
3. 1963 Trade Cases para. 70,812 at p. 78,267.

when it enacted the amended section 7. Congress determined to preserve our traditionally competitive economy. It therefore proscribed anti-competitive mergers, the benign and the malignant alike, fully aware we must assume, that some price might have to be paid". [1]

134. On the basis of the market share and concentration ratio test developed in the Philadelphia Bank case, mergers in which leading companies of a highly concentrated market participate are normally held to be illegal. Thus, in *United States v. Aluminum Co. of America* [2] the court took into account that Alcoa was the leading company in its market which produced 32.5% of bare aluminum conductor, 11.6% of insulated aluminum conductor, and 27% of aluminum conductor, and together with its three largest competitors controlled more than 76% of the market. In *United States v. Continental Can Co.* [3] the six leading producers controlled 70% of the relevant market in which the Continental Can Co. was the second largest producer with 21.9% and the Hazel-Atlas Glass Co., the acquired company, the sixth largest producer with 3.1%. This tendency of the Supreme Court, in markets with a relatively high aggregate share possessed by the largest companies, to consider small increases in the market share of one of the leading companies by merger as a violation of section 7 was then further developed in the Von's Grocery and Pabst Brewing cases.

135. In *United States v. Von's Grocery Co.* [4] the Court held that the merger between two grocery chains in the Los Angeles metropolitan area, Von's Grocery with approximately 4.7% of total retail sales and Shopping Bag with approximately 4.2%, was likely to substantially lessen competition in this area. It is important to note that no retailer in the area had a market share of more than 10%; the largest had about 8%, the 4 largest about 25%, the 8 largest about 41% and the 12 largest about 49%. But the Court found that there was a trend toward concentration, the aggregate share of the 8 largest companies in Los Angeles having risen from 33.7% in 1948 to 40.9% in 1958 and the number of independent retailers having dropped from 5,365 in 1950 to 3,590 in 1963, and that the merger would have substantially increased concentration. The Court did not consider it necessary to refute the defendant's argument that the merger between the two grocery chains was not prohibited by section 7 because "the Los Angeles grocery market was competitive before the merger, has been since, and may continue to be in the future". The Court citing *Philadelphia National Bank* emphasized that

"it is enough for us that Congress feared that a market marked by both a continuous decline in the number of small businesses and a large number of mergers, would slowly but inevitably gravitate from a market of many small competitors to one dominated by one or a few giants, and competition would thereby be destroyed. Congress passed the Celler-Kefauver Act to

1. 1963 Trade Cases para. 70,812 at p. 78,271.
2. 377 U.S. 271, 1964 Trade Cases para. 71,116.
3. 378 U.S. 441, 1964 Trade Cases para. 71,146.
4. 384 U.S. 270, 1966 Trade Cases para. 71,780.

prevent such a destruction of competition. Our cases since the passage of the Act have faithfully endeavoured to enforce this congressional command." [1]

136. In *United States v. Pabst Brewing Co.* [2] at issue was the merger between Pabst, the tenth largest brewer in the country and Blatz, the eighteenth. In 1957, the two companies had accounted for 23.9% of the beer sales in Wisconsin, 11.32% of the sales in the three-state area of Wisconsin, Illinois, and Michigan and 4.49% of the sales throughout the country. The Supreme Court pointed out that the merger took place in an industry marked by a steady trend toward economic concentration and concluded that the

"probable effect of the merger on competition in Wisconsin, the three-state area, and in the entire country was amply sufficient to show a violation of section 7 in each and all of these three areas". [3]

137. The Court explicitly held that it was not necessary to show that the trend toward concentration in the beer industry was due to mergers. It stated that

"Congress, in passing section 7 and in amending it with the Celler-Kefauver Anti-Merger amendment was concerned with arresting concentration in the American economy, whatever its cause, in its incipiency. It passed and amended section 7 on the premise that mergers do tend to accelerate concentration in an industry. Many believe that this assumption of Congress is wrong, and that the disappearance of small business with a correlative concentration of business in the hands of a few is bound to occur whether mergers are prohibited or not. But it is not for the courts to review the policy decision of Congress that mergers which may substantially lessen competition are forbidden, which in effect the courts would be doing should they now require proof of the congressional premise that mergers are a major cause of concentration. We hold that a trend toward concentration in an industry, whatever its causes, is a highly relevant factor in deciding how substantial the anti-competitive effect of a merger may be". [4]

138. The *Merger Guidelines of the Department of Justice*, [5] announced "solely as a statement of current Department policy", reflect the market share and concentration *ratio* test developed by the Supreme Court since the Philadelphia Bank decision. In these Guidelines the enforcement policy of the Department of Justice with respect to horizontal mergers is characterized as follows:

1. *Ibid.*, at p. 82,599.
2. 384 U.S. 546, 1966 Trade Cases para. 71,790.
3. *Ibid.*, at p. 82,661.
4. *Ibid.*, at p. 82,661.
5. ICCH – Trade Regulation Reporter para. 4,430. It should be noted that the guidelines may be amended from time to time to reflect changes in enforcement policy and that such changes may also precede the issuance of amended guidelines.

71

"In enforcing section 7 against horizontal mergers, the Department accords primary significance to the size of the market share held by both the acquiring and the acquired firms... The larger the market share held by the acquired firm, the more likely it is that the firm has been a substantial competitive influence in the market or that concentration in the market will be significantly increased. The larger the market share held by the acquiring firm, the more likely it is that an acquisition will move it toward, or further entrench it in, a position of dominance or of shared market power. Accordingly, the standards most often applied by the Department in determining whether to challenge horizontal mergers can be stated in terms of the sizes of the merging firms' market shares".[1]

139. Based on these considerations the Department of Justice will ordinarily challenge the following horizontal mergers: in a highly concentrated market, i.e., a market in which the shares of the four largest firms amount to approximately 75% or more, where the acquiring firm (i.e. the firm with the larger market share) and the acquired firm (i.e. the firm with the smaller market share) account for, approximately, the following percentages of the market:

Acquiring Firm	Acquired Firm
4 %	4 % or more
10 %	2 % or more
15 % or more	1 % or more

140. In less highly concentrated markets, i.e., markets in which the shares of the 4 largest firms amount to less than approximately 75%, the Department of Justice will normally challenge mergers between firms accounting for, approximately, the following percentages of the market:

Acquiring Firm	Acquired Firm
5 %	5 % or more
10 %	4 % or more
15 %	3 % or more
20 %	2 % or more
25 % or more	1 % or more

141. In markets with a trend toward concentration, i.e., when the aggregate market share of any grouping of the largest firms in the market, from the two largest to the eight largest, has increased by approximately 7% or more within 5-10 years prior to the merger, the Department of Justice will normally challenge any acquisition by any firm in such a grouping of any firm whose market share amounts to approximately 2% or more.

1. *Ibid.*, at No. 4.

142. In addition to these three situations the Guidelines state that a challenge by the Department of Justice can ordinarily be anticipated in the following two instances:

a) acquisition of a competitor which is a particularly "disturbing", "disruptive", or otherwise unusually competitive factor in the market; and

b) a merger involving a substantial firm and a firm which despite an insubstantial market share, possesses an unusual competitive potential or has an asset that confers an unusual competitive advantage (for example, the acquisition by a leading firm of a newcomer having a patent on a significantly improved product or production process).

143. The Guidelines also reflect the great hesitancy of the Courts to accept as justification economies alleged to be produced by the merger in question. The reasons why this justification will normally be rejected are stated in the Guidelines as follows:

i) the Department's adherence to the standards will usually result in no challenge being made to mergers of the kind most likely to involve companies operating significantly below the size necessary to achieve significant economies of scale;

ii) where substantial economies are potentially available to a firm, they can normally be realized through internal expansion; and

iii) there usually are severe difficulties in accurately establishing the existence and magnitude of economies claimed for a merger.

The Guidelines also restate the Failing Company Doctrine under which the acquisition of a firm with no reasonable prospect of remaining viable is considered by different standards. [1]

b) *Vertical Mergers*

144. The first big vertical merger case was *United States v. E.I. Du Pont de Nemours and Co.* [2] In this case the acquisition of 23% of the stock of General Motors by Du Pont was held by the Supreme Court to violate section 7 of the Clayton Act. The anti-competitive effects of this acquisition were seen in Du Pont's achievement of a commanding position as a supplier of automobile finishes and fabrics to General Motors which was considered to have been promoted by its stock interest and not gained solely on competitive merit. The Court found "that Du Pont purposely employed its stock to pry open the General Motors' market to entrench itself as the primary supplier of General Motors' requirements for automobile finishes and fabrics". [3] The Court thus considered the foreclosure of competitors of the acquiring company in supplying to the acquired company as the

1. *Ibid.*, at No. 9.
2. 353 U.S. 586, 1957 Trade Cases para. 68,723.
3. 1957 Trade Cases para. 68,723 at p. 72,927.

relevant anti-competitive effect, but did not develop any further criteria in terms of market shares for the appraisal of this effect in the particular case. The shares of Du Pont in the supply to General Motors in 1947 before the action was started were: finishes 68.4%, and fabrics 38.5%. General Motors being the leading purchaser of automobile finishes and fabrics, the effect of a foreclosure of competitors supplying such materials to General Motors was in any case substantial.

145. In *United States v. Brown Shoe Co.*[1] the Supreme Court described the possible anti-competitive effects of vertical mergers in the following general terms:

"The primary vice of a vertical merger or other arrangement tying a customer to a supplier is that, by foreclosing the competitors of either party from a segment of the market otherwise open to them, the arrangement may act as a 'clog on competition', Standard Oil Co. of California v. United States (1948-1949 Trade Cases p. 62, 432), 337 United States 293, 314 which 'deprive(s) ... rivals of a fair opportunity to compete'. H.R. Rep. No. 1191, 81st Cong., 1st Sess. 8. Every extended vertical arrangement by its very nature, for at least a time, denies to competitors of the suppliers the opportunity to compete for part or all of the trade of the customer-party to the vertical arrangement".[2]

146. In holding that the merger between Brown Shoe and Kinney injured competition by foreclosing other suppliers of shoes the Court took into account that Kinney was the largest independent chain of family shoe stores making about 1.2% of all national retail shoe sales by dollar volume, that Brown Shoe followed a policy of forcing its own shoes on its subsidiaries (as indicated by the fact that while Kinney bought no shoes from Brown prior to the merger, its purchases from Brown at the time of trial had reached about 7.9%), and there was a general trend toward vertical integration in the shoe industry.

147. In the recent case *United States v. Ford Motor Co.*[3] the District Court for the Eastern District of Michigan, Southern Division, held that Ford's acquisition from the Electric Autolite Co. of properties including spark plug and battery plants, the trademark "Autolite", and sales facilities violated section 7 of the Clayton Act because it foreclosed Ford as a possible spark plug competitor and as a potential customer of spark plug and battery manufacturers. As to batteries the Court reasoned that the acquired plant would supply most of Ford's battery needs, which were 6.2% of the market, and that it was likely that Ford would build more plants, thus excluding the remainder of its needs as targets of suppliers. The same conclusion was made with respect to spark plugs where Ford bought about 10% of total production. Although Ford had a long standing commitment with Champion, the biggest of the three large producers (General

---

1. 370 U.S. 294, 1962 Trade Cases para. 70,366.
2. 1962 Trade Cases para. 70,366 at p. 76,492.
3. 1968 Trade Cases para. 72,492.

Motors and Autolite being the other two), the Court regarded Ford as a potential customer of the smaller producers, because Ford was known to have been shopping for a private brand. The merger in the Court's view therefore destroyed the smaller plug firms' motive to work a change leading to deconcentration.

148. In the *Merger Guidelines of the Department of Justice* the jurisprudence of the courts with respect to vertical mergers is reflected by the Department's statement that significant anti-competitive consequences can be expected to occur "whenever a particular vertical acquisition, or series of acquisitions, by one or more of the firms in a supplying or purchasing market, tends significantly to raise barriers to entry in either market or to disadvantage existing non-integrated or partly integrated firms in either market in ways unrelated to economic efficiency".[1] Although this jurisprudence has not developed the same type of market share and concentration ratio test as in the case of horizontal mergers, the Department in its Guidelines attempted to frame its enforcement policy primarily in terms of the market shares of the merging firms and the conditions of entry which already exist in the relevant market, which may be the supplying firm's market or the purchasing firm's market or both.

149. In determining whether a vertical merger may significantly lessen existing or potential competition in the supplying firm's market the Department under its Merger Guidelines attaches primary significance to (*i*) the market share of the supplying firm; (*ii*) the market share of the purchasing firm or firms, and (*iii*) the conditions of entry in the purchasing firm's market. Accordingly, the Department will ordinarily challenge a merger or series of mergers between a supplying firm, accounting for approximately 10% or more of the sales in its market, and one or more purchasing firms, accounting *in toto* for approximately 6% or more of the total purchases in that market, unless it clearly appears that there are no significant barriers to entry into the business of the purchasing firm or firms.

150. As regards the anti-competitive effects on the purchasing firm's market the Department of Justice believes that adherence to the standard for the determination of anti-competitive effects on the supplying firm's market will result in challenges being made to most of the vertical mergers which may have adverse effects in the purchasing firm's market. In any case, however, where a product supplied by one of the merging firms is a significant feature or ingredient of the end product manufactured by the purchasing firm and its competitors, the Department of Justice will ordinarily challenge a merger or series of mergers between a supplying firm, accounting for approximately 20% or more of the sales in its market and a purchasing firm or firms accounting *in toto* for approximately 10% or more of the sales in the market in which it sells the product whose manufacture requires the supplying firm's product.

151. Finally, the Guidelines have named as the most common instances in which, apart from the market share tests, a challenge can

1. *Guidelines*, No. 11.

75

ordinarily be expected "acquisitions of suppliers or customers by major firms in an industry in which (i) there has been, or is developing, a significant trend toward vertical integration by merger such that the trend, if unchallenged, would probably raise barriers to entry or impose a competitive disadvantage on unintegrated or partly integrated firms, and (ii) it does not clearly appear that the particular acquisition will result in significant economies of production or distribution unrelated to advertising or other promotional economies".

c) Conglomerate Mergers

152. As was already noted, the main types of possible anti-competitive effects of conglomerate mergers are the danger of reciprocal buying and, where the merger involves a potential entrant, a reduction or exclusion of potential competition.

153. The first aspect was dealt with by the Supreme Court in *FTC v. Consolidated Foods Corporation.* [1] In this case Consolidated Foods, a large food wholesaler and retailer, had acquired Gentry Inc., a producer of dehydrated onion and garlic with about a 32% market share. The challenge of this merger by the FTC was based on the theory that since the products supplied by Gentry were mainly used by food processors which supplied a significant part of their production to Consolidated Foods in its capacity as food wholesaler and retailer, Consolidated using this purchasing power could force these firms to purchase their onion and garlic needs from Gentry rather than from Gentry's competitors. The Supreme Court held that the reciprocity made possible by the present merger was "one of the congeries of anti-competitive practices at which the antitrust laws are aimed. The practice results in an 'irrelevant and alien factor' ... intruding into the choice among competing products, creating at least 'a priority on the business at equal prices' ". [2]

154. It stated that "where, as here, the acquisition is of a company that commands a substantial share of a market, a finding of probability of reciprocal buying by the Commission, whose expertise the Congress trusts, should be honoured if there is substantial evidence to support it". [3] The Court concluded that the Commission's view that Gentry, as a result of the merger, could obtain sales that might otherwise go to its competitors and that thereby "the two-firm oligopoly structure of the industry is strengthened and solidified and new entry by others is discouraged" was supported by such evidence.

155. Under its *Merger Guidelines* the Department of Justice will ordinarily challenge any merger which creates "a significant danger of reciprocal buying". [4] Such a danger is normally considered to be present "whenever approximately 15% or more of the total purchase in a market in which one of the merging firms' ("the selling firm") sales are accounted for by firms which also make substantial sales

1. 380 U.S. 592, 1965 Trade Cases para. 71,432.
2. *Ibid.*, at p. 80,868.
3. *Ibid.*, at p. 80,871.
4. *Guidelines*, No. 19.

in markets where the other merging firm ("the buying firm") is both a substantial buyer and a more substantial buyer than all or most of the competitors of the selling firm". In addition, the Department will ordinarily challenge "(i) any merger undertaken for the purpose of facilitating the creation of reciprocal buying arrangements, and (ii) any merger creating the possibility of any substantial reciprocal buying where one (or both) of the merging firms has within the recent past, or the merged firm has after consummation of the merger, actually engaged in reciprocal buying, or attempted directly or indirectly to induce firms with which it deals to engage in reciprocal buying, in the product markets in which the possibility of reciprocal buying has been created".[1]

156. The potential entry aspect was dealt with by the Supreme Court in *FTC v. Procter and Gamble Co.*[2] In this case the acquisition of the Clorox Chemical Co., the largest manufacturer of household bleach with a market share of about 50%, by Procter and Gamble, the leading producer of soap, detergents, and cleansers and the country's largest advertiser was challenged by the FTC under section 7 of the Clayton Act.[3] The Supreme Court, regarding this acquisition as a "product extension merger" since household bleach was closely related to P and G's line of business, considered the anti-competitive effects of the merger under the following two aspects: (1) the increase of power of Clorox on its market as a result of its merger with a financially powerful giant and the deterrent effect of this increase on the other bleach producers and potential new entrants, (2) the diminution of potential competition as a result of P and G's disappearance as a probable new entrant by way of internal expansion or acquisition and expansion of a small firm. On the first aspect the Court agreed with the FTC that the substitution of a powerful giant (P and G) for a smaller, but already dominant, firm (Clorox) may substantially reduce the competitive structure of the household bleach industry by raising entry barriers and by dissuading smaller firms from aggressive competition. Special attention was given to P and G's much larger advertising budget and its ability to use its volume discounts to the advantage of Clorox products giving them a further advantage over competing products and making market entry of new firms more difficult. On the second aspect the Court was satisfied with the Commission's findings that P and G was the most likely new entrant into the liquid bleach market and that its existence at the edge of the industry exerted considerable influence on the market.

157. In its *Merger Guidelines* the Department of Justice has announced that it will ordinarily challenge any merger between one of the most likely entrants and

     i) any firm with approximately 25% or more of the market;

1. *Ibid.*
2. 386 U.S. 568, 1967 Trade Cases para. 72,061.
3. CCH Trade Reg. Rep. para. 16,673 (1963).

ii) one of the two largest firms in a market in which the shares of the two largest firms amount to approximately 50 % or more;

iii) one of the four largest firms in a market in which the shares of the eight largest firms amount to approximately 75 % or more, provided the merging firm's share of the market amounts to approximately 10 % or more; or

iv) one of the eight largest firms in a market in which the shares of these firms amount to approximately 75 % or more, provided either (*a*) the merging firm's share of the market is not insubstantial and there are not more than one or two likely entrants into the market, or (*b*) the merging firm is a rapidly growing firm. [1]

158. The likelihood of potential entry of a firm will be determined mainly by its "capability of entering on a competitively significant scale relative to the capability of other firms (i.e., the technological and financial resources available to it) " and its " economic incentive to enter (evidenced by, for example, the general attractiveness of the market in terms of risk and profit; or any special relationship of the firm to the market; of the firm's manifested interest in entry; or the natural expansion pattern of the firm; or the like) ".

d) *Joint Ventures* [2]

159. The basic rules for the appraisal of possible anti-competitive effects of joint ventures under section 7 of the Clayton Act were laid down by the Supreme Court in *United States v. Penn-Olin Chemical Co.* [3] The Penn-Olin Chemical Company was formed as a joint venture by two large chemical companies (Olin Mathieson and Pennsalt) to manufacture and sell sodium chlorate in the southeastern United States. The Supreme Court held that section 7 of the Clayton Act was also applicable to the formation of joint ventures and that such a formation may be considered to substantially lessen competition where there is a reasonable probability that either firm would have entered the market while the other remained a significant potential competitor. [4]

160. Penn-Olin was the only case of a joint venture to reach the Supreme Court, but a few other cases were settled by consent judg-

1. *Guidelines,* No. 18.

2. Since joint ventures normally involve both a horizontal aspect (potential competition between the parties to the joint venture) and a conglomerate aspect (entry to a new market), they are discussed here under a separate heading.

3. 378 U.S. 158, 1964 Trade Cases para. 71,147.

4. On demand, the district court held that the Government had not proved that, in the absence of the joint venture, independent entry by either Olin or Pennsalt was reasonably probable and again it dismissed the complaint. The Government again appealed to the Supreme Court urging that the district court applied an erroneous standard in determining that neither Pennsalt nor Olin was a likely entrant. The Government argued that the district court had accorded primary weight to " subjective " evidence of the firms' intention to enter the relevant market. The Government also asked the Supreme Court to decide whether, assuming that either Pennsalt or Olin would have entered the market, the elimination of the potential competition of the non-entering firm by the joint

ments or orders.[1] It is even more difficult here to derive from the cases general criteria in terms of market shares and concentration ratios than in the case of vertical and conglomerate mergers.

*

*   *

161. *Japan* uses essentially the same criterion for the appraisal of mergers as the United States ("... where the effect of a merger may be to substantially restrain competition in a particular field of trade",[2] but differs in its interpretation and application. Neither has it developed precise market share and concentration ratio standards as was done in the United States with respect to horizontal mergers, nor has it followed the American prophylactic approach of intervening against "incipient" concentration trends. This is clearly reflected by the few cases of FTC intervention so far.

162. In *Toho Co. Ltd. v. Fair Trade Commission*[3] it was held that an acquisition of two cinemas by way of lease, giving Toho 57.9% of audience capacity in all cinemas in the area considered to be the relevant market, substantially restrained competition. The Tokyo High Court, confirming the order of the FTC held that it was immaterial whether the substantial restraint of competition was reasonable or not, and that it was not necessary to prove particular conduct such as raising admission charges because such conduct was only one of many factors to determine whether competition was substantially restrained or not. Substantial restraint of competition meant that the situation appeared or at least was likely to appear in which competition itself was diminished so much that particular entrepreneurs or trade associations could control their market to some extent by fixing prices, quality or other conditions.

163. In 1957 the Fair Trade Commission ordered *Nippon Gakki Company* to dispose of the shares which it had acquired, in the name of a third company, in another company operating in the same market.[4] Nippon Gakki was the leading firm in the musical instruments field with the following market shares: 54% for pianos, 64% for organs, and 28% for harmonicas. The company in which it had acquired an approximate 25% share of the capital was the second largest firm in the field with market shares of 16%, 13% and 7% respectively. The Commission found that the acquisition tended substantially to restrain competition in the production and sale of musical

venture may have substantially lessened competition within the meaning of section 7. In a *per curiam* opinion, dated 11th December 1967, the Supreme Court affirmed the judgment of the district court by an equally divided court. 1967 Trade Cases para. 72,301.

　　1. See, e.g. United States v. Mobay Chemical Co., 1967 Trade Cases, para. 72,001; F.T.C. v. Phillips Petroleum Co., CCH Trade Reg. Rep., para. 17,640 (1966).

　　2. Section 15(1)(i) of the Antimonopoly Act. This criterion applies not only to mergers in the technical sense covered by section 15, but under section 16 also to the other forms of concentration stated there.

　　3. *Guide,* Japan, Sec. 3.1, Case No. 1.

　　4. *Guide,* Japan, Sec. 3.0, Case No. 6.

instruments and ordered the leading firm to dispose of a part of the shares it had acquired.

164. A few cases of approved mergers may further illustrate the interpretation of the substantial-restraint-of-competition criterion.

165. The merger of the *Tshikawajima Heavy Industries Co.* and the *Harima Shipbuilding Co.* was approved because of the existence of strong rivals and for other reasons. The combined market share of 10.12 % in ship construction still ranked second behind the 16.04 % market share of the largest firm. Still more important was the merger between the three Mitsubishi Heavy Industry companies with its strong position in shipbuilding and with a dominant share in the production of machines for making paper pulp. The merger was allowed because of the existence of strong rivals and powerful buyers and for other reasons.

166. In the case of the merger between *Nippon-Kana-ami Co.* and *Kyoto Kana-ami Kogyo Co.* which had a combined market share of 90 % for wire-netting used for paper-making, the FTC held that no substantial restraint of competition would result because the latter company had been substantially under the control of the former and was not regarded as an independent competitor and the buyers of the two companies were mainly large paper manufacturing enterprises, while the two companies themselves were relatively small in size. [1]

167. In *Canada,* the criterion for judging the legality of mergers is whether, as a result of the merger in question, competition "is or is likely to be lessened to the detriment or against the interest of the public, whether consumers, producers or others". [2] Two cases of mergers have been adjudicated under this criterion so far. In *Regina v. Canadian Breweries Ltd.,* [3] the defendant company had acquired, by a series of mergers, 60.9 % of beer sales in Ontario and 48 % in the whole of Canada. The Supreme Court of Ontario acquitted the accused, largely on its finding of fact that the price of beer in Ontario had always been fixed, throughout the whole period in question, by the provincial Liquor Control Board. A considerable control over sale and prices in other provinces was likewise exercised by the respective provincial board or commission. Such government control meant, in effect, that price competition between breweries was eliminated. Apart from matters affected by government control the court found that there was no restraint of competition.

168. In *Regina v. British Columbia Sugar Refining Co.* [4] the defendant company had a complete sugar monopoly in British Columbia, Alberta and the western part of Saskatchewan. By acquiring the Manitoba Sugar Co. its share of the market in eastern Saskatchewan was slightly increased and its share of the Manitoba market was greatly increased. However, eastern refineries were still able to sell in Mani-

---

1. Mergers and Cartels in Japan, Japan Industry Series, *Trade Bulletin Corporation,* at pp. 8 and 13.
2. Section 2(e) of the Combines Investigation Act.
3. 1960, 126 C.C.C. 133, *Guide,* Canada, Sec. 3.1, Case No. 2.
4. 32 WWR (New Series) 577, *Guide,* Canada, Sec. 3.1, Case No. 3.

toba and eastern Saskatchewan. The trial Court of Manitoba rejected the Government's action finding i.a. that "the price-fixing procedure, and indeed the whole method of operation of the accused, had come into existence long before the merger complained of and, therefore, cannot in any way be attributed to the merger. Nor has the prosecution satisfied me that there has been any real change since the merger".[1] The Court also emphasized that "preventing or lessening competition is not enough. The Crown must go further with its proof and show the activities complained of (had) operated or (are) likely to operate to the detriment or against the interest of the public...".[2]

169. The two cases just described clearly express a tendency of the courts to interpret the merger criterion of section 2(e) of the Combines Investigation Act rather narrowly, a tendency which may be partly explained by the criminal law character of the procedure and sanctions under this provision.[3] However, the Director of Investigation and Research, in his informal consultations with representatives of enterprises participating in proposed mergers, has indicated that the law on this point requires clarification either by the Supreme Court of Canada or by the legislator.[4] He does not therefore necessarily follow the "virtual-monopoly test" applied in the breweries and sugar cases. Some indications of the Director's attitude toward mergers may be derived from the reasons that have led to the discontinuance of inquiries into recent merger cases.

170. In the *Electric Signs Case*,[5] a merger between two manufacturers of electrically illuminated advertising signs created a firm accounting for something over 50% of the market. The Director found that market entry was relatively easy, that the source of the most disturbing price reductions appeared to be the medium-sized firms, one of which had doubled its sales volume within a relatively short period of time, and that there was "no indication that the dominant position of the acquiring firm had been used in a manner detrimental to advertisers or competing sign manufacturers".[6]

171. A similar case involved a series of mergers in the field of *food distribution*[7] whereby a company accounting for approximately 50% of the total wholesale and retail food sales in the market area was created while the rest of the market was shared by a number of relatively small companies. It was found that "the control already exercised by the company over retail outlets in the particular area presents an important barrier to the entry of new wholesalers and the dominance of the firm in the retail food distribution market undoubtedly makes retailers reluctant to engage in price competition

1. *Ibid.*, at p. 606.
2. *Ibid.*, at p. 585.
3. For details see paras. 323 and 324 infra.
4. Cf. Report of the Director of Investigation and Research for the Year Ended March 31, 1966, at pp. 19 and 21.
5. *Ibid.*, at pp. 39, 40.
6. *Ibid.*, at p. 41.
7. Report of the Director of Investigation and Research for the Year Ended March 31, 1967, at p. 37.

for fear of retaliation ". Considering the possibility of applying to the courts for an order [1] prohibiting any further acquisitions by the dominant firm in the relevant market, the Director concluded that " substantial evidence of monopolistic misbehaviour and of likelihood of further acquisitions" necessary to persuade a court to make an order of prohibition was not available and therefore discontinued the inquiry.

172. What could already be observed in the analysis of Japanese law may also be said with respect to Canada: the threshold where competition may be held to be lessened substantially is definitely higher and the evidence required greater than in the United States. Nothing further may be said generally except that the Director for Investigation and Research in assessing the effects of particular mergers takes into account all relevant factors, such as market structure and behaviour, government regulation of the particular industry, history of growth of the acquired firm, the probable effects of the merger on competition and market entry and the likelihood of increased efficiency as a result of the merger. [2]

---

1. Such an order is possible under section 31(2) of the Combines Investigation Act. The possibility of indictment under section 33 has not been discussed in the report.

2. See the following list of relevant questions stated by the Director for Investigation and Research in his Report for the Year Ended 31st March 1966, p. 19:

"1. Is there a sensibly defined product for which there are no close substitutes?

2. Is there evidence that a substantial market (even though this may be regional) is likely to be affected by the merger and is capable of fairly unambiguous definition?

3. In the absence of competition among domestic suppliers, is there evidence in the form of a substantial tariff or statistics showing that only a small proportion of the market is supplied by imports, that foreign suppliers cannot be looked to, to protect the public?

4. Is there reasonable assurance that there is no significant government regulation?

5. Is there evidence that existing concentration ratios are high or that there is a large size-differential between the acquiring company and its rivals?

6. Is there evidence that the barriers to entry in the industry are high or that they will be raised by the merger or that new firms have not in fact entered the industry for some significant period of time?

7. Is there evidence that competition remaining in the market is likely to be ineffective?

8. Does the acquiring firm have a history of growth by merger or a history of coercive or predatory action or any other anti-competitive behaviour?

9. Is there any evidence of intent to reduce competition or to dominate the industry?

10. Is there any likelihood that there will be foreclosure of an important market or source of supply to firms unconnected with the acquiring company?

11. To what extent is there evidence of a real possibility of increased efficiency via economies of scale or the transfer of assets from incapable into capable hands?

12. Is there direct evidence of detriment such as excessive profits or price enhancement following the merger?"

173. In the *United Kingdom* section 6 of the Monopolies and Mergers Act 1965 authorizes the Board of Trade — in accordance with the recommendations of the Monopolies Commission — to prohibit a merger where

  a) the combined market share of the participating enterprises would exceed one-third, or where the value of the assets taken over exceed five million pounds and

  b) the merger "operates or may be expected to operate against the public interest". So far, two mergers have been prohibited under this provision. [1]

174. In the *Fisheries case* [2] the Monopolies Commission considered the prospective influence of the combined firm in the cod fish market:

"In this respect there is no doubt that the combined company would be in a very strong position. They would own 117 distant water trawlers of the total British distant water fleet of 196. In 1964 their landings of cod at Hull and Grimsby accounted for 54% of total Humber cod landings. In other words they would, immediately following the merger, be a great deal larger than any other company operating in this field. More than half the supplies would be under their control and, if they chose, they would be able to take advantage of their dominant position. This does not mean that they would always be free to set a price for distant water cod to suit themselves; the quantities landed by other trawler owners would still be substantial, there would still be some supplies of cod from other ports and some price limitation would be imposed by the relative prices of other varieties of fish, of imports and of competing foods. But within this framework there would remain substantial scope for varying the price of cod". [3]

175. The Commission accepted the assertion of the participants that the present management would not abuse its dominant position. But it was concerned

"that a future management of the combined company might well seek to increase profits by using their dominant position in the market to secure higher prices. It seems likely that prices to the consumer will in any case tend to rise, particularly if supplies become more difficult, but we regard it as undesirable that the extent of such rise could be determined by one company instead of by the force of competition in the market". [4]

1. In July 1968 the Monopolies Commission, by a 6 to 4 majority, found that the merger between *Barclays Bank, Lloyds Bank, and Martins Bank* was against the public interest. See: The Monopolies Commission: Barclays Bank Ltd., Lloyds Bank Ltd. and Martins Bank Ltd., a report on the proposed merger, HMSO London 1968, Cmnd. 319. Since this case mainly involves special questions of banking, it is not discussed in this study.

2. The Monopolies Commission; Ross Group Limited and Associated Fisheries Limited, a report on the proposed merger, 1966, London, HMSO, Cmnd. 42.

3. *Ibid.*, at para. 119.

4. *Ibid.*, at para. 125.

176. The Commission then turned to the question of possible benefits to be derived from the merger. It was sceptical on any considerable rationalization improvements in trawling or in distribution as a result of the merger. But even assuming that the expected amounts of savings – which the Commission considered as unrealistic – could be secured these benefits would be negligible if they were to be passed on to the consumer and, in view of the present financial strength and profitability, would not put them in a significantly stronger financial position than the two companies separately would be in. The Commission finally evaluated the probable effects of the merger on the fish industry as a whole:

> " As regards the strengthening of the industry as a whole, the merger would contribute nothing to the solution of the problem of fragmentation. It would produce a situation in which the industry would contain one very large company, the remainder still being fragmented into many small enterprises, which could not offer effective competition ... The benefits of the competition now existing between two large companies would be lost and for this reason we think it unlikely that the merger would significantly accelerate the rate at which new methods are being introduced. Two companies of the size of Ross Group and Associated Fisheries ought individually to achieve improvements in efficiency, and it is our view that the spur of competition between them would be more effective in bringing this about ... In short, we think that the merger would not contribute significantly to increased efficiency in the industry, and would not materially improve the chances of creating an industry that would be viable, in the sense of being able to stand on its own and attract all the capital it needs without reliance on Government subsidies ". [1]

177. Stating that a number of other remedies would not effectively prevent the mischief expected as result of the merger the Monopolies Commission recommended the prohibition of the merger.

178. The second case was the proposed merger between *United Drapery Stores and Montague Burton*, [2] two retail chain stores for men's clothing with a combined turnover of £180 million in more than 1,700 retail stores. The Commission estimated the merger's share in the supply of men's suits at 35% and the share of low-priced men's suits at 45%. It expected from the merger a substantial weakening of competition at the retail level and an increase in the prices of the lower-priced men's suits, the sale of which had not been very profitable before. The argument of Montague Burton that it had no other choice but the merger because of its need for good management and for an improvement in productivity was rejected by the Commission which observed that this enterprise was not less successful than United Drapery Stores and that any existing management problems could be solved in other ways.

1.   *Ibid.,* at para. 142.

2.   The Monopolies Commission: United Drapery Stores Ltd., and Montague Burton Ltd., A report on the proposed merger, 1967, London, HMSO, Cmnd. 3397.

179. In the merger case between *The British Motor Corp. and the Pressed Steel Company* [1] B.M.C., with a market share of 35.8%, the largest producer of automobiles in the United Kingdom, had acquired Pressed Steel, with assets of approximately £55 million gross and £33 million net of liabilities, the largest independent motor car body and body tool manufacturer in the world. Pressed Steel produced bodies for about 40% of all passenger cars manufactured in Britain as well as bodies for commercial vehicles. The motor industry accounts for over 90% of Pressed Steel's turnover. In regard to its motor industry business Pressed Steel depended on B.M.C. for approximately 40% of its business by value and for about 61% in terms of body units. B.M.C. purchased roughly a third of its car body requirements from Pressed Steel. Three other automobiles producers, Rootes, Rover and Jaguar, were almost entirely dependent on Pressed Steel for their car bodies.

180. The Monopolies Commission found that a probable result of the merger would be some economic advantages of larger scale, integrated production and increased efficiency in the export of car bodies. [2] The main element, however, of the Commission's finding that the merger was not against the public interest, was the consideration that because of the trend toward vertical integration in the automobile industry the possibility could not be excluded that the two principal customers of Pressed Steel, B.M.C. and Rootes, might themselves start to manufacture car bodies, which account for 35-40% of the value of the finished car. Compared with an acquisition of Pressed Steel by Rootes in which Chrysler had a financial interest, the merger with the British-owned B.M.C. which could be expected to show "more consideration for the needs of Pressed Steel's existing customers than a foreign principal would necessarily feel obliged to do", was considered a more desirable solution. [3] It was also taken into account that the acquisition by a foreign firm might compel B.M.C. to set up additional manufacturing capacity of its own, a development which the Commission criticized as a wasteful duplication of national resources. [4] In view of the assurances given by the parties to the merger that they intended to supply B.M.C.'s competitors as in the past and in the event of a shortage of materials, to make allocations to all customers on a *pro rata* basis in accordance with the practice followed on previous occasions, the Commission saw no danger for the other customers of Pressed Steel resulting from the merger. At the invitation of the Commission B.M.C. and Pressed Steel have put these undertakings in more specific terms. [5]

181. In the case of the merger between *Guest, Keen and Nettlefolds Ltd. (GKN)* and *Birfield Ltd.,* [6] bringing together a major steel concern

1. The Monopolies Commission; The British Motor Corporation Ltd., and the Pressed Steel Company Ltd., A report on the merger, 1966, London, HMSO.
2. *Ibid.,* at paras. 51-53.
3. *Ibid.,* at para. 54.
4. *Ibid.,* at para. 57.
5. *Ibid.,* at paras. 60, 61.
6. The Monopolies Commission Guest, Keen and Nettlefolds Ltd., and Birfield Ltd., A report on the merger, 1967, London, HMSO, Cmnd. 3186.

and a producer of component parts for the transmission system of automobiles, a major aspect was that the joint company became virtually the sole manufacturer in the United Kingdom of propeller shafts and of constant velocity joints. Before the merger there had been increasing competition between the two firms in the field of propeller shafts while Birfield had a monopoly in constant velocity joints. They were, however, confronted with the considerable market power of the six big automobile firms which buy the major part of the products concerned. The Commission concluded from this situation

> "that if the company seeks to improve the margin on the sale of propeller shafts for initial equipment it must do so by reducing costs rather than raising prices. We are satisfied that the bargaining power of the buyers in this case is sufficient to ensure that the merged company will always be under the strongest pressure to keep its costs and its profit margins as low as possible. We do not necessarily accept all that has been said by G.K.N. in this connection about the effects of potential competition. We do not think that any large motor manufacturer would contemplate relying upon imported propeller shafts. Motor manufacturers are, of course, technically competent to make their own propeller shafts or they might (as they did in 1959) encourage some other engineering concern to undertake production of them in competition with the existing monopoly, but we do not think it likely that they would adopt either of these courses unless convinced that the prices they were being charged were very much higher than they ought to be or that the monopolist was seriously at fault in some other respect. We accept, nevertheless, that this ultimate ability of manufacturers to enter the market reinforces the bargaining power of the buyers to which we have referred above ...

> We note that all the customers think Birfield's prices for propeller shafts, when it had the field to itself before 1960, were reasonable and that, particularly in view of G.K.N.'s co-operative attitude in matters of price negotiation and access to plant and drawings, they are not worried by the possibility that the merged company might abuse its position in this respect. For these reasons we see no likely detriment to the public interest arising from this merger as regards the costs of propeller shafts and constant velocity joints ... ". [1]

182. Considering the question whether the new firm would abuse its monopoly in the sale of replacement parts where the ultimate customer is not the motor manufacturer but the owner of the vehicle, the Commission accepted the argument of G.K.N. that the interest of both the components and the motor manufacturers in deterring manufacturers of "spurious" components from entering the market would provide a sufficient check. [2] In viewing the merger as a whole the Commission pointed to the possibility that Birfield might not have

1. *Ibid.,* at paras. 131-133.
2. *Ibid.,* at paras. 134-136.

had a chance to continue on its own in the long run anyway and that a possible take-over by a foreign components producer or a domestic motor concern (both of which had been rumoured) would provide no obvious advantages over the merger with G.K.N.

183. Another merger approved by the Monopolies Commission involved two major producers of *mineral insulated cable*.[1] Before the merger, the market had been divided about equally between the two participants whereas the merged firm, with a market share in excess of 90%, enjoyed an almost complete monopoly. In addition, one of the participants held a dominant position in the cables industry as a whole. Though competition from substitutes and potential entrants, in the Commission's view, placed some check on the market power of the merged firm, the Commission saw a danger that the new enterprise might ask excessive prices, might use its monopoly in the supply of mineral insulated cables in order to gain advantages in the sale of other types of electric cables, and might, based on its large financial resources, choose a price policy designed to drive the remaining small competitor out of the market.[2] In order to safeguard against such a development the Monopolies Commission sought and was given a number of assurances as to the future market conduct of the merging firm (B.I.C.C.).[3] On the other hand, the Monopolies Commission expected a substantial improvement in the export of mineral insulated cables as a result of the merger, because it rendered unnecessary the former duplication of overseas sales organisations. In view of these advantages and of the assurances given by the parties to the merger, the Commission concluded that the merger was not to be expected to operate against the public interest.[4]

184. Mergers of newpapers are governed by the special provisions of section 8 of the Monopolies and Mergers Act 1965. The transfer of a newspaper or of newspaper assets to a newspaper proprietor whose newspapers have an average circulation per day of publication amounting, with that of the newspaper concerned, to five hundred thousand or more copies is unlawful unless the Board of Trade gives express consent after having received a report on the matter from the Monopolies Commission on

"whether or not the transfer may be expected to operate against the public interest, taking into account all matters which

1. Monopolies Commission: British Insulated Callender's Cables Ltd., and Pyrotenax Ltd., A report on the proposed merger, 1967, London, HMSO, Cmnd. 490.

2. *Ibid.*, at paras 149-156.

3. *Ibid.*, Appendix 5. BICC gave, i.a., the assurance that "the cost reductions achieved as a result of the merger will be used to promote the use of and expand the sale of mineral insulated cable and to reduce net selling prices to customers (or to avoid increases that would otherwise have been necessary)", "BICC will continue to supply other cable makers with mineral insulated cable, and will do so at prices and on terms, and with service and continuity of supply, which will make it commercially practicable for them to participate in sales of mineral insulated cable" and "if at any time the Board of Trade should so request, BICC will grant licences under any patents relating to mineral insulated cable, including accessories, on reasonable terms".

4. *Ibid.*, at paras. 160-162.

appear in the particular circumstances to be relevant and having regard (amongst other things) to the need for accurate presentation of news and free expression of opinion ".

Consent may be given without a report in the case of a transfer of small newspapers or in some circumstances of uneconomic newspapers [proviso to section 8(1) of the 1965 Act].

185. Since the application of section 8 involves for the most part questions outside the scope of this study, no further analysis can be given.[1]

186. In the *ECSC* there is a general prohibition of all mergers of a certain size[2] unless they are authorized by the High Authority (article 66, section 1, ECSC-Treaty). The conditions under which such authorization is granted are that the High Authority finds

"... that the transactions in question will not give to the interested persons or enterprises, as concerns the products subject to its jurisdiction, the power:

— to determine prices, to control or restrict production or distribution, or to prevent the maintenance of effective competition in a substantial part of the market for such products; or

— to evade the rules of competition as they result from the execution of this Treaty, in particular by establishing an artificially privileged position involving a substantial advantage in access to supplies or markets " [article 66, section 1(1)].

187. The Treaty continues:

"in arriving at its decision and acting in accordance with the principle of non-discrimination set forth in sub-paragraph b) of article 4, the High Authority shall take account of the size of enterprises of the same kind existing in the Community, as far as it finds this justified to avoid or correct the disadvantages resulting from an inequality in the conditions of competition ".

188. The Court of the European Communities[3] has interpreted the term "power to determine prices" in its application to cartels[4] as well as to mergers by referring to the purpose of the rules on competition established by the Treaty:

"The technological and economic development leading to greater and greater economic units and every day reinforcing the oligopolistic character of the coal and steel market has not been

1. For further details see the two reports of the Monopolies Commission on the Mergers Times/Sunday Times and Thomson Newspapers/Crusha.

2. The requirements are stated in the Decision No. 25/67 *Official Journal* No. 154 of 7th July 1967.

3. Decision No. 13/60 of 18th May 1962, Collection of the Decisions of the Court of the European Communities, German edition, Vol. VIII, pp. 183-237'

4. Cf. Art. 65 para. 2c ECSC–Treaty according to which one of the requirements of authorization of a *cartel* is that the High Authority finds that the agreement "is not capable of giving the interested enterprises the power to determine prices, or to control or limit the production or selling of a substantial part of the products in question within the common market, or of protecting them from effective competition by other enterprises within the common market ".

ignored by the crafters of the ECSC-Treaty; instead, the provisions of article 65, para. 2 and 66, para. 2 justify the conclusion that they did not intend to oppose this development, provided that it serves the purposes of the Treaty and does not eliminate the minimum of competition that is necessary to satisfy the fundamental requirements of article 2, namely 'progressively to establish the conditions which by themselves safeguard the most economic apportionment of the production at the highest standard of efficiency' and to 'safeguard, that there will be no interruption in employment and to avoid heavy and lasting disturbances in the economies of the Member states'". [1]

"... nothing justifies the argument that the Treaty intended to prohibit the large production and sales units typical for the coal and steel market or at least to object to their formation. It would be closing one's eyes to reality and denying the necessities of technical progress to attempt the restauration of an atomistic market in this realm, which is quite unthinkable for the products in question".

189. Turning to the case at bar concerning the authorization under article 65, para. 2 of a common sales pool for the entire coal production of the Ruhr area, the Court continued:

"At the present stage the problem is to decide from which quantity upward the supply controlled by a cartel constitutes so substantial a part of the respective products in the common market that it renders competition in that market incomplete to an extent that impairs the aims of the Treaty". [2]

190. Referring to the duty of the High Authority "to avoid or correct the disadvantages resulting from an inequality in the conditions of competition" as provided in article 66, para. 2, the Court went on to explain that the relative size of the competing units in the market is more significant than the absolute volume of supply of a single organisation. The Court concluded from the fact that the sales pool in question would control twice the production of the next largest competitor (Charbonnages de France), that there was a "discrepancy" in the size of the pool and the other existing organisations, which justified the conclusion that the cartel controlled a substantial part of the products in the common market. [3]

191. The High Authority has interpreted this decision of the Court as approval of its policy of authorizing mergers even if they resulted in quite substantial market shares and in a further strengthening of the oligopolistic market structure but provided these shares were not out of proportion to the market shares of already existing firms. Thus it has stated its conviction that the comparatively equal size of the iron producing firms has kept the concentration movement in this industry

1. *Op. cit.,* at pp. 226/227.
2. *Ibid.,* at p. 231.
3. *Ibid.,* at p. 233.

within the limits of article 66.[1] The underlying philosophy is that a further concentration of the already oligopolistic market "is not equivalent to a respective lessening of competition. On the contrary, a smaller number of stronger competitors may even result in intensified competition".[2] This view is reflected especially in the more recent decisions of the High Authority.

192. In the merger case of *August-Thyssen-Hütte AG* and the *Phoenix-Rheinrohr AG*,[3] authorized by the High Authority under certain conditions, the two merging enterprises controlled 10% of the raw steel production and 7.5%[4] of rolled products within the Community. The High Authority found that the combined market shares resulting from the merger were "in no instance a danger to competition, because there is always a large number of competitors controlling shares that constitute a counterweight sufficient for the maintenance of competition".[5] The High Authority furthermore found the following requirements satisfied to a degree sufficient for an authorization of the merger:

> *a)* independence of the firms operating in the market
>
> *b)* the incentive for independent action must not disappear by a knowledge of mutual market reaction
>
> *c)* single enterprises or a group of enterprises must not be in a position to evade the application of the Treaty provisions on competition.[6]

193. The conditions for authorization were the following:

> *a)* an existing long-term supply contract with a firm belonging to a competing group had to be modified as to term of notice and as to volume
>
> *b)* interlocking personal relationships between the new firm and other firms in the market were prohibited.[7]

194. Another important merger was the *Hoesch/Dortmund-Hörder Hütten-union/Hoogovens*[8] by which the combined firms became the second largest producer of iron and raw steel in the Community with market shares of 9.3 and 9.9% respectively. More specifically, the two firms became the largest producer of steel piles with a production share of about one-third. The emerging firm also held the first place in the production of hot rolled strip steel and a second place in the production of steel sheet. The High Authority held that

1. Die Politik der Hohen Behörde bei Kartellen und Zusammenschlüssen (The Policy of the High Authority on cartels and concentration) *Bulletin of the ECSC*, cited in Handbuch der Montanunion, B 71, at p. 413.

2. *Ibid.*, at p. 411.

3. Haute Autorité: 12e Rapport Général sur l'activité de la Communauté (1er février 1963 – 31 janvier 1964) No. 240.

4. *Ibid.*, Table p. 212.

5. Die Politik der Hohen Behörde bei Kartellen und Zusammenschlüssen, *loc. cit.* at p. 418.

6. *Ibid.*, at p. 418.

7. 12e Rapport Général, at No. 240.

8. 15e Rapport Général, (1er février 1966-31 janvier 1967), Nos. 226-231.

the strong market position of competitors and the characteristics of the market for steel piles assured a sufficient degree of competition with this product. For the other products the High Authority had no objections "having regard to the strong position of the following producers... and taking account of the high degree of concentration generally existing in these sectors".[1] Again the merging firms were required to terminate personal connections with third firms in the market.

195. The interpretation of the effective competition criterion in article 66, para. 2 may also be seen from the decisions applying article 65, para. 2 to cartels. This inference is justified because the relevant criterion in article 65, para. 2 has practically the same wording and, as was already said, has been interpreted by the Court of Justice as equivalent. The most important recent authorization decision under article 65, para. 2 concerned the 4 common sales pools of the German steel industry. In its decision authorizing the *Walzstahlkontor West* [2] (the decisions concerning the three other pools follow the same lines of reasoning) the High Authority, in determining whether the requirements of article 65, para. 2(c) were met, found that the production shares of the pool were 17.6% for raw steel and ranged from 8.1% up to 29.3% for particular steel products.[3] It was pointed out that some of the larger production shares were, for various reasons, not indicative of the market influence of the syndicate and concluded that the cartel, taken by itself, met the requirements of article 65, para. 2(c). The High Authority furthermore investigated "how the market position of the Walzstahlkontor West relative to the other important producers of rolled steel in the Community has to be judged with regard to the degree of competition which is required by the Treaty".[4]

196. For this purpose the High Authority referred to the table [5] shown on the following page.

197. On the basis of this table the High Authority reached the following conclusions:

> "The table shows the oligopolistic structure of the common steel market. It can be concluded from this survey that the Walzstahlkontor West for some important product groups has the largest market share, for some others however ranks behind other suppliers. From a general point of view it appears that the pool acquires an important market position as a supplier of rolled products, but that there remains also a sufficient number of suppliers of comparable size. The decisive question is whether in an oligopolistic market there is a balance between

---

1.   *Ibid.,* at No. 230.

2.   Decision No. 3/67 of 5th March 1967, Official Journal No. 76 of 21st April 1967, pp. 1373/67–1384/67.

3.   *Ibid.,* at p. 1379/67.

4.   *Ibid.,* at p. 1380/67.

5.   *Ibid.* at p. 1380/67. The production shares of the other syndicates, Walzstahlkontor Westfalen, Walzstahlkontor Nord und Walzstahlkontor Süd have also been identified, cf. *ibid.,* pp. 1391/67, 1402/67 and 1413/67.

THE EIGHT LARGEST PRODUCERS' SHARE OF THE COMMUNITIES' PRODUCTION
AFTER FORMATION OF THE ROLLED STEEL SYNDICATES

(Percentages)

	1	2	3	4	5	6	7	8	Total
Raw Steel	17.6 West	11.6 Westf.	9.5 Süd	9.2 Nord	8.9	7.8	7.3	3.2	75.1
Hot rolled wide strip (total)	18.0 West	16.4 West	15.9 Westf.	13.7	13.0	8.3 Nord	7.7	6.8	99.8
Hot rolled wide strip products	22.8 West	21.3 Westf.	13.4	12.7 Nord	10.5	7.1	6.7	5.3	99.8
Railway tracks	24.1 West	14.2	11.0	9.7	9.2	8.1 Nord	7.4	6.6 Süd	90.3
Wire rod	16.5 West	15.1	14.7 Nord	12.0 Süd	10.7	5.1	3.2	3.1	80.4
Steel bars	14.2 Süd	9.8 Nord	8.7	8.1 West	7.9	7.0 Westf.	6.0	4.8	66.5
Heavy sections	20.3 Süd	12.6 West	10.6 Nord	9.5 Westf.	9.2	6.8	5.9	5.6	80.5
Strip steel	33.8	23.0 West	13.0 Westf.	8.1	6.8 Süd	5.3	3.3	2.5	95.8
Wide flats	29.3 West	18.6 Westf.	14.6 Süd	11.4	11.0	3.4	3.3	3.1	94.7
Heavy plates	20.7 Westf.	16.9 Nord	13.2 West	10.1	9.4	6.5 Süd	4.0	3.9	84.7
Medium plates	14.7 Nord	13.6	12.6 West	10.9	10.2	9.7 Westf.	9.0	6.5	87.2
Steel sheets	15.3 Westf.	14.4 West	13.6	10.1	8.3	8.0	6.9	6.5 Nord	83.1
Tin plates	28.7	22.1 Westf.	17.1 West	9.5	6.3	4.3	3.6	3.6 Süd	95.2
Galvanised and lead-costed material	17.3 West	15.8	11.6	8.0	7.7 Westf.	6.4	6.3	5.6	78.7

the suppliers or whether this is disturbed by a tendency toward a monopoly. The High Authority has examined this question with the following result: the formation of the Walzstahlkontor West does not — taking into account the simultaneous formation of the three other (pools) — lead, within the oligopoly of the suppliers of rolled steel in the Community, to an imbalance that impairs efficient competition ". [1]

198. The High Authority concluded therefrom that the pool would not be able to determine prices of an important part of the rolled steel products in the Common Market nor would it be able to control production or distribution nor protect these products from effective competition with the products of other enterprises.

199. Although there are no practical cases yet, two further possibilities for taking action against mergers should be mentioned.

200. In *Belgium,* under section 15 of the Act on Protection Against the Abuse of Economic Power, the King may prohibit mergers involving a body corporate against which a recommendation establishing the existence of an abuse of economic power has already been issued and which commits a further abuse.

201. In the *EEC* the Commission has announced that article 86 of the EEC Treaty prohibiting abuses of dominant enterprises may, under special circumstances, also be applied to mergers. [2] In the Commission's view article 86 may apply to mergers if a market dominating enterprise "strengthens its position to such an extent that — in contradiction to the conception on which the Treaty and especially article 86(b) is based and to the disadvantage of consumers, suppliers and dealers — a monopoly situation is created which prevents the functioning of competition ". [3] After publication of the Commission's memorandum the German Federal Cartel Office has announced that it will have to be examined whether section 22 of the German law may be applied to mergers under similar circumstances. [4] As in the EEC, no practical cases have as yet arisen.

CONCLUSION

202. Compared with the other legislations just examined, the United States has the most advanced practice of merger control, as is reflected by the great number of cases which have been decided involving all types of mergers — horizontal, vertical, conglomerate, and joint ventures — and their various effects on competition. The United

1. *Ibid.,* at p. 1381/67.
2. See the Memorandum of the EEC Commission on Concentration in the Common Market of 1st December 1965, Doc. SEC(65)3500, 2 CCH-Common Market Reporter, para. 9081.
3. *Ibid.,* at No. 27.
4. See BKA Activity Report 1966 at pp. 11-12.

States also goes much further than any other country in preventing mergers with anti-competitive effects. Although under the other laws no general criteria in terms of market shares and concentration ratios as in the United States have been developed, it is safe to say that the threshold where mergers are considered to be illegal or against the public interest is in all cases substantially higher than in the United States. Even on the assumption that in the particular case no beneficial effects in terms of economies or of some other kind could be ascertained, it is unlikely that mergers like Brown Shoe/Kinney or Von's Grocery/Shopping Bag would have been challenged under the other laws.

203. The United States approach is basically a prophylactic one. As expressed in the wording of section 7 ("... *may be* substantially to lessen competition or *tend* to create a monopoly") the American merger law is concerned with probable dangers to competition and the likelihood of such dangers is already seen at a relatively early stage of concentration of the market or, as the Supreme Court said in Brown Shoe, "at a time when the trend to a lessening of competition in a line of commerce was still in its incipiency".[1] This prophylactic character of the American antimerger policy is made especially clear by its strong emphasis on the potential competition aspect, an aspect which may by itself cause a merger to be held illegal.[2] One of the reasons is of course that the purpose of section 7, as amended in 1950, and as interpreted by the Supreme Court, is not only to preserve effective competition but also to arrest concentration and the correlative disappearance of small business as a goal of social policy.[3]

204. In the ECSC the primary concern of the High Authority (now the E.C. Commission) and of the Court of Justice in applying article 66 of the ECSC Treaty was not so much, as is the case in the United States, the prevention of probable adverse effects on competition as the actual maintenance of effective competition in order to ensure the achievement of the fundamental aims of article 2 of the Treaty. In pursuing this goal the High Authority in its merger decisions has in particular seen to it that the oligopolistic market conditions largely prevailing in the coal and steel fields are not changed by mergers in such a way that there would be no longer a larger number of independent suppliers, none of which has a substantially stronger market position than his competitors. This concern with maintaining "balanced" market structures may be seen particularly from the Thyssen/Phoenix Rheinrohr and Hoesch/Hoogovens decisions and the decisions concerning the German steel pools. Considering that the "balance" in those cases was still maintained the High Authority

1. 1962 Trade Cases 70,366 at p. 76,489.

2. This applies in particular to market extension mergers, e.g. F.T.C. v. Procter and Gamble, and joint ventures. See also United States v. Gillette Co., Civil Action No. 68-141-W, D. Mass., 1968, where the acquisition of the German firm Braun AG was attacked under section 7 of the Clayton Act, although Braun was only a potential supplier of electric shavers to the United States.

3. See especially the Von's Grocery and Pabst Brewing opinions of the Supreme Court (paras. 135 to 137 supra).

has not opposed further concentration on markets with an already significant oligopolistic character."

205. While it is clear that in the United States and in the ECSC a merger which has anti-competitive effects, as specified in the law, can normally not be justified by beneficial economic effects (e.g., economies) or other reasons, the contrary is true with respect to, at least, the United Kingdom. The broad admission of justifying reasons in the United Kingdom, made possible by the "public interest" criterion, explains why in some cases (e.g., in the cases G.K.N./ Birfield and B.I.C.C./Pyrotenax) dominant positions and even complete monopolies resulting from the merger were accepted. The reasons for which mergers with even substantial anti-competitive effects may be justified range from economies of scale to the prevention of foreign control.[1] An essential element in some cases was that the merging companies gave assurances as to their good performance after the merger. Obviously the maintenance of competition under such a system is but one factor to be considered together with other factors of economic policy.

206. In Canada, as in the United States and in the ECSC, the only statutory criterion is the effect of the merger on competition. It seems, however, that beneficial effects are taken into account, though apparently not to such an extent that monopolistic situations or market dominating positions would be accepted. In Canada this balancing of effects is made possible by the requirement that competition must be lessened "to the detriment of the public".

207. The foregoing examination of the merger laws confirms what could already be observed from the analysis of the concept of market power under the "conduct" laws: that foreign product alternatives are taken into account in determining whether actionable market power exists or is likely to result from the merger in question. No case was found where the existence of significant imports was disregarded. While, normally, the presence of imports is taken into consideration when determining whether a merger of domestic enterprises results in undesirable market power on the domestic market,[2] some recent United States cases involving mergers between domestic and foreign enterprises have extensively dealt with the effects of imports on domestic competition.

208. Thus, in *United States v. Jos. Schlitz Brewing Co.*,[3] involving a merger between the second largest brewing company in the United States and the third largest in Canada (Labatt), section 7 of the Clayton Act was held to be applicable not only because Labatt controlled a smaller American brewing firm, but also because of the elimination of Labatt as a potential direct entrant to the American

1. Cf. B.M.C./Pressed Steel, Amalgamated Dental Co./Dental Supply Co. and Dentists Supply Co. of New York, and Thorn Electrical Industries of Radio Rentals.

2. See, e.g., the report of the British Monopolies Commission on the merger between Ross Group and Associated Fisheries *op. cit.,* at paras. 34-42.

3. 253 F. Supp. 129, 1966 Trade Cases para. 71,725 (D.C.N.D.Cal); affirmed *per curiam* 385 U.S. 37, 1966 Trade Cases para. 71,916.

market.[1] In *United States v. Mobay Chemical Co.*[2] a joint venture for the production of plastic foam set up by an American (Monsanto) and a German chemical firm (Farbenfabriken Bayer) was prohibited under section 7 on the ground that Bayer was eliminated as an important actual and potential competitor on the American market. Similarly, in *United States v. The Gillette Co.*,[3] a merger of an American enterprise with a foreign competitor was challenged on the sole ground that the merger would prevent competition from imports to the domestic market.[4]

209. As is illustrated by these cases, the fact that the domestic market is large does not exclude the fact that imports from foreign countries are an important factor in the assessment of the competitive situation on this market. The existence of imports may mean that in a particular case a merger between domestic enterprises will not be considered to have serious anti-competitive effects. On the other hand, a merger between a domestic and a foreign enterprise may also contain anti-competitive features, if the acquired foreign firm has a significant actual or potential capacity to enter the domestic market independently. The cases just mentioned thus show that the geographic extension of the market is as such irrelevant for the question whether in a given case foreign product alternatives have to be taken into account and, further, that the application of national law to mergers between domestic and foreign enterprises does not necessitate an extension of the relevant geographic market beyond national boundaries. All that can be generally said is that foreign product alternatives will normally play a more important role in small countries with a relatively higher share of foreign trade in national product than in larger countries. But the decision in a particular case will always depend on whether and to what extent such alternatives do in fact exist, irrespective of the size of the market.

B. MONOPOLIZATION

210. Section A dealt with the acquisition of undesirable market power by means of mergers. The present section will deal essentially with the achievement of such power by single enterprises. The provisions

1. The Court found that Labatt "had the desire, the intention and the resourcefulness to enter the United States market" and that, in view of the fact that entry of new American firms into beer brewing was highly unlikely, "the large established Canadian breweries represent the most probable sources of potential competition in the United States markets". *Ibid.* at p. 82,258.

2. 1967 Trade Cases para. 72,001.

3. Civil Action No. 68-141-W (D. Mass); 5 Trade Regulation Reporter para. 45,068, Case No. 1988.

4. Since Braun, the acquired German firm, had not yet in fact exported electric shavers to the United States, the anti-competitive effect of the merger was exclusively seen in the disappearance of a *potential* foreign supplier as an independent firm.

on monopolization, at least in the United States, are an instrument of structure control in the sense that the remedy normally involves a dissolution of the monopoly power, in many cases requiring some divestiture by the company holding such power. In Canada and Japan, on the other hand, the monopolization provisions are at least in part instruments of a conduct control approach directed against the monopolizing firm's practices whether they are employed to achieve a powerful position (e.g. predatory practices to eliminate competitors) or whether they take the form of an abuse of the acquired market power, especially in relation to buyers or sellers on the other side of the market. Such an interpretation of the monopolization concept means that only certain practices of the monopolist are prosecuted while its position of power, i.e. the market structure, is left unaffected. This approach is substantially identical to the system of conduct control under the "conduct" laws to be studied in chapter II of Part II.

211. In the *United States* the term "monopolize, or attempt to monopolize" in section 2 of the Sherman Act is not defined in the law itself. The Courts have interpreted it as "(1) the possession of monopoly power in the relevant market and (2) the wilful acquisition or maintenance of that power as distinguished from growth or development as a consequence of a superior product, business acumen, or historic accident".[1]

212. The first of these two elements – monopoly power – has been defined by the Supreme Court as "the power to control prices or exclude competition".[2] Its presence is primarily determined in terms of market share. Thus, in *American Tobacco Co. v. United States* the Supreme Court stated that "over two-thirds of the entire domestic field of cigarettes and ... over 80% of the field of comparable cigarettes" constituted "a substantial monopoly".[3] In *United States v. Aluminum Co. of America*[4] 90% of the market was held to constitute monopoly power. As was noted by Judge Hand in this case 90% control of output "is enough to constitute a monopoly, it is doubtful whether 60 or 64% would be enough; and certainly 33% is not".[5] In the *Grinnell Case,* 87% of the accredited central station service (the relevant market) was held to constitute monopoly power.[6] On the other hand, in the *Cellophane Case*[7] the Supreme Court denied the presence of monopoly power after finding that Du Pont, though producing almost 75% of the entire supply of cellophane, had only 17.9% share in the larger flexible packaging materials market. It may

    1. United States v. Grinnell Co., 384 U.S. 563 at pp. 570-1, 1966 Trade Cases, para. 71,789 at p. 82,648.
    2. United States v. E.I. Du Pont de Nemours and Co., 351 U.S. 377, 391, 1956 Trade Cases, para. 68,369.
    3. 328 U.S. 781, 797 (1946).
    4. 148 F.2d. 416, 1944-1945 Trade Cases, para. 57,342.
    5. 1944-1945 Trade Cases para. 57,342 at p. 52,679.
    6. 1966 Trade Cases para. 71,789 at p. 82,648.
    7. United States v. E.I. Du Pont de Nemours and Co., 351 U.S. 377, 1956 Trade Cases, para. 68,369.

therefore be said that ordinarily a relatively high (predominant) market share must be attained, certainly much higher than the combined market shares in horizontal merger cases, before market power in the sense of section 2 of the Sherman Act can be inferred.

213. The finding of such market power must however be accompanied by the additional element of "deliberateness" to constitute monopolization. The Courts have consistently emphasized that "mere size" was not enough.[1] Essentially the proof of deliberateness involves a conclusion as to how the monopoly power was acquired, maintained or used, i.e. whether the acquisition, maintenance or use of monopoly power was a result of an inevitable market development, "thrust upon" the monopolist, or of a deliberate strategy to achieve a monopoly position, by unlawful practices such as unlawful mergers or restraints of trade or even by trade practices which are by themselves lawful. In the *Alcoa Case* the Court said that Alcoa in 1940 was not

" ... the passive beneficiary of a monopoly, following upon an involuntary elimination of competitors by automatically operative economic forces. Already in 1909, when its last lawful monopoly ended, it sought to strengthen its position by unlawful practices, and these concededly continued until 1912. In that year it had two plants in New York, at which it produced less than 42 million pounds of ingot; in 1934 it had five plants (the original two, enlarged; one in Tennessee; one in North Carolina; one in Washington), and its production had risen to about 327 million pounds, an increase of almost eight-fold. Meanwhile not a pound of ingot had been produced by anyone else in the United States. This increase and this continued and undisturbed control did not fall undesigned into "Alcoa's" lap; obviously it could not have done so. It could only have resulted, as it did result, from a persistent determination to maintain the control with which it found itself vested in 1912. There were at least one or two abortive attempts to enter the industry, but "Alcoa" effectively anticipated and forestalled all competition, and succeeded in holding the field alone. True, it stimulated demand and opened new uses for the metal, but not without making sure that it could supply what it had evoked. There is no dispute as to this; "Alcoa" avows it as evidence of the skill, energy and initiative with which it has always conducted its business; as a reason why, having won its way by fair means, it should be commended, and not dismembered. We need charge it with no moral derelictions after 1912; we may assume that all it claims for itself is true. The only question is whether it falls within the exception established in favour of those who

---

1. Some lower courts have, however, held that once monopoly power in terms of predominant size is established, the burden of proof is on the monopolist to show that it was not achieved or maintained by improper means. See e.g. United States v. Grinnell Corp., 1964 Trade Cases para. 71,298 at p. 80,246 (D.C.R.J. 1964). The Supreme Court in the same case did not pass judgment on this issue stating that the record had clearly shown that Grinnell's monopoly power was consciously acquired.

do not seek, but cannot avoid, the control of a market. It seems to us that that question scarcely survives its statement. It was not inevitable that it should always anticipate increases in the demand for ingot and be prepared to supply them. Nothing compelled it to keep doubling and redoubling its capacity before others entered the field. It insists that it never excluded competitors; but we can think of no more effective exclusion than progressively to embrace each new opportunity as it opened, and to face every newcomer with new capacity already geared into a great organisation, having the advantage of experience, trade connections and the elite of personnel. Only in case we interpret "exclusion" as limited to manoeuvres not honestly industrial, but actuated solely by a desire to prevent competition, can such a course, indefatigably pursued, be deemed not "exclusionary". So to limit it would in our judgment emasculate the Act; would permit just such consolidations as it was designed to prevent".[1]

214. In *United States v. United Shoe Machinery Corp.*[2] the conclusion that United Shoe, a manufacturer of shoe machinery with more than 75% of the market, had monopolized its market was mainly based on the finding that United Shoe's market position was not only a result of the superiority of its products and services, but also of its policy of never selling but only leasing its machines to shoe manufacturers. The Court found that the complex long-term (10 years) lease contracts "deter a shoe manufacturer from disposing of a United machine and acquiring a competitor's machine. He is deterred more than if he owned that same machine, or if he held it on a short lease carrying simple rental provisions and a reasonable charge for cancellation before the end of the term".[3] While recognizing that the leasing practices of United Shoe, were in one sense "normal methods of industrial development", in other words not in themselves illegal restraints of trade, the Court stated that

> "they are not practices which can be properly described as the inevitable consequences of ability, natural forces, or law ... They are contracts, arrangements and policies which instead of encouraging competition based on pure merit, further the dominance of a particular firm. In this sense they are unnatural barriers: they unnecessarily exclude actual and potential competition: they restrict a free market. While the law allows many enterprises to use such practices, the Sherman Act is now construed by superior courts to forbid the continuance of effective market control based in part upon such practices".[4]

215. Finally, in the *Grinnell Case,* the conclusion as to a deliberate acquisition of monopoly power was mainly based on the finding of

1. *United States v. Aluminum Co. of America,* 1944-45 Trade Cases, para. 37,342 at p. 57684/5.

2. 110 F. Supp. 295, 1953 Trade Cases para. 67,436 (D.C. Mass. 1953) affirmed *per curiam* 347 U.S. 521, 1954 Trade Cases, para. 67,755 (U.S. Sup. Ct., 1954).

3. *Ibid.,* at p. 68,183.

4. *Ibid.,* at p. 68,188.

restrictive agreements and pricing practices applied in the past and on Grinnell's record of buying up competitors. "By those acquisitions it perfected the monopoly power to exclude competitors and fix prices".[1]

216. The cases discussed so far clearly involved single-firm monopolies. The same principles would, however, apply to a group of enterprises acting in concert which deliberately acquires and maintains monopoly power, because section 2 of the Sherman Act expressly covers combinations and conspiracies to monopolize.[2] On the other hand, the question whether section 2 applies to oligopolies, i.e. a group of enterprises pursuing a policy of parallel conduct without acting in concert, is still open. Some commentators[3] have suggested that section 2 should be applied to oligopoly situations as well, but to date no actions under section 2 against the acquisition or use of monopoly power of a group of oligopolies not acting in concert were brought.

217. It should be noted that section 2 also covers attempts to monopolize. Such an attempt means "the employment of methods and practices which are utilized for the specific purpose and with the specific intent to achieve and build a monopoly, and which, if successful, would be likely to accomplish such monopolization".[4] This provision permits action against powerful enterprises which have not yet achieved monopoly power in the sense of the law, but which apply their market power to exclude competitors from a substantial part of commerce.[5]

218. Canada prohibits the "formation of monopoly" (section 33 of the Combines Investigation Act), a monopoly being defined in the law as "a situation where one or more persons either substantially or completely control throughout Canada or any area thereof the class or species of business in which they are engaged and have operated such business or are likely to operate it to the detriment or against the interest of the public, whether consumers, producers or others..." [section 2(f)].

1. 1966 Trade Cases para. 71,789 at p. 82,641.

2. For examples of such collective monopolization see, e.g. American Tobacco Co. v. United States, 328 U.S. 781, 1946-1947, Trade Cases para. 57,468 (U.S. Sup. Ct. 1946); United States v. Paramount Pictures 334 U.S. 131, 1948-1949 Trade Cases, paras. 62, 244.

3. See, e.g., Neale, *The Antitrust Laws of the United States of America* 182 (1960) Edwards, *Control of the Single Firm: Its Place in Antitrust Policy,* 30 Law and Contemp. Prob. 465 (1965).

4. Kansas City Star v. United States, 240 F.2d. 643, 1957 Trade Cases para. 68,601.

5. See, e.g. Lessig v. Tidewater Oil Co., 327 F.2d.459, 1964 Trade Cases, para. 70,993, at p. 78,938: "If the jury found that Tidewater intended to fix the price at which 2,700 independent service station operators resold gasoline, and to exclude other suppliers of petroleum products and sponsored T.B.A. items from competing for the patronage of these operators, and took steps to accomplish that purpose, it could properly conclude that Tidewater attempted to monopolize a part of interstate commerce in violation of Section 2 of the Sherman Act".

219. In the only case so far decided under this provision, *Eddy Match Co. Ltd. v. The Queen* [1] the Eddy Match company was found guilty of having formed a monopoly in the wooden match industry. After a merger in 1927 of the three firms then engaged in the manufacture of wooden matches in Canada, a number of independent match companies were established, but each was acquired by the Eddy Match group after some time, so that the monopoly was always re-established after a period of competition. In eliminating rivals and maintaining its monopoly position the group employed such practices as preferred pricing, special discounts, "fighting-brands", and flooding the market with matches. As stated in the report of the Commissioner:

> "When competition re-appeared, as new businesses were started, it did not last long because the new productive facilities were soon brought under the same control as Eddy Match. Moreover, it was competition of a limited nature. Eddy Match took steps to induce wholesalers to restrict sales of competitive lines and to keep the prices of them to retailers in line with the prices of Eddy Match. When these independent manufacturers quoted lower prices Eddy Match generally met their competition not by lowering the price of its standard products, but by introducing special brands, sometimes called "fighting brands", at reduced prices. They were sold only in the areas affected by the new competition, and only in limited quantities and for limited periods". [2]

220. As to the question of "control of business" within the meaning of section 2(f) the Court said:

> "When a group of companies engaged in the same business are alone in the field; when they work together as a unit; when they are free to supply the market or to withhold their product; when there is no restriction on the prices which they charge, save their own self-interest; when their freedom to exclude individuals as customers is restricted only by their interpretation of existing penal laws, then, by all normal standards, those companies are in control of the business in which they are engaged". [3]

221. The issue of the public interest was stated by the court in the following general terms:

> "Such a condition (viz. complete control of a business) creates a presumption that the public is being deprived of all the benefits of free competition and this deprivation, being the negation of the public right, is necessarily to the detriment or against the interest of the public.
>
> This presumption however may be rebutted and it does not seem unreasonable to suggest that some "control" might in

1. 1953, 109 C.C.C. 1 (appeal decision), *Guide,* Canada, Section 3.1, Decision No. 1.

2. Manufacture, Distribution and Sale of Matches in Canada, Report of Commissioner 1949 at p. 124.

3. (1953) 109 C.C.C. 1 at p. 18.

exceptional circumstances be more advantageous to the public than if the business had been left free. But when faced with facts which disclose the systematic elimination of competition, the presumption of detriment becomes violent. In these circumstances, the burden of showing absence of detriment must surely rest on the shoulders of those against whom the presumption plays ". [1]

222. The predatory practices engaged in by the group were considered to be relevant in this connection in that they

"... testify with great eloquence as to the power which appellants could and did exercise, as to their determination to be alone in the field, as to the helpless position of the public and, in short as to the inevitability of the very evil which the Act seeks to prevent. Thus even if one cannot infer from the fact of complete control that there existed the likelihood of detriment to the public, this inference can and must be drawn from the acts that were done during the acquisition, development and exercise of that control ... ". [2]

223. *Japan* prohibits "private monopolization" (section 3 of the Antimonopoly Act), defined in the law as

"such business activities, by which any entrepreneur, individually, by combination or conspiracy with other entrepreneurs, or in any other manner, excludes or controls the business activities of other entrepreneurs, thereby causing, contrary to the public interest, a substantial restraint of competition in any particular field of trade "[3] [Section 2(5)].

224. In the *Soy Sauce Case*[4] the practices applied by the leading producer Noda Soy Sauce Co. (36.7% supply of all soy sauce) to effect compliance of retailers with its price list was considered as private monopolzation. By exerting pressure upon the wholesalers and through them upon the entire line of distribution, dissident retailers were forced to adhere to Noda's list prices. Noda being the price leader of the four large manufacturers, the prices of the other three (with a combined market share of 31.7%) were brought to the same level following Noda's action.

CONCLUSION

225. The monopolization concept in the three countries just studied is not uniform. In the United States monopolization is essentially a phenomenon of market structure, i.e. the deliberate acquisition or

1. *Ibid.* at pp. 20-21.
2. *Ibid.* at p. 22.
3. Section 19 of the Antimonopoly Act prohibits the employment of unfair business practices by any entrepreneur and is applicable also to the conduct of market-dominating enterprises.
4. 7 F.T.C. Decision Reports 108 (F.T.C., 27th December 1955).

maintenance of monopoly power on the market. It is not the way in which such power is applied in particular instances which constitutes the offence (though of course such practices are important indicia of "deliberateness"), but its existence without being "thrust upon the monopolist". It is logical therefore that the law in this case is primarily concerned with the dissolution of the monopoly rather than with remedying its operation, as will be seen in further detail in Part III when the legal measures are studied.

226. Though the Canadian monopolization concept describes a market situation (substantial or complete control of a business), the law is essentially concerned with the operation of such a situation. If such a situation is operated against the public interest, the monopolist may be fined, but his position remains unchanged. This concern of the law with harmful business conduct rather than with undesirable market structure is brought out in Japan in the text of the law which expressly speaks of "business activities". As was illustrated by the Soy Sauce Case, monopolization refers to individual business practices (in this case: obligation to adhere to retail list prices) rather than to the possession of monopoly power as such. Again, as will be seen later, the legal measures which may be taken against monopolization are not aimed at the dissolution of such power. It should be noted that in the United States such individual practices could still come under section 2 of the Sherman Act as "attempts to monopolize", when they are applied with the intention to eliminate competitors as a means of acquiring monopoly power. To this extent, section 2 includes also aspects of conduct control.

227. Monopoly power in the United States is primarily defined in terms of market shares, the shares required to establish monopoly power being comparatively high (no case under 75 %). This clearly shows that the market power which may be "deliberately" acquired by a single firm is substantially higher than that which may be achieved by a merger of two or more firms. In the only Canadian case adjudicated so far, the market share was practically 100 %, and from the reasoning of the court it may be inferred that at least similarly high market shares as in the United States would be required to establish "control of business". In contrast, the Japanese Soy Sauce Case involved much lower market shares (36.7 %). But apparently the fact that the "monopolist" was the price-leader of the three other major producers with a combined market share of 31.8 % was taken into consideration. The Soy Sauce Case may therefore be regarded as an oligopoly case similar to the situation of the German Petrol Price Case, a problem which under the Canadian and United States monopolization laws has not yet been adjudicated. Obviously the application of these laws to oligopolies would present special problems if more than a control of individual business practices of the oligopolists is intended. Since the market power of a group of oligopolists rests on the extent to which they follow a policy of market behaviour, structural measures against the position of market power of the group would have to aim at the termination of parallel conduct of the oligopolists. Whether this aim could be achieved by splitting up the individual oligopolists cannot be predicted with any certainty at

present due to the lack of relevant experience under any of the laws just studied.

228. As to the foreign trade aspects the same comment may be made as was made in the case of mergers, viz. that foreign product alternatives are taken into account in determining whether a domestic firm has monopoly power. An example of this is the Alcoa case where the Court found that

> "it was the threat of greater foreign imports which kept "Alcoa's" prices where they were, and prevented it from exploiting its advantage as sole domestic producer; indeed, it is hard to resist the conclusion that potential imports did put a "ceiling" upon those prices. Nevertheless, within the limits afforded by the tariff and the cost of transportation, "Alcoa" was free to raise its prices as it chose, since it was free from domestic competition, save as it drew other metals into the market as substitutes" [1]

1. United States v. Aluminum Co. of America, 148 F.2d.416, 1944-1945 Trade Cases, para. 57,342 at p. 57,681.

CRITERIA UNDER THE "CONDUCT" LAWS

229. The "conduct" laws which will be analysed in the following pages deal with specific acts of powerful enterprises without interfering with the position of market power as such. It will be shown what substantive law criteria are used in these laws to determine undesirable acts and to permit action to be taken against them. These criteria are the following:

A. Abuse of a market dominating position (Germany, the EEC, Spain and EFTA),

B. Activities contrary to the public interest (United Kingdom, Belgium, the Netherlands, Switzerland and Norway),

C. Interference with the normal operation of the market (France),

D. Unreasonable prices, unfair business conditions, refusals to to sell, etc. (Denmark) and

E. Use of dominant position for purposes contrary to the ECSC Treaty.

A. ABUSE OF A MARKET DOMINATING POSITION

230. In *Germany,* section 22(3) of the Act against Restraints of Competition empowers the Cartel Authority to intervene against market dominating enterprises which "abuse their dominating position". The following cases illustrate the meaning of such an "abuse".

231. In the *Zementkontor Unterelbe case,*[1] a limited liability company acting as a common selling agency for the North-German cement producers, practised a system of geographic price differentials: customers located in the area to the right of the Elbe river had to pay 4.- DM (about 1 U.S. dollar), per ton more than those located

---

1. German Federal Supreme Court, Decision of 17th May, 1965, WuW/E BGH 667; *Guide,* Germany, Section 3, Case No. 43.

on the other side of the river. The Federal Cartel Office prohibited the continuation of this price differential and ordered the agency to reduce its higher price to the level prevailing in the lower price area.[1] Although the order was essentially one of abuse supervision of a legalized cartel, the Federal Supreme Court stated that the same principles would apply even if the suppliers had not been linked by a cartel agreement, since due to parallel market conduct they were market dominating within the meaning of section 22(2).

232. The Federal Supreme Court confirmed the Federal Cartel Office's view that not only the price differentiation but also the higher price in itself was abusive. The Court pointed out that replacement costs cannot be used as a criterion to determine whether a price was abusive or not. Stating that higher prices than those obtainable under competitive conditions were abusive, the Court held that the Federal Cartel Office was justified in basing its order on a comparison with the prices in the competitive South German market. This conclusion, the Court continued, "cannot be refuted by the argument that even if a common sales agency did not exist, the enterprises forming it would not enter into effective competition as intended by section 1, because they constituted an oligopoly and their prices would therefore be determined by the peculiarities of an oligopolistic market. For, if there existed no substantial competition between these enterprises and if their prices were indisputably higher than the prices that would prevail under conditions of effective competition, the Federal Cartel Office would also be empowered to intervene with the aim to prevent the manufacturers from charging higher prices. In this case, it would derive its powers from section 22(1), (2), (3), No. 1, and (4)".[2]

233. In the *Meto Case*[3] the practice of a dominant manufacturer of manual labelling machines selling his machines only on the condition that the buyer agrees to purchase his entire requirements of labels for a period of 5 years exclusively from the machine manufacturer was considered by the Federal Cartel Office as an abusive practice of a market dominating enterprise. Stating generally that "every

1. Decisions of 17th September 1962, WuW/E BKartA 508, and of 10th April 1963, WuW/EB BKartA 656.

2. WuW/E BGH 667,673.

3. Federal Cartel Office, Decision of 2nd October 1967, WuW/E BKartA 1189. Affirmed by Berlin Court of Appeals, judgment of 18th February 1969, Kart V 34/67. Stating generally that the criteria for the definition of abuse had to be taken from the principles underlying a competitive economic system, the court held that "economic power has to be eliminated where it impairs the effectiveness of competition and its inherent tendencies to promote efficiency and optimal satisfaction of consumers' demands. The supervision of market dominating enterprises for abuses, therefore "has as its prime purpose to keep open the market access of other enterprises". The court considered tying agreements as "typical cases of abuse of power in the meaning of section 22(3) because they fortify a market dominating position by means other than greater efficiency and strangle competition of tomorrow". The abuse was seen not only in relation to the tied buyers – who were offered less because they had to use more expensive labels – but also in relation to the other sellers of labels who were excluded from part of the market. The argument of the manufacturer that the exclusive use of his own labelling material was necessary for a successful distribution of

practice of a market dominating enterprise was abusive which produces market results which could definitely not have been obtained in effective competition ",[1] the Office said that the requirement clause in question could not have been practised under conditions of effective competition, because (a) it was unusual even in the sale of more complicated machines, (b) the prices of the labels were excessive as compared with the 30 to 40 % lower prices of other label suppliers, and (c) the value of the labels to be purchased normally exceeded substantially the value of the machine. The argument of the manufacturer that the exclusive use of his own labelling material was necessary to maintain his five-year free servicing of the machines during this period was rejected on the grounds that (a) the other sellers offered labelling material of a like quality and (b) the value of the free service was so far exceeded by the additional costs resulting from the machine manufacturer's higher prices compared with the prices of his competitors during the five year period.

234. The abuse was seen not only in relation to the tied buyers, but also in relation to the other sellers of labels, the latter conclusion being based on the premise that "market dominating enterprises which apply, on another market than the dominated market, competitive means which are not available to their competitors for the sole reason that they do not possess the necessary market power, act abusively ".[2]

235. In the *Sporting Goods Fair case*[3] the organiser of the only specialized fair for winter sports goods was found to have abused its dominant position by admitting only those producers who sell their products exclusively to specialized retailers. The purpose of section 22 was outlined by the Federal Cartel Office as follows:

> "The object of section 22 of the Act against Restraints of Competition is the protection against the exploitation of market power by enterprises both in the dominated market and in markets where the market dominating position produces effects (third markets). In the dominated market protection is sought, on the one hand, for enterprises belonging to the preceding or

the machines was rejected on the grounds that even if a justification of this kind were at all acceptable:

a) the defendant did not in fact render free services to the extent claimed,
b) the cost of the services actually rendered was by far exceeded by the additional income resulting from the buyers' obligation to use only defendant's expensive labels,
c) free maintenance service was not necessary to satisfy the needs of buyers and to promote the machines, and
d) labels produced by other firms did not affect the proper functioning of defendant's machines.

1. *Ibid.* at p. 1,193.
2. *Ibid.* at p. 1,195.
3. Federal Cartel Office, Decision of 31st May 1968 BM 76/67. That part of the order made by the Federal Cartel Office which prohibited the respondents from refusing admission to the fair on the ground that the applicant did not exclusively sell to specialized retailers has since been affirmed by the Berlin Court of Appeals. Judgment of 22nd July 1968, WuW/E OLG 907. The Federal Supreme Court rejected the appeal of the respondents against this judgment.

subsequent economic levels against restrictions of their economic freedom of action and against economic exploitation which would not be possible or would not produce the same detrimental effects if there existed substantial competition. Enterprises belonging to the same economic level as the market dominating one (competitors), on the other hand, should be protected against unjustified interference with their competition. One of the most important tasks of the supervision of abuses of market dominating enterprises is to keep open the access of other enterprises to the market".[1]

236. The Office held that under conditions of substantial competition the respondent company could not have applied the restriction on access to its fair, a restriction which in the absence of equivalent exhibition opportunities hindered the excluded companies in their competition with those admitted to the fair. The Office rejected the respondent's argument that since the exhibition company was an organisation established by specialized dealers to promote their business interests, it would make no sense to admit producers who, by directly selling to consumers, acted to the detriment of those who organised the fair. It was held that the defendant, by offering the opportunity to exhibit, was not handling an internal matter of the dealers' organisation but in dealing with non-member enterprises acted as an enterprise and was thus subject to the rules governing enterpreneurial conduct.

237. In the *Petrol Case*[2] the abuse was seen in the fact that the oil companies involved had maintained the high prices, which they had justified by the shortage of supplies and increased transportation costs, although the supply situation had meanwhile, in Autumn 1967, considerably improved and transportation costs had gone down substantially. On the basis of its own calculations which differed from those submitted by the oil companies, the Federal Cartel Office came to the conclusion that at this time all companies involved were in a position to lower their petrol prices though each to a different degree, and that therefore, under conditions of substantial competition, they could not have maintained the high prices. The further charging of these prices was thus an abuse of a dominant position under section 22. No order was made, however, after the Esso Company lowered its prices by an average of about 2.4 Pfenning and the others followed suit.

238. It should be noted, finally, that section 26(2), *inter alia,* subjects market dominating enterprises to a prohibition of unfair hindrance in the business activities of other enterprises and unjustified discrimination against other enterprises. This provision is often concurrently applied to cases of abuses of dominant enterprises, for example in the Meto case just discussed. It may be said generally that both unfair hindrance of business and unjustified differentiation between other enterprises constitutes an abuse under section 22.

1. *Ibid.*
2. Bundeskartellamt Activity Report 1967, pp. 41–42.

239. In *Spain,* section 2 of the Act against Restraints of Competition 1963 prohibits abusive practices which enable enterprises "to exploit a dominant position in such a manner as to cause unjustified damage to the national economy, the interests of consumers or those of other competitors". Section 3 of the Act specifies the following examples of such practices:

a) Directly or indirectly fixing buying or selling prices or other trading terms.

b) Limiting production, distribution, technical development or capital investment to the detriment of the national economy.

c) Effecting the sharing of markets; of territorial delivery areas or sectors or of the sources of supply.

d) Pursuing a commercial policy aimed at eliminating competitors by means of unfair competition.

e) Applying, in trading with third parties, different terms for similar or equivalent goods or services, thereby placing such parties in a position of unequal competitiveness.

f) Making the conclusion of a contract subject to the acceptance of additional goods or services or commercial transactions which, by their nature and the custom of the trade, have no connection with the subject-matter of such contract.

240. In the case of the *Carbonell y Cia., S.A.,*[1] the only one so far decided under section 2, an abuse of dominant buying power was at issue. The Carbonell Co., the only producer of olive oil in the Castro del Rio area, had obtained oral undertakings from the farmers of that area for the sale of all their olive extract grease at a price ultimately to be unilaterally determined by Carbonell. The prices for the farmers' products, which were determined on the basis of the volume of the olive crop, were very low, especially in 1964, when the crop was unusually large. Carbonell's pricing policy also affected prices in the surrounding areas because the prices paid by the defendant were followed by other processors. The Court held that Carbonell had abused its dominant position in fixing sales prices contrary to article 3, para. (a) of the Act and ordered it to change its buying policy, so as to give each farmer the possibility to supply on the basis of a written contract at a price agreed upon in advance.

241. In the *EEC,* article 86 prohibits "so far as trade between Member States may be thereby affected... one or more firms to abuse a dominant position in the Common Market or any substantial part thereof". As examples of abuses article 86 lists the following practices:

a) the direct or indirect imposition of unfair buying or selling prices or other unfair trading terms;

b) the limitation of production, marketing or technical development to the prejudice of consumers;

1. Decision of 11th November 1967.

109

c) the application to trade partners of unequal conditions in respect of equivalent transactions, thereby placing them at a competitive disadvantage;

d) subjecting the conclusion of a contract to the acceptance by trade partners of additional goods or services which are by their nature or by the custom of the trade related to the subject matter of such contract.

242. The Commission has not yet applied article 86 in practical cases. In its Memorandum on Concentration in the Common Market the Commission has merely stated in general terms that the abuse must be understood as an objective misconduct in the light of the aims of the Treaty and that it may be committed against actual and potential competitors, suppliers and consumers.[1] In a recent interpretation of article 177, the Court of Justice held that neither the bringing of a patent infringement action against the importation of the same product from other Member countries where no patent protection existed, nor the fact that the price of the patented product in the country where the action was brought was higher than the price of the product coming from the patent-free country were necessarily abusive.[2]

243. In the *EFTA*, article 15(1)(b) of the Convention recognizes as incompatible with the Convention, "insofar as they frustrate the benefits expected from the removal or absence of duties and quantitative restrictions on trade between Member States, ... actions by which one or more enterprises take unfair advantage of a dominant position within the Area of the Association or a substantial part of it". The EFTA working party on restrictive business practices has clarified certain technical terms referred to in this article which were endorsed by the EFTA Council on 25th September 1968. In particular "taking unfair advantage of a dominant position" was defined as meaning that the dominant position must be abused and that the establishment or holding of a dominant position is not in itself contrary to para. 1(b) of article 15.[3]

B. ACTIVITIES CONTRARY TO THE PUBLIC INTEREST

244. In the *United Kingdom* the criterion for taking action against the conduct of powerful enterprises as defined in the law is whether "the conditions exist or things are done which, according to the report of the Commission as laid before Parliament, operate or may be expected to operate against the public interest".[4] The Monopolies

1. Doc. EEC(65)3500, No. 25.
2. Judgment of 29th February 1968, Case 24/67, in the matter Parke, Davis and Co.
3. See Annex I for further details of the working party's interpretations of Article 15(1)(b).
4. Section 3(1) of the Monopolies and Mergers Act 1965.

Commission has published about 30 reports on different products in which such "operations against the public interest" of various kinds were dealt with. Some of the important reports will be described in the following paragraphs.

245. In the case of the *British Oxygen Co.*,[1] which sold over 98% of the oxygen supplies as well as of the supplies of dissolved acetylene in the United Kingdom, a number of practices were found by the Monopolies Commission to be contrary to the public interest. One of these practices was BOC's policy of obtaining exclusive control over the provision of plant and equipment to other suppliers or to consumers who might wish to make their own gas.[2] It was also found to be contrary to the public interest "that a monopoly such as BOC should take advantage of its position to eliminate competitors by making local and selective reductions in prices instead of extending to all consumers the benefits of any price reductions which may be possible".[3] The Commission also criticized the rule that the consumer must take from BOC his total requirements of gases if BOC had installed and maintained any necessary apparatus free of charge, in cases where this requirement included gases for which the apparatus was not used. "Its purpose can only be to preserve BOC's monopoly position, and in our view it limits the customer's freedom of choice to an extent which is contrary to the public interest".[4]

246. The Commission also dealt with BOC's prices. It found that the profit rate on capital employed (using the historical basis) in the production of the gases in question had been 23 to 24% in 1952 to 1954, roughly one-third to one half higher than the weighted average for all manufacturing industries in the sample examined by the Commission. The Commission also considered that BOC enjoyed to a very high degree the advantages of a monopoly position and that the element of risk involved in its operations was confined mainly to the risks involved in changes in the general level of industrial activity. In respect of BOC's business in the gases under reference, therefore, the Commission thought that BOC should be in a position to raise money on more favourable terms than if it were bearing normal trading risks; they considered that it should be able to obtain a considerable part of the capital required for the expansion of its business from debentures and similar forms of borrowing which would require a somewhat lower rate of interest. It did not need, therefore, "to earn the same return on capital as a company in a competitive industry".[5]

> "BOC differs from firms which are in competitive industries in the extent to which it is able to set its price at whatever levels suit it best. We note that both before and since the war BOC

1.   Report on the Supply of Certain Industrial and Medical Gases, 1956, London, HMSO, Cmnd. No. 13.
2.   *Ibid.* at para. 248.
3.   *Ibid.* at para. 251.
4.   *Ibid.* at para. 252.
5.   *Ibid.* at para. 259.

has aimed at and secured profits in the region of 23 to 25% on capital employed and that even in 1952 to 1954, which were prosperous years for industry generally, its profits were well above the average level in manufacturing industry. After making full allowance for the seller's market which has prevailed during most of the post-war period we consider that BOC's profits have been unjustifiably high for an almost complete monopoly facing a limited financial risk. It follows that the prices charged by BOC for oxygen and dissolved acetylene are too high. While it may be that some economies could be made, we have no evidence upon which we could base any general finding that BOC's costs are too high, but to the extent that BOC's profits are too high there is scope for reduction in the prices charged to consumers. We should not consider it any answer to this to say that it would involve BOC having recourse to the market in future for a greater proportion of the capital which it may require for the extension of its business as distinct from the replacement of its existing assets. We do not think that a monopoly should take advantage of its position to charge current consumers with the cost of its future expansion as distinct from replacement. As an illustration of the scope for reduction, if the profit on capital employed had been limited to 15% in 1954, prices could have been reduced on average by nearly 7%. If a reduction in price of the order of 7% had been uniformly applied, the average price of liquid oxygen would have fallen from 13s. 4d. to 12s. 5d. a 1,000 cubic foot; of industrial compressed oxygen from 33s. 9d. to 31s. 6d.; and of dissolved acetylene from 148s. 6d. to 138s. 4d.

We find that BOC charges unjustifiably high prices for oxygen and dissolved acetylene and that this operates and may be expected to operate against the public interest". [1]

247. Finally, while BOC's practice of charging delivered prices on a national basis was not challenged by the Commission, the fact that BOC did not disclose its price lists was found to be against the public interest. The Commission said:

"In our view the underlying principles should be that there should be no discrimination either between individual consumers or between classes of consumers in similar circumstances; that the scales of charges should be based on relevant costs; and that they should be made known to all consumers. BOC's present methods of charging for oxygen and dissolved acetylene do not satisfy these conditions, and we find that in this way they operate and may be expected to operate against the public interest". [2]

248. In its *Wallpaper-Report* [3] the Commission dealt with the business conduct of the Wallpaper Manufacturers Ltd. (W.P.M.), which, together

1. *Ibid.* at paras. 261, 262.
2. *Ibid.* at para. 275.
3. Report on the Supply of Wallpaper, 1964, London, HMSO, Cmnd. No. 59.

with its manufacturing subsidiaries (The Group), supplied 79% of wallpaper in the United Kingdom. The Commission considered, i.a. the Group's constant practice of acquiring interests in competing firms. It concluded

"... that the Group's manufacturing acquisitions over the years have helped materially to maintain its command over the wallpaper market and have severely limited the effectiveness of the competition it encounters. We take the view that such a course of action is against the public interest unless it can be shown that the monopoly position so established and maintained is used to the public benefit, for example, in promoting efficiency and so reducing costs and prices. We have not found the Group's arguments on this subject convincing. Its twelve mills are said to compete with one another in design, new ideas and service and, subject to central control, in price but nevertheless to enjoy most of the advantages to be expected in an organisation of its size. We do not regard limited internal competition of this kind as a substitute for external competition ... these considerations lead us to the conclusion that the Group's acquisitions of wallpaper manufacturing businesses have not been shown to result in any such advantages to the public interest as might outweigh the disadvantages inherent in the suppression of competition ". [1]

249. The Commission also found that the exclusive dealing arrangements with the majority of the merchants and of the larger retailers of wallpaper not to handle any wallpapers other than the Group's products had operated against the public interest:

"We do not think that this system either promoted efficiency in distribution or stimulated competition. It is difficult to believe that it led to any overall economy in distribution. One effect may well have been to increase the number of distributors handling wallpaper, since independent manufacturers inevitably had to seek new outlets. Moreover, the independent manufacturers in order to obtain outlets were obliged to give higher margins than were obtainable from the Group; and we think it probable that this tendency was strengthened by the artificial and unequal division of the market between "combine" and "non-combine" distributors. The effect of the system on the independent manufacturers was to set a severe limit on their opportunity to compete "value for value, price for price and service for service". Exclusive trading, if practised by a supplier with so large a share of the market as that enjoyed by the Group, is calculated to consolidate and perpetuate his dominant position. We think that the Group's exclusive arrangements had this effect in the sense that they helped to regard that decline in its share of the trade which appears to have been a feature of its history in the absence of new acquisitions ". [2]

1.   Ibid. at para. 169.
2.   Ibid. at para 174.

250. The Commission finally objected to the Group's practice of maintaining resale prices of pattern book ways. Considering the relatively high distributive margin of about 60% of the retail price the Commission held:

" ...this is a trade in which any practice tending to remove or ease the pressure of competition upon retail prices is, *prima facie*, undesirable. We should, therefore, need to be convinced that abandonment of the practice would result in some obvious overriding disadvantage before we could conclude that the practice was not against the public interest ".[1]

The Commission saw no such disadvantage but, on the contrary, expected that the pressure of competition would have "a wholesome effect upon efficiency and costs in the distributive trade, and ultimately upon the retail prices ...". The Commission summarized its conclusions on this point as follows:

"Thus our judgment as to the effect of resale price maintenance in the wallpaper trade is considerably influenced by the facts that it is practised by the monopoly supplier and by no other supplier, that it is applied only to one-half of the monopoly supplier's products with a view to supporting a particular method of trading, and that some of the goods to which it is applied are nevertheless supplied through other channels where they exercise an influence on the price structure. We conclude, therefore, that the Group's practice of maintaining the resale prices of pattern book ways operates and may be expected to operate against the public interest ".[2]

251. In its *report on Petrol*[3] the Commission found that the *solus system* under which retailers were required by each of a number of the oil companies to sell only that supplier's brand or brands of motor fuel did not as such operate against the public interest. However, certain facets of the solus system as practised by the oil companies were considered detrimental.

252. The Commission stated that the length of term of the agreements, while giving the suppliers concerned a greater measure of security of outlet, was not in the public interest if it exceeded five years:

"Given sufficient security, the apportionment of the trade between the various suppliers would tend to become rigid and it would be increasingly difficult for new suppliers to enter the market except by building new stations. The established suppliers in such conditions would also feel freer to pursue what they regarded as their own interests and to control the trade of the retailers more strictly. As we make clear elsewhere ... we think that the suppliers are already exercising too much control over the retailers' trade in lubricants and that there is

1.   *Ibid.* at para. 178.
2.   *Ibid.* at paras. 180-181.
3.   A Report on the Supply of Petrol to Retailers in the United Kingdom, 1965, London, HMSO, Cmnd. No. 264.

114

a danger that they may interefere with their trade in other goods".[1]

253. The Commission criticized restrictions on the retailer in the sale of lubricants and other petroleum products in as far as brands competing with those of the oil company in question were involved. It found that the limitations on the freedom of the retailer would restrict the choice of the motorist in selecting the desired brand of lubricant.[2] Furthermore, it saw a real danger that the brands of the independent suppliers of lubricants might be partly or wholly excluded from the market.[3]

254. A further violation of the public interest was seen in the attempt of the oil companies to influence the trade of the retailers in tyres, batteries and accessories of other manufacturers:

> "We can see no advantage in petrol companies setting out to promote the sale of various brands of goods which are not petroleum products, and commissions ... on goods which it does not handle seem likely in the long run to add to the cost of distribution. The petrol company's intervention in this case appears to us objectionable because it is using its captive market – the solus retailers – to influence the distribution of products which it does not make without the expectation that this will bring about a saving in cost but solely for its own financial advantage. Any transactions of this nature relating to the businesses of retailers with whom the petrol suppliers have solus relationships are in our opinion against the public interest.
>
> In our view, therefore, no petrol supplier should accept any commission or other benefit in respect of the sales or purchases of tyres, batteries, accessories or other goods not being petroleum products by any retailer with whom he has a solus agreement, and any existing arrangement or agreement which has such an effect should be terminated".[4]

255. The same conclusions were made with regard to restrictive obligations on the retailer in relation to the purchase, sale, stocking, display or advertising of such goods.

256. Other features of the solus system found to operate against the public interest were the petrol supplier's right of preemption of the retailer's premises[5] and the insufficient security given to tenants as to the termination of their leases.[6]

257. Finally the Commission concluded that the acquisition of petrol stations by the petrol suppliers might be expected to operate against the public interest unless some limit were imposed.* The Commission

---

1. *Ibid.* at para. 382.
2. *Ibid.* at para. 396.
3. *Ibid.* at para. 397.
4. *Ibid.* at paras. 406, 407.
5. *Ibid.* at paras. 408-411.
6. *Ibid.* at para. 419.
7. *Ibid.* at paras. 412-419.

recommended that no supplier whose deliveries of petrol to company-owned stations exceeded 15% of his total deliveries to retailers and whose total deliveries exceeded 10 million gallons in any year should build or acquire further petrol stations.[1]

258. In the *report on Colour Film*,[2] the Commission dealt extensively with the prices of the Kodak Co., which with about 75% of the market was the dominant supplier in the United Kingdom. In determining whether the prices of colour film supplied by Kodak were excessive the Monopolies Commission compared (1) the rates of profit on capital employed earned by Kodak on its whole business (1964: 22.8%, calculated on the historic cost basis) with the indices of profit for the manufacturing industry as a whole (1963: 13.4%), and (2) the rates of profit on capital employed earned by Kodak on its colour film business (1964: 55.6%) with those earned upon the remainder of its business (1964: 17.6%) and upon its whole business (1964: 22.8%).[3] The Commission rejected the view of Kodak that so long as Kodak's *overall* profits were not unreasonably high, the company should be free to make on its *colour film* business a very high rate of profit. The Commission pointed out that according to this view a rate of profit, which would be regarded as objectionable if the company concerned had no business other than in reference goods, could not be condemned if the company happened to have other less profitable business outside the reference which was allowed to counterbalance the profit on reference goods. After finding that colour film, accounting for one-sixth of Kodak's business, provided one-third of its total net profits,[4] and considering that production and sale of colour film was not a very risky business for Kodak[5] the Commission arrived at the following conclusions:

"Kodak earns from its colour film trade a disproportionately large share of its total profits because its monopoly position in colour film affords it more discretion than it has in its other fields of activity. We have no objection to a successful competitor gaining a fair reward for his success; but when his success leads to a position of market dominance such as Kodak enjoys in colour film it involves him in responsibilities to the public interest. The public interest appears to us to require in the present case that the monopoly supplier should use his position to ensure that the consumer obtains good quality and efficient service at the lowest price consistent with a fair reward to the supplier. Although there is no reason why a part of that reward should not subsequently be devoted to financing the further expansion of the supplier's business, we do not think that his requirements for expansion should determine the size of the reward. We note that according to our figures for Kodak's

1. *Ibid.* at para. 415.
2. Colour Film, A Report on the Supply and Processing of Colour Film, 1966, London, HMSO, Cmnd. No. 1.
3. *Ibid.* at paras. 253, 254.
4. *Ibid.* at para. 257.
5. *Ibid.* at para. 258.

colour film business in 1964 ... an average reduction of 20% in the company's selling prices would still have left Kodak with a profit on this business of 20% on capital employed on the historic cost basis (sales being presumed to remain un-changed quantitatively). We make this point not in order to suggest that 20% is necessarily the desirable maximum rate of profit but to illustrate the room for manoeuvre which Kodak enjoys, and the quite significant effects that a change of pricing policy might bring about.

" Such a price reduction would, no doubt, strengthen Kodak's command of the market. The calculation we have made in the preceding paragraph is unrealistic in this sense. Had Kodak in fact been selling at prices 20% below the actual level in 1964, this would certainly have stimulated demand for its products and led to increased sales; these might eventually be expected in turn to provide scope for further economies of scale and still lower prices. As we have already indicated we do not regard it as a valid objection to such a process that it would tend to enhance Kodak's monopoly position. A monopoly can be advantageous to the public interest if it results in econo-mies of scale which are passed on to the consumer. This may also have the effect of strengthening the monopoly, but the monopoly can be regarded as justified so long as it continues to achieve and pass on further economies ".[1]

259. Another aspect of Kodak's price policy which was found to operate against the public interest was the fixed retail margin of 30% of the retail price. The Commission was struck in particular by the fact "that the retailer can earn two or three times as much by selling a colour film as by the more-or-less identical operation of selling a black and white film; and if the colour film is process-paid the margin is nearly doubled again without his being required to give any addi-tional service ".[2] The Commission further pointed out that there was no need for the retailer to finance any stock or to hire especially skilled personnel and concluded that the level of the retail margin was due primarily to the absence of any compelling stimulus to keep retail prices as low as possible.

260. The Commission finally condemned the practice of Kodak to restrict the sale of colour film to appointed dealers, because it had the effect of keeping the retailer's margin higher than it needed to be and was not an indispensable means to reduce distribution costs,[3] and it also condemned the practice of selling reversal colour film only on a process-paid basis.

261. The four reports just studied may suffice to show what types of practices have been regarded as operating against the public interest and on what considerations the findings of the Monopolies Commission were based. It is not possible in this study to analyse in detail all the reports of the Commission. The following survey of the

1. *Ibid.* at paras. 259-260.
2. *Ibid.* at para. 267.
3. *Ibid.* at paras. 270-274.

various types of practices that have been found to violate the public interest to date may, however, give some overall indication of the practical relevance of the British system although they do not claim to be exhaustive.

262. An important factor has been the *price level* of the dominant firm which was found in a number of instances to be against the public interest.[1] In determining whether prices were against the public interest the Commission has mainly relied on the rate of return on capital, its conclusions being based on a comparison of the rates of (*a*) the dominant firm with those of manufacturing industry as a whole, and (*b*) those of the dominant firm in its dominated business with those in its business as a whole. As was shown by the Kodak Report, the Commission emphasizes that the profits of the monopolist must not be excessively high not only as regards his entire business but also in the particular section of business with respect to which he has dominant power. This normally prevents excessive monopoly profits from being used to finance other less profitable activities of the dominant firm.

263. The Commission emphasized that it did not regard the indices of profits for manufacturing industry as a whole as a precise yard-stick for measuring the profits of individual companies, still less for measuring the profits earned by a company on a particular product, or group of products which represent only one section of its business. However, the Commission insisted that it was the best available. The Commission further pointed out that the use of the historic basis for the calculation of capital costs was the only one available which affords a comparison between the results of the dominant company and those of manufacturing industry as a whole.

264. Other *pricing practices* which were regarded by the Monopolies Commission as against the public interest were discriminatory prices,[2] excessively high distributors' margins,[3] distributors' bonuses and allowances which were not solely related to the individual distributor's turnover in the products of the manufacturer concerned,[4] resale price maintenance,[5] and price recommendations for other products or services.[6]

---

1. Cf., in addition to the British Oxygen and Kodak reports: Report on the Supply of Fertilizers (1959), Report on the Supply of Household Detergents (1966).

2. Cf., especially the reports on British Oxygen and on Electrical Equipment for Mechanically Propelled Land Vehicles (1963). See also the Report on the Supply of Chemical Fertilizer where some discriminations and uniform delivered prices were accepted by the Commission.

3. Cf., Kodak Report (retailers' margin of 30%).

4. Cf., Report on the Supply of Cigarettes and Tobacco and of Cigarette and Tobacco Machinery (1961).

5. Cf. Report on the Supply of Wallpaper. In the Cigarettes Report r.p.m. applied by the dominant manufacturer Imperial Tobacco Co. was accepted, mainly because of the retailer's low margins and the danger of loss-leader selling. Since the adoption of the Resale Prices Act of 1964 the question is governed exclusively by this law as stated by the Commission in its Kodak-Report.

6. Cf. Kodak Report (recommendation of prices to be charged for film processing).

265. Several reports dealt with *restrictions on distribution.* This field covers practices such as supplying only to certain categories of retailers [1] or to supply only to exclusive dealers, [2] to restrict or influence otherwise the sale of products of other manufacturers by retailers, [3] to impose a long-term duration of sole agency agreements, [4] the tying of the sale of one product with another product [5] or a service, [6] and discriminations in the supply of products to retailers. [7]

266. In some cases the Commission has considered that certain acquisitions of other companies by a dominant firm were against the public interest. Thus, in the Wallpaper Report the Commission stated that the dominant group should not further acquire competitors without the consent of the Board of Trade. In the Petrol Report the Commission recommended limitations on the distribution of petrol through company-owned stations. In the case of cigarettes and tobacco the Commission recommended that the dominant manufacturer Imperial Tobacco Co. divest itself of its 42.5 % financial interest in the second largest manufacturer Gallaher Ltd. Finally, in its Report on the Supply of Man-made Cellulosic Fibres [8] one of the recommendations of the Commission was that Courtaulds should not be allowed, without the permission of the Board of Trade, to make further acquisitions in any sector of the textile and clothing industry where its share exceeds a certain figure (e.g. 25 %).

267. In two cases the Commission dealt with *import restrictions.* In the first case, concerning copper semi-manufacturers, [9] the Commission found that the participation of British firms in the Lausanne Agreement, which provided, *inter alia,* for protection of home markets, was against the public interest. In the second case, concerning cellulosic fibres, the Commission condemned the mutual agency agreements which Courtaulds, the dominant supplier, admitted were made with producers in other EFTA countries for the purpose of preventing increased competition from imports from other EFTA countries after the reduction of tariffs within EFTA. [10]

1.   Cf. Kodak Report (confining the retail distribution of colour film to certain appointed outlets). In its Report on the Supply of Infant Milk Foods the Commission has accepted the practice of confining distribution of baby food to retail chemists.

2.   Cf. Wallpaper Report, Petrol-Report (solus system in petrol distribution as such not against the public interest, but subject to certain changes).

3.   Cf. Petrol Report (restrictions on the sale of lubricants, "promotion agreements" with T.B.A. manufacturers).

4.   Cf. Petrol Report (too long terms of solus agreements, too short terms of leases).

5.   Cf. Kodak Report (selling reversal colour films only at prices which include processing).

6.   Report on the Supply of Films for Exhibition in Cinemas (block-booking).

7.   Films Report ("bars" on the showing of films in other cinemas).

8.   Cmnd. 130, 1968.

9.   Report on the Supply and Export of Certain Semi-Manufactures of Copper and Copper-Based Alloys (1955).

10.   Report on the Supply of Man-made Cellulosic Fibres (1968) at paras. 33-52 and 219-230.

268. A final important problem dealt with by the Commission concerned *advertising expenditures.* In its Report on the Supply of Household Detergents, the Commission stated that the advertising and promotion policies of the two leading manufacturers, Unilever and Procter and Gamble, were against the public interest and recommended that the Board of Trade should encourage the two companies to agree to at least a 40% reduction of their selling expenses.[1]

269. In *Belgium* section 2 of the Act of 27th May 1960 on Protection against the Abuse of Economic Power defines an abuse of economic power as the power to "prejudice the public interest by practices which distort or restrict the normal play of competition or which interfere either with the economic freedom of producers, distributors or consumers or with the development of production or trade". To date this provision has not been applied in published decisions so that a practical illustration of this definition cannot be given.

270. In the *Netherlands,* the statutory criterion for taking action against dominant positions is that its "consequences conflict with the public interest".[2]

271. Two cases were so far decided on the basis of this criterion. In the *Sipkes case,*[3] a grocery wholesaler in Friesland who was a member of an affiliated group of wholesale grocers in that province, was boycotted by a number of cigarette manufacturers. The boycott was instituted after independent wholesale tobacconists informed the manufacturers that they did not approve of deliveries to the "affiliated" grocery wholesaler. The Minister found that only one of the manufacturers from whom the wholesaler Sipkes sought to purchase cigarettes would deliver to him, and further, that the refusal of all other manufacturers to sell to Sipkes was based in part on Sipkes' position as an affiliated rather than an independent wholesaler. Concluding that Sipkes was unable to conduct his cigarette trade "in a reasonable way" – i.e. by being allowed to purchase from a number of manufacturers while continuing the affiliated form in which he chose to operate his business – the Minister condemned the boycott as contrary to the public interest.

272. In the *Lijmar case,*[4] a number of cigar manufacturers had refused to sell to a wholesaler who was affiliated to a voluntary chain. It was found that the refusal to supply seriously hindered the distributor concerned in freely practising his wholesale cigars trade in the form he had chosen, i.e. that of a voluntary chain store. This effect of the refusal to sell was deemed incompatible with the prevailing system of production and distribution by individual enterprises, which is based on the principle that the individual firm is free to choose the form of trading which it considers best suited to the conduct of its business.

---

1. Whether and to what extent this recommendation and the others mentioned above have been carried out will be discussed in Part III.
2. Section 24(1) of the Economic Competition Act.
3. (1961) N.S. No. 118.
4. (1961) N.S. No. 151.

273. In *Norway,* the King may, with respect to dominant enterprises, amend or annul practices which are i.a. "detrimental to the public interest" [section 42(3) of the Act on Control of Prices, Profits and Restraints of Competition]. The criteria for intervention under this section concern restrictive practices which are deemed likely to have a harmful effect on production, distribution or other business activities in the realm, or are otherwise considered unreasonable or detrimental to the public interest.

274. The provision against refusals to deal, section 23, applies to all suppliers whether they are market dominating or not. As is illustrated, however, by the *Swiss Watches case,* the Price Directorate in its examination whether a refusal to deal "would be detrimental to the public interest or would have an unreasonable effect on the other party" takes into account whether the firm refusing to supply has a market dominating position. In this case the Price Council accepted after modification a selective sales system introduced by the producers of two well-known Swiss watches, noting that unless the supplier held a dominant position on the market, a selective sales system could normally be left unchallenged. [1]

275. In *Switzerland,* the statutory criteria for public intervention against a dominant enterprise are whether the conduct of such enterprise has effects that are "economically or socially detrimental" (section 20(1) Cartels Act) or whether it "prevents competition or interferes with it appreciably in any one branch of the economy or occupation, in a manner that is incompatible with the public interest, especially one detrimental to consumers" (section 22(1) Cartels Act). While the first criterion is used in the special investigations of the Cartel Commission which may issue recommendations to the market dominating enterprises, the latter criterion is relevant in the enforceable decisions of the Federal Court against such enterprises. In practice, however, the latter criterion is regarded as a precision of the formulation used in section 20(1) Cartels Act. [2]

276. In its report on the situation in the *Sanitary Trade* the Cartels Commission considered it as economically or socially detrimental that there was a too narrow legal or factual relationship between the concertedly acting producers and the cartel formed by the wholesalers, the result being that imports were restricted and the wholesalers protected against competition from outsiders. [3]

277. In the *Petrol and Fuel Oil Report* [4] the Cartels Commission did not conclude that the oil firms' conduct had results which were economically or socially detrimental but the Commission pointed out some "oligopolistic restraints of competition" which would meet the requirements of section 20(1) of the Cartels Act if

1. Pristidende No. 10 of 1963; *Guide,* Norway, Section 3.10.3; see also Pristidende No. 5 of 1956; No. 15 of 1968; No. 21 of 1959.
2. Cf. Report on the competitive situation in the sanitary trade, *loc. cit.,* at para. 220.
3. *Loc. cit.,* at paras. 220-223.
4. The competitive situation in the petrol and fuel oil market, *loc. cit.*

- they impaired the supply to Switzerland of oil or oil products
- they affected adversely the quality of oil products offered in Switzerland
- they impaired the distribution of petrol and fuel oil to consumers
- they resulted in price level for oil products that must be be regarded as excessive.

In this connection the Commission stated that it would regard as economically detrimental a tacitly co-ordinated conduct of the oligopoly whereby independent wholesale importers and wholesalers were hindered or driven out of business, because this would result in even greater losses of the intensity of competition. [2]

278. In addition, section 4 of the Act on Cartels prohibits subject to the exceptions listed in section 5, such coercive practices as black-listing of employers, discrimination concerning prices or terms of purchase, and undercutting aimed at a particular competitor, when their object is to eliminate outside competition or appreciably to inter-fere with its free exercise. There is no case yet in which the pro-hibition of section 4 has been applied to a market dominating enter-prise. [3] Since, however, the prohibition applies both to dominant enterprises and cartels, some indication as to its scope may be seen from a case involving a refusal by a cartel to supply to a wholesaler. In this case, *Walch v. Swiss Association of Wine and Spirit Merchants*, [4] numerous producers, importers and general agents in the spirits trade had made an agreement with the Swiss association of wine and spirits merchants to fix minimum resale prices and to see that these prices were observed by retailers. After Walch, a wholesaler, not being a party to the agreement, had offered spirits to several hotels at lower prices, the "arbitration board", appointed by the parties to the agreement to enforce it, decided that Walch be excluded from being supplied with the products covered by the agreement for a period of 12 months. The Court of first instance in the Canton of Berne held that this refusal was an appreciable hindrance of an outsider's ability to compete which was not justified by an overriding legitimate interest of the parties to the agreement. The Court stated that the pro-ducts covered by the agreement were amongst those most in demand and that a dealer in spirits could not keep his place in the market without selling them. Justification under section 5 was denied on the grounds that the refusal exceeded the *bona fide* aim of securing obser-vance of the agreed minimum resale prices because the cartel mem-bers were not prepared to resume supplies even if Walch agreed to observe these prices. The Court also took into account that there was

1. *Ibid.* at para. 101.
2. *Ibid.* at para. 103.
3. In Walch v. Navazza, ATF 91 II 489, Section 4 was found not to apply because the defendant, the sole agent in Switzerland of "Black and White" whisky and 'Martell'' cognac, was found to have no dominant position. (See paras. 71-72).
4. 2 *Publications de la Commission Suisse des Cartels* 327 (1967).

apparently a secret list of some 300 important customers to whom the signatories to the agreement had delivered merchandise at prices lower than the minimum selling prices prescribed for third parties, and that the signatories to the agreement delivered goods at reduced prices to their most worthwhile customers whilst compelling resale agents to pay the prices laid down in the agreement. Under the circumstances, the judge concluded that in this particular case genuine regulation of the market and, above all, the safeguarding of "fair competition and the prevention of its action from being distorted" could not be regarded as the purpose of the prohibition issued against the plaintiff.

C. INTERFERENCE WITH THE NORMAL OPERATION OF THE MARKET

279. In *France* article 59 bis of the Price Ordinance No. 45-1483 prohibits activities of dominant enterprises which "have the object or may have the effect of interfering with the *normal operation of the market*". There are, as yet, no practical cases from which the application of this criterion could be seen. In the case *Fédération Nationale des Cinémas Français contre Radiodiffusion Française*[1] a violation of article 59 bis was denied on the ground that ORTF, even if it had a dominant position as buyer of films, did not prevent other film exhibitors from obtaining supplies and from discussing freely the price for the renting of films.

D. UNREASONABLE PRICES AND BUSINESS CONDITIONS, UNREASONABLE RESTRAINT ON THE FREEDOM OF TRADE, ETC.

280. In *Denmark,* the criterion for administrative action against powerful enterprises is that their conduct "results in or must be deemed to result in unreasonable prices or business conditions, unreasonable restriction of the freedom of trade, or unreasonable discrimination in respect of the conditions of trading".[2]

281. In the enforcement practice of the Monopolies Control Authority this standard has mainly been applied to cases of refusal to sell and of refusal of delivery on equal terms.

282. In one case a dominant manufacturer of gas and electric kitchen ranges had discontinued supplies to the Consumers' Co-operative Chain of Copenhagen after this chain had started to quote and advertise net prices instead of the manufacturer's higher recommended

---

1. Judgment of 8th March 1965, (1965) Revue trim. dr. eur. 286.
2. Section 11(1) Monopoly Control Act.

resale prices.[1] The Monopolies Control Authority and the Appeal Tribunal held that the refusal to supply in this case was an unreasonable restraint of the freedom of trade within the meaning of section 11(1) as it obstructed the chain's pricing policy. The M.C.A. rejected the manufacturer's argument that it would be an unreasonable restriction of his own business interests if he could not protect himself against a reduction in sales to other dealers which had resulted from the chain's new pricing policy. The Appeal Tribunal further attached special importance to the fact that the chain sold at prices covering the relevant sales costs and a fair net profit. The Tribunal also found that considering the supplier's market position, it might constitute a significant restriction of the chain's trading conditions if it could not carry the products in question.

283. In another case a radio dealer complained to the Authority that he could not obtain delivery of radio and television sets from a leading Danish factory. Seeing that the complainant already sold two of the most well-known makes of radio and television sets in his shop and that he could obtain delivery of two more equally well-known makes, the Authority did not find sufficient grounds on which to order the factory to sell to the complainant.

284. The Appeal Tribunal, however, found that in being unable to carry the factory's make, the complainant's freedom of trade had been seriously hampered. For many years the complainant had been operating a medium-sized business, and after a time, the factory had delivered spare parts to the repair shop also operated by the complainant. The Tribunal therefore, ruled that the refusal to sell constituted a restriction on the complainant's freedom of trade and that the ensuing inequality in trading conditions was unreasonable. [2]

285. These cases show that the decision whether the refusal to supply constitutes an unreasonable restriction on the freedom of trade is mainly based on a balancing of the interests of the manufacturer and the affected dealer. In weighing the dealer's interests account is taken of the strength of the supplier's market position and of alternative sources of supply available to the dealer.

286. Although *Sweden* has no special provisions on market dominating enterprises, it may be useful in this context to mention section 5 of the Swedish Act to Counteract Restraints of Competition which authorizes the Freedom of Commerce Board to eliminate through negotiations harmful effects of restraints of competition. A restraint is considered to have a harmful effect, "if, contrary to the public interest, it unduly affects the formation of prices, restrains productivity in business, or impedes or prevents the trade of others".[3] In determining, whether a restraint has had effects which were contrary to the public interest, the question whether the restraints had been

1. *Meddelelser fra Monopoltilsynet,* 1962, pp. 267-277. See also Guide, Denmark, Section 3, Case No. 14.

2. *Meddelelser fra Monopoltilsynet,* 1965, pp. 283-286.

3. Section 5(2).

practised by a market dominating enterprise may be of some importance.

287. An example is the Board's decision to open negotiations with a larger producer of *household detergents*.[1] This producer had announced a "functional discount" of 2 % to distributors who regularly undertake distribution from their own warehouse to at least 25 retail establishments open to the public. The Board took exception to the fact that large department stores, chain-stores, and mail-order houses did not receive this discount. After finding that this practice involved a restraint of competition which affected business productivity, the Board, in determining whether this restraint had harmful effects, considered the fact that the products of the company consisted essentially of widely used everyday articles with well-known brands and that the company had a dominating position in the market for detergents. The Board found it to be against the public interest that different distribution systems were not allowed to compete on equal terms in the sale of the company's products.

E.   CONDUCT CONTRARY TO THE ECSC TREATY

288. Under article 66(7) of the *ECSC Treaty* the High Authority is authorized to intervene, where a market dominating enterprise makes use of its position "for purposes contrary to those of this Treaty". The decision against the *Oberrheinische Kohlenunion AG*[2] seems to be the only case where the conduct of a market dominating enterprise has been formally attacked by the High Authority. This company was practically the only supplier of coal to customers in the southern and southwestern parts of Germany. It had announced that it would in future supply directly to industrial consumers and public utilities with an annual consumption of 300,000 tons or more. The High Authority found that such a practice "would lead to division of the market between (the respondent) and the dealers and would hinder consumers in the free choice of their suppliers". The defendant would thus "use its market dominating position for purposes contrary to the Treaty, especially to its article 4".[3] The High Author-

---

1.   *Pris- och Kartellfragor*, No. 4/5 and No. 8, 1963; *Guide* Sweden, Section 3, Case No. 17.

2.   Recommendation of the High Authority, dated 11th July 1953; Official Journal 1953, p. 154.

3.   Article 4 of the ECSC Treaty reads as follows: "The following are recognized to be incompatible with the common market for coal and steel, and are, therefore, abolished and prohibited within the Community in the manner set forth in this Treaty: a) ...; b) measures or practices discriminating among producers, among buyers or among consumers, especially as concerns prices, delivery terms and transport rates, as well as measures or practices which hamper the buyer in the free choice of his supplier; c) ...; d) restrictive practices tending towards the division or the exploitation of the market".

ity directed a recommendation to the defendant to abstain from the illegal practice. [1]

F. CONCLUSION

289. The detrimental effects of the conduct of powerful enterprises, against which action may be taken under the "conduct" laws, are measured by such criteria as "abuse", "violation of the public interest", "interference with the normal operation of the market", "unreasonable prices, unfair business conditions", etc. The foregoing analysis of the application of these criteria has shown that it is not possible to include them in a single general formula. Not even in the country with the most developed practice, the United Kingdom, does such a formula exist. Before an attempt is nevertheless made to state a few general conclusions, the following summary of enforcement practice shows what main types of practices have been dealt with.

290. The most frequent practices – frequent not only as regards number of cases but also number of countries in which the cases have arisen – are *refusal to deal and differential treatment.* Cases of this type have been dealt with, under the above-mentioned standards, in Denmark, Germany, the Netherlands, Norway, Switzerland, the United Kingdom and in the ECSC. Although it may be generally said that these countries have recognized that powerful enterprises are under a special obligation due to their market power not to refuse to deal with others and not to differentiate between other enterprises, this obligation has in no case amounted to a *per se* condemnation. Instead, the finding that a refusal to sell or differential treatment was an "abuse" etc., was always based on a balancing of the various interests and effects involved.

291. Thus, in cases of refusal to sell a main point of consideration was whether the customer affected had other sources of supply and whether he needed the products concerned to stay in business or to enter the market. [2] On the other hand, legitimate interests of the refusing or differentiating supplier were accepted as justification. [3]

1. In connection with article 66, para. 7 of the ECSC Treaty, article 15 of the EFTA Convention should be mentioned which declares as "incompatible with this Convention in so far as they frustrate the benefits expected from the removal or absence of duties and quantitative restrictions on trade between Member States; ... *b*) actions by which one or more enterprises take unfair advantage of a dominant position within the Area of the Association or a substantial part of it". Although no cases have as yet been decided, it is clear from the text that Article 15 has to be interpreted in the light of the particular purpose of the Convention.

2. See, e.g. the German Sporting Goods Fair case (paras. 235 and 236), the Danish gas cookers case (para. 282), the Dutch Lijmar case (para. 272), the Swiss spirits case (para. 278) and the ECSC brown coal case (para. 288).

3. See the cases in the preceding footnote where such interests were weighed against the interests of the customers affected. See also the Monopolies Commission's Report on Chemical Fertilizer where some discrimination was accepted on the ground that the supplier pursued legitimate business interests.

In addition to these particular interests, the public interest in maintaining competition was taken into account, e.g. in free competitive pricing where refusals to sell were used to prevent retailers from selling below the manufacturer's recommended resale prices. [1]

292. It is clear that where there are special provisions against refusals to sell or differential treatment the cases will normally be dealt with under these provisions. This may explain that for example in France, where such special provisions exist, [2] no cases of refusals to sell or differential treatment have as yet been dealt with under the provision concerning dominant enterprises. Therefore, the extent to which cases of refusal to sell and of differential treatment have been dealt with under the laws on dominant enterprises does not indicate the particular country's complete attitude towards these practices.

293. A second group of practices which have been dealt with under the laws on dominant enterprises are *restrictions on distribution,* mainly in the form of restrictive agreements. This group includes sole agency and exclusive dealing agreements and tie-in clauses. The laws on dominant enterprises have been applied in practice to these restrictions only in Germany and the United Kingdom. The only German case (Meto) concerned a tie-in clause imposed by a dominant supplier which was found to be an unreasonable burden on buyers and an unfair hindrance to competitors entering the market. Access to the market was also the decisive consideration in the Monopolies Commission's finding in the Petrol case that the restrictions on the sale of lubricants of other suppliers and the "promotion" agreements with certain tyres, batteries and accessories manufacturers violated the public interest. The other types of practices restricting distribution which were considered as violating the public interest were already summarized earlier.

294. Again, as has already been shown with regard to refusal to deal and differential treatment, no *per se* rules concerning "abusive" practices or practices violating the public interest have been formulated. Instead, the assessment is made on the basis of the individual interests involved in the particular case and the general interest in the maintenance of effective competition, in particular, of free market access. It should also be noted that special provisions may exist enabling action to be taken against restrictive distribution agreements. The absence of particular provisions in the United Kingdom may explain in part the relatively frequent application of the law on powerful enterprises to such agreements and therefore does not fully indicate a particular country's general attitude towards such agreements. [3]

---

1. See, e.g., the Danish gas cookers case (paras. 235 and 236).

2. See Article 37 of the Price Ordinance No. 45-1,483.

3. In the United States the restrictions imposed on petrol retailers in the sale of tires, batteries and accessories have been dealt with under Section 5 of the Federal Trade Commission Act. See e.g., Atlantic Refining Co. v. F.T.C., 381 U.S. 357, 1965 Trade Cases para. 71,459. In Germany these restrictions were recently attacked under Section 18. See Federal Cartel Office Decision of 19th July 1968, BM – 46/67.

295. The third group of practices dealt with within various countries relates to *prices*. These practices may be considered from two aspects: (1) the prices of the dominant supplier himself, (2) his influence on the prices of other sellers (e.g., in the form of resale price maintenance).

296. The first aspect has been dealt with in Germany and the United Kingdom. The German case concerning Zementkontor Unterelbe was decided by comparing the prices asked on one market with those prevailing on another regional market for the same product where competition existed. Further, the fact that geographical price discrimination was involved, facilitated the finding that the prices concerned were abusive. In the Petrol Prices case the finding of abusively high prices was made with respect to a particular price increase only. It was held that since the additional costs justifying the increase were no longer being incurred by suppliers, it was abusive to continue to maintain the higher prices. No finding was made, however, as to whether or not the higher price level was abusive in the light of total costs.

297. The two German cases involved special situations. In the first case a comparable competitive market was available and in the second the finding of an abuse was limited to a particular price increase. However, the United Kingdom Monopolies Commission has based its findings that prices of dominant enterprises violated the public interest on total cost calculations. The Commission has mainly relied on the rate of return on capital in order to determine whether prices were against the public interest, its conclusions being based on a comparison of the rates of return of the dominant firm with those of manufacturing industry as a whole, and the dominant firm in business in which it has a dominant position with those in its business as a whole. On this basis the Commission calculated, for example, in the Kodak case, Kodak's profits in its colour film business (1964: 55.6 %) and compared them with the profits of Kodak's other business (1964: 17.6 %) and in Kodak's entire business (1964: 22.8 %) and with the profit level in manufacturing industry (1963: 13.4 %). After considering the arguments of Kodak in defence of its profits level the Commission concluded that Kodak's pricing policy, in the light of the high profit aimed at and obtained by that policy, operated and might be expected to operate against the public interest.

298. It is not possible to discuss in this study in detail the problems of cost and profit calculations and the question whether such calculations and comparisons with the profits in other industries are an adequate method to determine whether the prices and profits of a market dominating enterprise are abusive or not. For the purpose of this study it must be sufficient to state the two concepts on which this determination may be and have in fact been based: the hypothetical competitive market and the "reasonable" price calculated on the basis of costs and profits. Further practice must show to what extent these concepts are a sufficient basis for an effective control of the prices of market dominating enterprises. [1]

1. The same question arises in those legislations which have introduced a general system of price control, e.g. in Denmark under the Price Supervision Act of 25th May 1956.

299. Other pricing practices not already dealt with under the aspect of discrimination have involved mainly the application of resale price maintenance. The only country where r.p.m. was found to violate the criteria which were just studied is the United Kingdom. The issue has, however, lost its importance there, as resale price maintenance is now governed by the special provisions of the Resale Prices Act of 1964. This is a further confirmation of what was already said with respect to refusal to deal, differential treatment and restrictive distribution agreements that such special provisions have to be taken into account to see what a country's overall attitude with respect to a particular practice is.

300. In connection with resale price maintenance applied by dominant suppliers the recent German Melitta case[1] should be mentioned. In this case it was held that a dominant supplier with 91 to 94 % market share had to be considered *prima facie* to be the price leader in its market and was therefore presumed not to be in price competition with other suppliers of similar products. This being only a limited presumption applying to a supplier with almost a 100 % monopoly, it cannot be generally said that market dominating enterprises in Germany are barred from applying resale price maintenance.

301. *Acquisitions of other companies* were to date dealt with under the aspect of conduct control of dominant enterprises in only one country: the United Kingdom. In one case (cigarettes and tobacco) the Monopolies Commission recommended that the dominant firm divest itself of a financial interest in a competing enterprise, while in three cases (wallpaper, petrol and cellulosic fibres) restrictions as to future acquisitions of certain other firms were recommended. In the EEC and in Germany the application of the laws on dominant enterprises to mergers involving dominant enterprises has been discussed, but no cases have yet been decided. Similarly, no orders have been made under section 15 of the Belgian Act on Protection against the Abuse of Economic Power.

302. Finally, *import restrictions* and *advertising expenditures* should be mentioned. Again, as was the case with respect to acquisitions of other companies, the United Kingdom is the only country where these types of practices have been dealt with under the law on dominant enterprises.

303. *Summarizing,* it may be said that a great number of practices have been dealt with, the most frequent — as far as the number of cases and of countries in which the cases have arisen are concerned — being refusal to sell and differential treatment, but that no *per se* rules of "abusive" practices have been formulated. The frequency of these two practices in enforcement practice shows that there is however, a tendency to recognize that powerful enterprises are under a special obligation not to refuse to deal and not to discriminate. This is reflected, for example, in section 26(2) of the German Act against Restraints of Competition, which subjects market dominating

1. Berlin Court of Appeals, Judgment of 21st May 1968, Kart V 19 and 20/66.

enterprises to a particular duty not to discriminate and is also expressed in the lists of abusive practices contained in the Spanish law[1] and in the law of the EEC.[2] In general it may be concluded that practices of powerful enterprises which directly endanger the competitive position of other enterprises are at least to some extent presumed to be abusive. Further tentative rules applying to all "conduct" laws or at least to a majority of them cannot yet be formulated for lack of sufficient practical experience in most of these laws. This applies in particular to the question of "abusive" prices with respect to which only the United Kingdom has developed some general principles.

304. Apparently, the only attempt to base the enforcement of the law on dominant enterprises on some sort of general formula has been made in Germany where the Federal Cartel Office has generally stated that "every practice of a market dominating enterprise is abusive which produces market results which could definitely not have been obtained under effective competition".[3] The essence of this formula is to impose on market dominating enterprises a duty to act as if they were in effective competition with other enterprises. The finding of an abuse under such a formula is made on the basis of a comparison of the actual market conduct and market performance of the dominant enterprise in question with the "as if" situation of a competitive market. Where such a market does actually exist, as in the case Zementkontor Unterelbe, the application of the formula does not involve great practical difficulties. Where it does not, the comparison must be made with a hypothetical market situation which naturally contains uncertainties. To take the example of prices, a successful use of the "as if" concept presupposes that it is possible to determine what the prices on a market would be if effective competition prevailed. It seems that unless there are some comparable actual market situations, a solution to this problem can only be achieved on the basis of costs and profits calculations like those of the Monopolies Commission in the United Kingdom.

305. It is not possible, at this stage in the development of the laws on dominant enterprises, to state in more specific terms the essence of the concepts of "abuse", "violation of the public interest" etc. Basically it may be said that all laws aim at some correction of the market conduct or performance of dominant enterprises which are not subject to effective competition, but the enforcement practice in most countries is still too limited and scattered to permit the formulation of precise general principles at the present time. Further enforcement practice must be awaited before it can be seen more clearly whether such principles will be developed and what their content will be.

1. See Section 3(e) of the Act against Restraints of Competition.
2. See Article 86(c) of the EEC-Treaty.
3. See Meto case, (para. 233 supra).

Part Three

MEASURES AND PROCEDURES
TO CONTROL MARKET POWER

INTRODUCTION

306. Part II has described the substantive law criteria for taking action against the formation of undesirable market power by merger and monopolization and against specific business practices of existing powerful enterprises. Part III will describe in detail what sort of action may be taken and what procedures are applied.

307. The control of market power may be exercised either directly within the framework of the restrictive business practice laws or indirectly by other laws influencing either the formation or conduct of powerful enterprises. In the first chapter of this Part an analysis will be given of restrictive business practices laws pertaining to market power. The second chapter will then deal briefly with the influence of the various other laws.

Chapter I

DIRECT CONTROL OF MARKET POWER

308. Market power can be directly controlled in two basic ways: *i*) by aiming at preventing its formation or by dissolution (deconcentration) of existing market power, *ii*) by regulating or controlling the market conduct of powerful enterprises. These two procedures are not mutually exclusive and may be applied concurrently. Since the provisions against the formation or existence of market dominating enterprises cover, as a rule, only the collective formation of market dominating enterprises (by merger) and their individual formation by monopolization and similar means, even those countries with legislation of type *i*) are faced with the question of controlling the market conduct of existing powerful enterprises. This is not only the case where a single market dominating enterprise is the result of normal growth without merger with other enterprises, but also where a group of enterprises practising conscious parallel conduct such as price leadership is considered a market dominating group (oligopoly problem).

A. LAWS CONTROLLING THE FORMATION
OF MARKET POWER

309. Mergers and monopolization are, as far as can be seen, the only means of forming market power over which direct control is exercised under the restrictive business practice laws. The formation of such power by normal business growth or by parallel conduct of a group of enterprises is not directly restricted in the legislations covered by this study.

1. *MERGERS*

Control Measures

310. The measures which may be taken against mergers having the detrimental effects described in Part II may be either of an admin-

istrative or criminal character or both. While administrative measures are immediately directed at preventing undesirable mergers, including preliminary prevention until final clearance, and at remedying the situation where an illegal or unauthorized merger has been carried out, criminal sanctions in merger cases are intended to achieve these aims indirectly, by means of the threat of being criminally sanctioned for carrying out a merger.

Administrative Measures

311. The main examples where the measures which may be taken against undesirable mergers are primarily of an administrative character are the United States, United Kingdom, Japan and the ECSC. Under these legislations, mergers not conforming to the standards of legality may be declared illegal and prohibited by court or administrative orders.

312. In the *United States*, under section 15 of the Clayton Act, the district courts are invested with jurisdiction to prevent and restrain violations of section 7 of this Act. The proceedings are in equity, giving the courts vast powers to grant whatever relief they deem appropriate, including temporary restraining orders, and, after a consummated merger has been found illegal, to order dissolution and divestiture. A violation of any decree in a proceeding under section 15 is considered a contempt of court. [1]

313. In addition to the powers given to the courts under section 15, section 11 authorizes the Federal Trade Commission to enforce compliance with section 7 by issuing cease and desist orders and requiring divestiture. Where orders of this kind are violated, the Commission may apply to the competent Court of Appeals for the enforcement of its order. Final judgments or decrees of this court are subject to the aforesaid contempt of court rules. As has now been recognized by the United States Supreme Court, the Federal Trade Commission has also the power to seek temporary injunctive relief against the consummation of a merger pending proceedings under section 7 of the Clayton Act before the Commission, and the competent Court of Appeals has the power to grant such relief. [2]

314. In practice, many charges of violation of section 7 of the Clayton Act are settled by a consent decree of a court or by a consent order of the Federal Trade Commission. In both instances it is possible, with the consent of the defendant or respondent, to grant injunctive relief by a final decision without a trial or adjudication of the issues involved in the case. Both consent decrees and consent orders have steadily increased in importance as a means of enforcing section 7 of the Clayton Act and the antitrust laws in general.

1. Cf. e.g., First Security National Bank and Trust Co. v. United States, 382 U.S. 34, 1965 Trade Cases, para. 71,572 (United States Supreme Court).
2. Federal Trade Commission v. Dean Foods Co., 384 U.S. 597, 1966 Trade Cases, para. 71,788.

315. Where an agreement cannot be reached the courts and the Commission "determine the equitable relief necessary and appropriate in the public interest to dominate the effects of the acquisition offensive to section 7 of the Clayton Act". [1] While the primary object of decrees and orders granting relief in merger cases, whether litigated or not, is divestiture and dissolution, the courts and the Federal Trade Commission have frequently used additional remedies to eliminate any increase of market power that may have resulted from the merger. Thus, a firm which has violated section 7 of the Clayton Act will, in addition to an order of divestiture, generally be prohibited from making future acquisitions of stocks or assets, at least for a certain period, [2] or further acquisitions will be made subject to the consent of the government or leave of the court. [3] The defendant may also be ordered to grant non-exclusive licences on a reasonable royalty basis to competitors. [4] In a consent order, the Federal Trade Commission not only ordered the largest producer of household consumer products to sell one of several plants of an acquired coffee producer, but also ordered him not to:

"... Accept from media any discounts or rate reductions on coffee advertising which result from advertising for its other products, for the next five years.

Conduct any coffee promotion in conjunction with any of its other products in the same promotion for a similar five-year period.

Discriminate in price in the sale of coffee products unless such price differences are cost justified or the lower price is granted in good faith to meet an equally low price of a competitor". [5]

316. In another order the defendant was required — in addition to divestiture — to make available to other domestic producers and consumers at reasonable, nondiscriminatory prices a semi-finished product (crude lactose) so long as he held a share of or above 30 % of the sales of a processed product (lactose). [6]

317. In the *United Kingdom*, under the Monopolies and Mergers Act 1965, the Board of Trade may, not later than 6 months after consummation of a merger which either involves at least one third of a market for the supply of goods or entails assets being taken over

1. U.S. v. Kimberly-Clark Corp., 264 F.Supp. 439, 1967 Trade Cases, para. 72,018 (D.C. Cal.) at p. 83,621.

2. See e.g., U.S. v. General Shoe Corp., 1956 Trade Cases, para. 68,271 (D.C. Tenn.); U.S. v. American Smelting and Refining Co. et al., 1967 Trade Cases, para. 72,003 (D.C.N.Y.)

3. See, e.g., U.S. v. Anheuser-Busch Inc., 1960 Trade Cases, para. 69,599 (D.C. Fla.).

4. U.S. v. General Shoe Corp., 1956 Trade Cases, para. 68,271 (D.C. Tenn.).

5. F.T.C. v. Procter and Gamble, 3 CCH–Trade Regulation Reporter, para. 17,858 (1967).

6. F.T.C. v. Foremost Dairies Inc., 3 CCH–Trade Regulation Reporter, para. 17,835 (1967); apparently no analogous orders have been entered in litigated cases.

exceeding 5 million pounds, refer the matter to the Monopolies Commission for investigation. If the Commission finds that the merger operates or may be expected to operate against the public interest, the Board of Trade may prohibit or restrict the merger (section 3(5) and 6(10) Monopolies and Mergers Act 1965). It is further empowered to order divestiture (section 3(6) Monopolies and Mergers Act 1965). Finally, the Board of Trade may issue temporary restraining orders ("standstill orders") until the Monopolies Commission has completed its investigation (section 6(11) Monopolies and Mergers Act 1965).[1] All these orders may be enforced by civil proceedings (injunction or other appropriate relief) only. Violation of a court order would be a case of contempt of court. To date, the Monopolies Commission has considered two mergers to be against the public interest.[2] No further action was taken as the participants did not pursue their merger plans.

318. In a number of cases the Monopolies Commission approved mergers only after the participating enterprises had given undertakings and assurances concerning the future conduct of the combined enterprise's business conduct. For example, in the BMC/Pressed Steel merger an assurance was given by BMC to continue to supply car bodies to other car firms on customary terms.[3] Further, assurances designed to prevent potential abuses of the economic power acquired by the merger were given on the following points: to develop the monopoly product commercially, to pass on to customers the savings achieved by economies of scale resulting from the merger, to continue to supply the monopolized product to specified groups of enterprises, to refrain from any discrimination in price, to publish its prices, and to grant licences under any patents relating to the dominated product on reasonable terms.[4]

319. A special procedure applies in the United Kingdom to newspaper mergers involving a daily circulation of 500,000 or more copies. In this case the written consent of the Board of Trade is required (section 8(1) Monopolies and Mergers Act 1965).[5] Effecting an unauthorized newspaper merger is a criminal offence subject to imprisonment of up to two years or to a fine or both (section 8(5) Monopolies and Mergers Act 1965).

320. In *Japan,* under section 15(2) of the Antimonopoly Act, intended mergers have to be reported to the Fair Trade Commission.

1. Such orders were issued in the cases Ross Group Ltd./Associated Fisheries Ltd. and Dental Manufacturing Co. Ltd. or The Dentists Supply Co. of New York/Amalgamated Dental Company Ltd.

2. The Monopolies Commission, Ross Group Limited and Associated Fisheries Limited, A report on a proposed merger, London 1966; The Monopolies Commission, United Drapery Stores Limited and Montague Burton Limited, A report on the proposed merger, London 1967.

3. The British Motor Corp. Ltd. and the Pressed Steel Company Ltd., *loc. cit.,* at paras. 60–61.

4. See especially British Insulated Callender's Cables Ltd. and Pyrotenax Ltd., *loc. cit.,* Appendix 5.

5. For an example of such a proceeding see: The Monopolies Commission. The Times Newspaper and the Sunday Times paper proprietor. 1966, London, HMSO, Cmnd. 273.

Consummation of the merger in these cases in prohibited for a period of 30 days after the report has been received, unless the Commission has shortened or extended this period. Within this period, the Commission may file a complaint and initiate thereby a complaint procedure upon which, in case of a merger in violation of section 15(1), the necessary measure may be ordered (section 15(4), 17-2 and 54). Further, the courts may, upon application of the Fair Trade Commission, issue temporary injunctions in cases of urgent necessity [section 67(1)]. Violations of orders under section 54(1) and 67(1) are subject to penal servitude or administrative fines (sections 96, 97 and 98). So far these powers have been applied in very rare cases only.

321. In the *ECSC*, under article 66(1) of the ECSC Treaty, mergers are made subject to prior authorisation by the High Authority. In the case of an unauthorized merger the High Authority can either – subject to the payment of a fine by the participants – grant a subsequent approval if it finds that the merger meets the substantive requirements of a lawful merger [article 66(2)], or declare the merger illegal and order its dissolution [article 66(5)]. Further, temporary measures may be taken (article 66(5), subsection 3). The High Authority has specific powers to execute its decision, e.g. to organise the forced sale of illegally acquired assets. The sanction for effecting an unauthorized merger is a fine of up to 10% of the value of the assets acquired or regrouped. No criminal sanctions are provided for in the ECSC Treaty.

322. *In summary*, two legislations, those of the ECSC and – with respect to newspaper mergers – United Kingdom, require prior authorisation of mergers. Unauthorized mergers are illegal and subject to criminal sanctions (United Kingdom with respect to newspapers) or fines (ECSC) and may be dissolved. In the other legislations, either the courts (United States) or the administration may prohibit mergers which are contrary to the substantive standard of legality, as described in Part II, and eventually order their dissolution. Such orders may be enforced either by administrative sanctions (e.g., forced sale of assets), fines, or criminal sanctions (imprisonment in cases of contempt of court). In all legislations temporary measures until final clearance may be taken.

Criminal Measures

323. The only merger control system of a primarily criminal law character can be found in the Canadian Combines Investigation Act. According to section 33 of this Act every person who is a party or privy to or knowingly assists in, or in the formation of, an illegal merger as defined in section 2(e) of the Act is guilty of an offence and liable to imprisonment of up to two years. Where after investigation and report by the appropriate agencies a merger is considered to be in violation of the statute the only way to act against it is to bring a criminal action against the participants. However, the courts have the power to intervene against intended or recently consummated mergers before criminal proceedings have led to conviction (section

139

31(2) Combines Investigation Act). Where a conviction under section 33 has been secured, the Court may direct the participants to dissolve the merger (section 31(1) Combines Investigation Act). Failure to comply with, or contraventions of, orders under section 31 are subject to imprisonment up to two years or to a fine at the discretion of the Court.

324. The criminal character of the Canadian merger provisions has to be seen in the context of the particular constitutional situation in Canada under the British North America Act of 1867, under which the only constitutional basis for the Parliament of Canada to provide for sanctions in the field of restrictive business practices is its power to enact criminal law provisions.[1] It is difficult to judge whether and to what extent this criminal law character of the merger provisions has burdened their effectiveness. The fact that in all 4 cases adjudged under section 33 so far, the companies and persons charged were acquitted[2] may be an indication that the courts, in view of the criminal nature of the offence, are hesitant to hold a merger illegal under sections 2(e) and 33. To what extent this deficiency, if it exists, may be overcome by the practice of informal consultations between the Director for Investigation and Research and the representatives of enterprises participating in a proposed merger, is equally difficult to judge.

325. The only other legislation of a primarily criminal character which may apply to mergers is article 59 bis, para 1, of the French Price Ordinance No. 45-1483. Since there have been, however, as yet no practical merger cases under this provision. the question will not be further discussed in the present context[3]. Likewise, no further analysis is made here of the provisions against restrictive agreements, monopolization or dominant positions insofar as they may, in some legislations, also apply, under certain circumstances, to mergers.

Control Procedures

326. It is important to distinguish between the administrative or criminal law character of the merger provisions which have just been examined and whether the enforcement of these provisions is primarily entrusted to courts or administrative agencies. Thus, as has been pointed out already, section 7 of the Clayton Act has an administrative (civil) character in that it does not create a punishable offence but provides for powers to prevent mergers the effect of which may be to substantially lessen competition or to tend to create a monopoly.

1. For Details see Gosse, *The Law on Competition in Canada,* Toronto 1962, pp. 226 seq.
2. Rex v. Canadian Import Co., 61 C.C.C. 114 (1933); Rex v. Staples, (1940) D.L.R. 699; Regina v. Canadian Breweries Ltd., (1960) O.R. 601; Regina v. The British Columbia Refining Co. Ltd., (1960) 129 C.C.C. 7.
3. This problem is discussed by Blaise, *Le Statut Juridique des Ententes Economiques dans le Droit Français et le Droit des Communautés Européennes,* Paris 1964, pp. 145 seq.

But, as far as enforcement by the Antitrust Division is concerned, these powers can only be applied in the form of a court decision. Only the Federal Trade Commission can make its own decision by holding a merger illegal and prohibiting its consummation or require its dissolution, a decision which is, however, subject to court review (section 11 Clayton Act). The same procedure, i.e. initial administrative decision subject to court review, applies in Japan (section 77 Antimonopoly Act) and in the ECSC (article 66, para. 5(2) of the Treaty). On the other hand a purely administrative procedure is followed in the United Kingdom where orders with respect to mergers under the Monopolies and Mergers Act 1965 are not open to judicial review. On the other hand, a purely judicial solution is found in Canada, which, as a consequence of the criminal law character of its merger provisions, only provides for a court procedure. The only administrative aspect is the investigation by the Restrictive Trade Practices Commission whose findings are, however, neither binding on the Government, when deciding to bring an indictment, nor on the courts.

327. It seems obvious that a system of enforcement by the courts as exists in the United States and Canada would be difficult to apply where the criteria of control are merely phrased in general terms of public interest as is the case under the British Monopolies and Mergers Act 1965. To the extent that the decision whether a merger is against the public interest is considered a measure of economic policy, court decisions, whether they are initial or in review of administrative orders, may seem inappropriate. This is true whether the standard of legality in a particular case is previously examined by an independent expert body such as the British Monopolies Commission or the Canadian Restrictive Trade Practices Commission, or decided by the administration without prior examination by an independent body, as, for example, in the ECSC under article 66 of the ECSC Treaty. Naturally, where judicial review of administrative decisions in merger cases is admitted, as in Federal Trade Commission cases in the United States and in the ECSC, its practical impact depends largely on the scope of the powers of review conceded to the courts in cases of this type.

328. This interrelation between the political or judicial character of the substantive legality test and the system of enforcement must be borne in mind when looking at the purely administrative enforcement system under the British Monopolies and Mergers Act 1965 and the limitations as to the scope of judicial review of decisions of the Federal Trade Commission in the United States,[1] in Japan,[2] and

1. Under section 11(3) of the Federal Trade Commission Act as amended by the Celler-Kefauver Antimerger Act of 29th December 1950, the court's review power is limited to determining whether the F.T.C.'s findings of fact are supported by substantial evidence. So far, the Supreme Court has shown a strong tendency to confirm the findings and rulings of the Commission on the grounds that it is primarily the function of the expert authority in the field to make policy evaluations and judgments.

2. According to section 80(1) of the Antimonopoly Act the findings of fact made by the Fair Trade Commission are binding upon the court, if supported by substantial evidence.

in the ECSC.[1] Of course, whether an administrative or court enforcement system is more appropriate in merger cases and what should be the scope of the review powers given to the courts has to be seen in the context of the general constitutional and legal situation in each particular country. For this reason it is not intended to make any value judgment for or against one or the other of the systems just examined.

329. A second important procedural aspect in merger cases is the question of timing of actions brought against mergers. This question is relevant both in a system of prior authorisation (ECSC and − as regards newspaper mergers − the United Kingdom) and in a system of intervention as applied in the United States, the United Kingdom, Canada, and Japan. As to the first system, the ECSC Treaty specifies no period of time within which the High Authority has to decide whether to grant or refuse authorisation of a merger after it has been brought to its attention. On the other hand, in cases of newspaper mergers under the British Monopolies and Mergers Act 1965, after an application for consent has been received, the Board of Trade must refer the matter to the Monopolies Commission within one month and the Commission must present its report within three months of the matter being referred to them or, if there are special reasons why this cannot be done, within another three months at the latest [section 8(3)]. No time limit for the decision of the Board of Trade to permit or reject the merger is specified in the Act.

330. Of the other legislations, Japan is the only one with a general statutory time limit for action against mergers. After it has received a report on the merger from the participants (section 15(2) Antimonopoly Act), the Commission has to decide within 30 days whether or not to intervene (section 15(4) Antimonopoly Act). A similar system has been recently introduced in the United States with respect to bank mergers. Under section 1 of the Bank Merger Act Amendment of 1966, amending section 18(c) of the Federal Deposit Insurance Act, an action based on section 7 of the Clayton Act must be commenced during the waiting period provided in paragraph 6 of section 18(c) as amended (i.e. within 30 days or 5 days where an emergency exists).[2] In all other cases the only limitation for bringing an action against a merger is the general statute of limitation period, unless this period starts to run from the time the merger was consummated. This latter limitation does not seem to apply in Canada and in the United States. Thus, in the famous case United States v. E.I. Du Pont de Nemours and Co.,[3] it was possible to attack in 1949 a merger which had been effected in 1919.

---

1.   Under article 33(1) of the ECSC Treaty, the Court of Justice may not review the High Authority's evaluation of the situation, based on economic facts and circumstances, which led to such decisions or recommendations, except where the High Authority is alleged to have misused its powers or to have clearly misinterpreted the provisions of the Treaty or of a rule of law relating to its application.

2.   See 1 CCH-Trade Regulation Reporter, para. 1,282.

3.   353 U.S. 586, 1957 Trade Cases, para. 68,723.

331. It is obvious that the absence of a reasonable time limit for bringing an action against a merger must create in most cases not only a state of insecurity for the enterprises involved but also serious practical difficulties in implementing a subsequent dissolution. This is why some legislations have provided for a compulsory and binding pre-merger clearance (ECSC and the United Kingdom in the case of newspaper mergers) and others for time limits excluding later actions against mergers, and why all legislations permit preliminary measures to prevent the consummation of mergers until final clearance.

332. Legal security, which is brought about by formal premerger clearance and time limits for actions, can in practice to a certain extent also be achieved by an informal clearance procedure. Such procedures are applied in the United States both by the Federal Trade Commission and by the Antitrust Division and in Canada by the Director of Investigation and Research. Although negative clearance given in such cases is neither binding on the administration nor on the courts, it seems that in practice in only very rare cases was action taken by the administration contrary to its prior opinion given to the parties. An evaluation of the precise extent and impact of such informal proceedings, which are also frequently applied as regards other types of restrictive practices, must be left to a future special study.

333. A final procedural aspect which should be mentioned here is the admission of action by private parties in merger cases. This naturally depends on the extent to which the decision on the legality of a merger is considered to be a measure of economic policy rather than a legal judgment in a suit between private parties. Consequently, in the United Kingdom where, of all legislations discussed here, the political nature of decisions on mergers is the most obvious, no private actions or formal interventions by private parties in merger proceedings are admitted. Neither do such actions seem to be admissible in Canada[1] or in Japan.[2] In the ECSC, on the other hand, an affected party may sue the High Authority before the European Court if the High Authority fails to proceed against an illegal merger (section 35 of the ECSC Treaty). However, it does not seem that third enterprises could attack an authorisation of a merger by the High Authority.[3] The only legislation expressly admitting private actions in merger cases is that of the United States. Under section 16 of the Clayton Act private parties may sue for injunctive relief (including preliminary and temporary injunctions) against threatened loss or damage as a consequence of a merger violating section 7. The question whether in such a case a private right of action for treble damages (section 4 Clayton Act) may also accrue has not yet been

---

1. Part IV of the Combines Investigation Act providing for special remedies gives no rights to private parties.
2. See sections 25 and 26 of the Antimonopoly Act.
3. Article 33(2) of the ECSC Treaty requires that the plaintiff has been "affected" by the decision of the High Authority. This is interpreted as covering only those enterprises against which the decision was directed.

finally decided.[1] In practice, however, actions by private parties against mergers are rare.

2. *MONOPOLIZATION*

334. Three member States – Canada, Japan, and the United States – prohibit monopolization or the formation of a monopoly. The meaning of these concepts has already been discussed in Part II. Since in the United States, at least, which has the most extended practical experience with cases of this type, the measures taken against unlawful monopolization are mainly directed against the existence of the "monopoly" rather than merely against specific acts of a monopoly, it seems advisable to deal with these measures in close connection with antimerger cases, since the same measures are used in both merger and monopolization cases to prevent or to limit the formation of market power.

335. In the *United States*, monopolization is a criminal offence subject to fines of up to $50,000 or to imprisonment of up to one year, or both. In practice, however, the enforcement authorities proceed against monopolization by civil actions based on section 4 of the Sherman Act which empowers the Federal courts to prevent and restrain violations of this Act. Due to the particular nature of the offence of monopolization under section 2 of the Sherman Act which is constituted by the possession of monopoly power with the intent or purpose to exercise that power, such actions are normally not directed against particular acts of the "monopolist", but against his possession of monopoly power as such. The measures ordered by the courts in civil cases concerning monopolization under section 2 of the Sherman Act were, therefore, primarily dissolution and divestiture.[2]

336. The courts may, however, in addition to divestiture of financial interests or instead of it, order less drastic measures against the business behaviour of the monopolist to ensure that there remain no practices likely to result in monopolization in the future. Thus, in the United Shoe Machinery case, the monopolist was ordered to divest himself of certain subsidiaries and branches and also to terminate his lease-only policy and to offer his customers a choice of leasing or purchasing shoe machines. He was also ordered to modify the

---

1.   See e.g., Highland Supply Corp. v. Reynolds Metals Co., 245 F. 2d. 510, 1965 Trade Cases 71,561.

2.   See e.g., United States v. Aluminum Co. of America, 148 F. 2d. 416, 1944-1945 Trade Cases, para. 57,342 (Dissolution order against Alcoa. The question whether this was the appropriate remedy in this case was extensively discussed by the Court of Appeals); United States v. Grinnell Corp., 384 U.S. 563, 1966 Trade Cases, para. 71,789 (divestiture order concerning affiliated companies). These cases were dealt with in detail in Part II supra. See also United States v. United Shoe Machinery Corp., 968 Trade Cases, para. 72,457.

leasing contracts in several regards e.g. to shorten their term.[1] In another case, a producer of chemicals charged with the acquisition of a competitor, in violation of sections 1 and 2 of the Sherman Act and section 7 of the Clayton Act, was not only ordered to divest himself of a production plant, but also not to expand his production capacity and output beyond certain limits and was required to buy certain products for further processing from its competitors.[2] In both cases the defendants were compelled to license their patents to competitors.[3]

337. Where section 2 of the Sherman Act has been violated by an *attempt to monopolize*, control of the future conduct of the defendant may in fact be the only remedy available. An example is the case *Lorain Journal Co. et al. v. U.S.*[4] where the defendant newspaper company had attempted to monopolize advertising by refusing to accept advertisements from any local advertiser advertising through a newly established independent radio station. The purpose of this refusal was to destroy the radio station and to regain its monopoly in the dissemination of all news and advertising. The judgment enjoined the defendant from refusing to accept for publication or discriminating as to terms of publication where the reason for such refusal or discrimination is that the person submitting the advertisement has been or is advertising through any other advertising medium.

338. In *Canada*, the formation of a monopoly as defined in section 2(f) is a criminal offence punishable by a fine at the discretion of the Court or imprisonment for two years (section 33 of the Combines Investigation Act). So far, only one such case has been brought before the courts.[5] In this case, the defendant companies which had gained a monopoly position by various practices aiming at driving competitors out of the market and by mergers were fined. An order prohibiting the continuation of the offence and to dissolve the monopoly was not asked for by the Government on the grounds that the amendment to the Combines Investigation Act providing for such an order (section 31) had not come into force until after the conviction. Under this provision, where a conviction for unlawful formation of a

---

1. United States v. United Shoe Machinery Corp. 110 F. Supp. 295., 1952-1953 Trade Cases, para. 67,436. Affirmed United Shoe Machinery Corp. v. United States, 347 U.S. 521, 1954 Trade Cases, para. 67,755. The Government is presently seeking a modification of the decree of the District Court which in 1953 had refused to order the main relief requested − to dissolve United Shoe into three separate companies. The refusal of the District Court to grant the modification and order a reconstitution of United Shoe's business so as to form two fully competing companies on the shoe machinery market was reversed by the Supreme Court. See United States v. United Shoe Corp., 1968 Trade Cases, para. 72,457.

2. United States v. American Cyanamid Co. 1964 Trade Cases, para. 71,166 (consent judgment).

3. This aspect will be dealt with in more detail in paras. 429 to 443, infra.

4. 1950-51 Trade Cases, para. 62,957.

5. R. v. Eddy Match Co. (1951) 13 C.R. 217 (trial); 18 C.R. 357 (CA). Cf. Combines Investigation Act, Annual Report, 1955, p. 29.

monopoly is made, the court may direct the dissolution of the monopoly.

339. In *Japan*, private monopolization is prohibited by section 3 of the Antimonopoly Act. Violation of this provision may be sanctioned by cease and desist orders of the Fair Trade Commission (section 7) and by imprisonment for up to three years or by fines of up to 500,000 Yen (section 89). The cases brought before the Fair Trade Commission indicate that, contrary to the situation in the United States and possibly in Canada, the measures taken against private monopolization are not primarily directed against the deliberate possession of monopoly power but against specific acts of the "monopolist".[1]

340. The *procedural aspects* of actions against unlawful monopolization in Canada and in the United States are to a very large extent the same as those examined above with regard to mergers. The fact that in the United States section 2 of the Sherman Act is a criminal provision, thus being distinguished from section 7 of the Clayton Act which only provides a civil sanction, is apparently of no great practical importance because the enforcement authorities usually proceed against cases of unlawful monopolization by civil actions. What has been said above on the question of timing of actions with regard to mergers applies also to actions against unlawful monopolization. But it would be more difficult than in merger cases to provide a time limit since monopolization is frequently constituted by a series of acts and practices stretching over a long period of time, so that a point from which the time limit for bringing an action would run can hardly be definitely fixed.

341. What has been pointed out before with regard to criminal actions and private enforcement in merger cases is also relevant to monopolization cases and need not be repeated.

B. LAWS CONTROLLING THE CONDUCT OF MARKET DOMINATING ENTERPRISES

342. There are two basic ways to proceed against the conduct of market dominating enterprises having detrimental effects as described in Part II: *i*) such conduct may be directly prohibited under the law, subject to criminal, quasi-criminal or administrative sanctions in cases of violation, *ii*) the law may merely provide for administrative powers to intervene in particular cases of such conduct, e.g., by declaring it unlawful and calling upon the enterprises concerned to desist from their abusive conduct, or to act in a specific way in order to put an end to the abuse or violation of the public interest.

1.   See, e.g., the case of the Noda Soy Sauce Co., 9 F.T.C. Decision Reports 57 (F.T.C., 27th December 1955) where the prices policy of a powerful supplier was attacked. Cf. Ariga and Rieke, the Antimonopoly Law of Japan and its Enforcement, 39 *Washington Law Review* 437, 451 (1964).

343. The main difference between these two systems is the following. In the first case, the practices concerned are automatically illegal *ab initio*, no prior intervention of the enforcement authority being required, and the statutory measures to be taken are primarily criminal or quasi-criminal sanctions (mainly monetary fines) against the violation of the statutory prohibition. In the second case, the practices concerned are lawful until such time as the enforcement authority intervenes and declares them unlawful, and the measures to be taken are primarily of a regulatory character (orders to desist from certain conduct, e.g., from a discriminatory sales policy, or to do certain acts, e.g., to supply to a certain enterprise or to lower abusively high prices).

344. The practical consequences of this difference can be observed, for instance, in private litigations concerning abusive practices of market dominating enterprises. If such practices are directly prohibited under the law, the courts are bound to consider them unlawful, regardless of whether administrative or criminal measures have already been taken against the particular practice in question. On the other hand, under the intervention system, it is only after such measures have been finally taken that the rights and obligations of the parties involved are affected, and the injured party seeking relief against an abusive practice of a market dominating enterprise has to ask for the intervention of the enforcement authority or has to wait until the authority intervenes on its own initiative.

345. While the difference as to private enforcement between the two systems is thus considerable, it may be of less importance as far as public enforcement is concerned. Under the prohibition system, the statutory prohibition of abusive practices may be enforced by the authorities with the primary objective of making the enterprises concerned abstain from their conduct on the understanding that no sanctions for past violations of the law will be imposed if the enterprises comply with the suggestions or recommendations of the enforcement authority. This procedure is likely to be followed in particular when the enforcement authorities have a wide discretion whether or not to prosecute after a violation of the law has occurred. The practice of prosecuting only after unsuccessful attempts by the enforcement authority to stop the abusive practice is, from a practical point of view, not much different from an intervention system.

346. Both systems will now be analysed in detail with reference to the various national and Community laws. Part 1 will deal with the various measures which may be or have been taken, part 2 with a number of procedural aspects of public enforcement and part 3 with private enforcement.

1.   *MEASURES OF PUBLIC ENFORCEMENT*

a)   *The Prohibition System*

347. A general prohibition of abusive practices of market dominating enterprises applies in Spain (section 2(1) of the Act against Re-

147

straints of Competition) and in the EEC (article 86 EEC Treaty). A similar prohibition is contained in article 59 bis, para. 4, of the French Price Ordinance No. 45-1483 as amended by the Act No. 63-628 of 2nd July, 1963, which prohibits practices of market dominating enterprises or groups "where such practices have the object or may have the effect of interfering with the normal operation of the market". Further, a prohibition more limited in extent, covering only specific practices (unfair hindrance and unjustified differential treatment), is contained in section 26(2) of the German Act against Restraints of Competition. Another partial prohibition is contained in section 4 of the Swiss Cartel Act which prohibits a number of coercive practices against outside competitors. This prohibition not only applies to cartels but also to individual enterprises with a market dominating position and to market dominating groups (section 3 of the Cartel Act).

348. In *Spain*, if a violation of a prohibition has been found by the Court for the Protection of Competition, the Court enjoins the participants to desist from their abusive practices [section 15(1)(a)]. Thus, in the Carbonell case the dominant enterprise which had followed a policy of buying its raw material requirements from small enterprises at prices which it determined unilaterally after the sale took place was ordered to discontinue this practice.[1] The Court may further propose to the Council of Ministers the imposition of a fine up to 30% of the total amounts involved for the sale of the product or the performance of the service which was the subject of the practices concerned (section 28).

349. In the EEC, wilful or negligent violations of the prohibition in article 86 of the EEC Treaty are subject to fines of from 1,000 to 1,000,000 units of account or up to 10% of the turnover of the preceding business year of each of the participating enterprises (article 15(2)(a) of Regulation No. 17). In addition, the Commission may order that the participants desist from their abusive conduct (article 3 of Regulation No. 17). In order to enforce compliance with such a decision, penalties of from 50 to 100 units of account per day of delay, reckoned from the date fixed in the decision, may be imposed. No measures for violation of article 86 have been taken so far.

350. In *France*, criminal sanctions are applicable to violations of the prohibition of article 59 bis, para. 4, of the Price Ordinance No. 45-1483. If, after an investigation by the Technical Commission for Cartels and Dominant Positions a violation has been found to exist, the Minister for Economic Affairs may start a criminal action before the criminal courts which, on conviction, may impose imprisonment of from 2 months to 2 years or fines of from 60 to 200,000 N.F. or both (article 40 of Ordinance No. 45-1484 of 30th June, 1945 as amended by the Act No. 65-549 of 9th July, 1965). No case under article 59 bis, para. 4, has yet been brought before the Technical

1. Judgment of the Court for the Protection of Competition of 11th November 1967 in the matter Carbonell y Cia., S.A.

Commission. In all but 2 of about 80 cartel cases investigated so far by the Commission, the Commission's recommendations were settled informally. This procedure, which has recently been given statutory authorisation by article 4 of the Ordinance No. 67-835 of 28th September, 1967 [1] provides that the Minister may propose to the enterprises concerned an amicable settlement consisting of an engagement on their part to effect the necessary changes in their conduct. The settlement becomes invalid, i.e. compulsory measures may be taken, if the engagement is not carried out.

351. In *Germany*, wilful violations of the prohibition contained in section 26(2) of the Act against Restraints of Competition are subjected to fines of up to 100,000 DM or up to three times the additional profits obtained as a result of the infringement [section 38(1) No. 8 and section 38(4)]. No such fines have been imposed so far. A large number of cases under section 26(2), mostly involving discriminatory refusals to sell, were, however, settled informally, after the practices attacked had been abandoned (e.g., after supplies to a particular enterprise had been resumed or after discriminatory conditions of sale had been eliminated). [2] The court cases under section 26(2) involving practices of market dominating enterprises will be dealt with later, together with the analysis of private enforcement.

352. In *Switzerland*, violations of the prohibition contained in section 4 of the Cartel Act are only subject to private enforcement measures. If such a violation has been found, the competent court of the Canton (section 7) may, upon the request of the aggrieved party, hold that the practice is unlawful, order its cessation, the removal of the unlawful state of affairs, and the payment of damages (section 6). As was said earlier, section 4 has not yet been applied to market dominating enterprises. In the cartel case Walch v. Swiss Association of Wine and Spirit Merchants, [3] which was dealt with in Part II, the Court ordered the defendants on the basis of section 4 to cease withholding supplies from the plaintiff. In another cartel case where a violation of section 4 was seen in a refusal to grant a customary discount to a wholesaler, the Court ordered the cartel to grant this discount and to pay damages for the injury caused. [4]

1. *Official Journal* of 29th September 1967.

2. Between 1st January 1958 and 31st December 1967, 581 proceedings under Section 26(2) were initiated by the Federal Cartel Office, 114 of which were terminated upon cessation of the conduct complained of (1967 Annual Report, p. 214, Table M). Most of these proceedings concerned enterprises practising resale price maintenance. Proceedings against market dominating enterprises were terminated, for instance, upon resumption of supplies (Annual Report 1963 p. 56 and 1964 p. 44), upon termination of tie-ins effected by preferential prices and discounts (Annual Report 1963 p. 60) and upon admission to an exhibition (Annual Report 1962 p. 35).

3. Judgment of the Court of First Instance in the Canton of Berne of 25th July 1966, 2 *Publications de la Commission Suisse des Cartels* 327-333 (1967). See also *Guide,* Switzerland, Section 3.0, Case No. 4.

4. Judgment of 16th March 1965, 1 *Publication de la Commission Suisse des Cartels* 194-209 (1966). See also *Guide,* Switzerland, Section 3.0, Case No. 1.

The possibility of public action against practices of market dominating enterprises (section 22 of the Cartel Act) will be discussed in the following subsection.

353. In view of the fact that in only two of the legislations just considered (Germany and Spain) has the prohibition been enforced by public action, it is hardly possible at this time to draw any general conclusions as to the effectiveness of the prohibition system as far as it is applied to practices of market dominating enterprises. The experience acquired in Germany seems to indicate that the prohibition is primarily enforced in an informal way with a view to eliminating the detrimental effects of the prohibited conduct; by asking the enterprises concerned to desist from it, rather than by imposing the statutory sanctions by way of formal decisions.

354. It may be assumed that in the other legislations the enforcement authorities would follow the same policy. This would confirm what was suggested in the introductory remarks that, as far as public enforcement practice is concerned, the difference between the legislations following the prohibition system and those adhering to the intervention system is of minor importance. It is doubtful whether the threat of an immediately applicable public sanction has under these circumstances a greater repressive effect than the possibility of the enforcement authority's intervention under the intervention system. From the point of view of public enforcement it does seem, therefore, to be irrelevant whether a statutory prohibition or merely powers of intervention by the enforcement authorities against practices of market dominating enterprises are adopted. Both systems in this respect seem apt to yield the same results. The influence of private enforcement (especially of private damage suits) which in the legislations following the prohibition principle may be of considerable importance will be discussed later.

b)   The Intervention System

355. The legislations belonging to the intervention system do not automatically render unlawful and prohibit abusive or otherwise detrimental practices of market dominating enterprises, but merely provide for powers to intervene against particular cases of such practices. These powers may either be specially designed to deal with these practices (Belgium, Germany, United Kingdom and the Netherlands) or they may be applicable against anticompetitive practices in general, insofar as practices of market dominating enterprises are covered by this term (Denmark, Norway, and Switzerland). A further distinction can be made according to whether the powers of intervention are limited to the prohibition of certain acts or agreements or whether they permit direct regulation of the conduct of market dominating enterprises, e.g. by prescribing maximum prices or by ordering such enterprises to supply to certain buyers, etc.

356. In the following pages, the powers under the various legislations belonging to the intervention system and their application will be analysed in detail.

357. In the *United Kingdom*, once a practice adopted by a "monopoly" has been found to be against the public interest, section 10 of the Monopolies and Restrictive Trade Practices (Inquiry and Control) Act 1948 and section 3 of the Monopolies and Mergers Act 1965 provide for broad statutory powers to deal with the situation. The Board of Trade is empowered to declare unlawful, or require termination of, agreements or arrangements entered into by the "monopoly" (section 3(3)(a) and (b) Monopolies and Mergers Act 1965), to declare unlawful refusal to deal and tie-ins (section 3(3)(c) and (d) Monopolies and Mergers Act 1965), to declare unlawful discriminatory practices (section 3(4)(a) Monopolies and Mergers Act 1965), to require publication or notification of prices (section 3 (4)(b) Monopolies and Mergers Act 1965), and to regulate prices charged for goods or services (section 3(4)(c) Monopolies and Mergers Act 1965). Orders to this effect have to be made by statutory instrument requiring Parliamentary approval within 28 days after being made (section 3(11) Monopolies and Mergers Act 1965). The orders may authorise the Board of Trade to give directions to the persons or enterprises concerned in order to secure compliance with the orders. These directions may, upon the application of the Board, be judicially enforced.

358. In practice, the powers just described have rarely been applied. Instead, the Board of Trade has normally enforced the recommendations of the Monopolies Commission by securing voluntary action by the enterprises concerned in carrying out these recommendations or by obtaining from them undertakins that they will act in accordance with the recommendations. Since, 1948, when the first antimonopoly law was enacted, about 30 investigations by the Monopolies Commission have been carried out. In its reports the Commission has recommended inter alia, termination of resale price maintenance, [1] termination of selective or exclusive selling, [2] limitations as to the duration of sole agency agreements, [3] termination of restrictions in sole agency agreements as to the sale of products of other enterprises, [4] termination of allowing bonuses to retailers conditional on their granting to the supplier a proportion of their display, [5] lowering of prices considered to yield excessive profits, [6] limitation of advertising expenses, [7] abolition of import duties, [8] limitations on the

---

1. Report on the supply of electrical equipment for mechanically propelled land vehicles (1963), Report on the supply of wallpaper (1964).

2. Report on the supply and processing of colour firm (1966).

3. Report on the supply of petrol (1965).

4. *Ibidem.*

5. Report on the supply of cigarettes and tobacco and of cigarettes and tobacco machinery (1961).

6. Report on the supply of chemical fertilizers (1960), Report on Colour Film, *op. cit.*, Report on the supply of household detergents (1966).

7. Report on household detergents, *op. cit.*

8. Report on Colour film, *op. cit.* Report on Man-made Cellulosic fibres (1968).

acquisition of competitors[1] or retail outlets[2] and divestiture of financial interests in competitors.[3]

359. In the majority of cases these recommendations of the Monopolies Commission were accepted by the Board of Trade and, after negotiations, complied with voluntarily by the enterprises concerned. It appears, however, that the Board of Trade has shown some reluctance to accept recommendations in as far as they were not limited to the termination of the detrimental conduct itself. For example, the Board of Trade has not accepted recommendations for strict direct price control,[4] for divestiture of a dominant firm's stock-holding in a competitor,[5] for lowering import duties,[6] for a reduction of advertising expenses[7] and for a limitation of producer-owned retail outlets.[8]

360. The procedure of securing voluntary undertakings rather than employing the statutory powers specified in the law has given the Board of Trade a flexible instrument which enables it in particular to take reformative action going beyond a mere declaration of unlawfulness of past conduct and to give specific guidelines to the future business behaviour of the enterprises concerned. Thus, in the Petrol report it was not only stated that the usual 25 year term of solus agreements between petrol companies and petrol station owners was excessive but also that the terms of the contracts should be limited to a maximum of 5 years and the Board of Trade secured an undertaking from the oil companies to this effect. With respect to prices the Kodak case is a good illustration. The Monopolies Commission not only found Kodak's prices to be excessively high but recommended specifically a 20% reduction which was effected by Kodak

1.   Report on wallpaper, op. cit., Report on Man-made Cellulosic Fibres (1968).

2.   Report on petrol, op. cit.

3.   Report on cigarettes and tobacco, op. cit.

4.   Report on the Supply and Export of Matches and the Supply of Match-Making-Machinery, 1953, London HMSO Cmnd. 161, cf. Annual Report of the Board of Trade for year ended 31st March 1953. Oxygen-Report, Loc. cit., cf. Rowley, The British Monopolies Commission, London, 1966, at p. 338.

5.   Report on cigarettes and tobacco, op. cit.; Rowley, op. cit. at p. 341. No decision was yet made on the recommendation of the Commission in its report on cellulosic fibres to impose on Courtaulds some restrictions as to mergers with competing textile firms.

6.   Report on colour film, op. cit., Board of Trade, Press Notice of 3rd October 1964, Ref. 361. No decision was yet made on the cellulosic fibres report.

7.   Report on household detergents, op. cit. Cf. Board of Trade, Press Notice of 26th April 1967, Ref. 151, where the Board indicated that, before action was taken on the Commission's recommendation concerning advertising, the economic effects of the advertising in general and its relationship to competition were to be made the object of independent research.

8.   Report on petrol, op. cit. While the Commission had recommended a limit on the acquisition and building of petrol stations by oil companies with annual trade in excess of 10 million gallons, the turnover limit was set at 50 million gallons in the undertakings which were accepted by the Board of Trade. Cf. Board of Trade, Press Notice of 19th July, 1966, Ref. 274. Meanwhile, the ban on increases in the holding of company-owned sites has been lifted completely by the Board of Trade. Cf. The Financial Times, 5th September 1968, at p. 6.

after the Board of Trade had made a request based on the Commission's report.

361. In *Germany,* the cartel authority is empowered to prohibit abusive exploitation of market dominating positions and to declare contracts which are the result of an abuse to be of no effect (section 22(4) Act against Restraints of Competition). Such orders may be enforced by administrative sanctions; their wilful or negligent violation is an administrative offence subject to administrative fines (section 38(1) No. 2 and 4).

362. In the 4 cases of abuse which were decided so far the following measures were taken: In the Zementkontor Unterelbe case the original order of the Federal Cartel Office was to reduce the price level in the higher price area to that of the lower price area. The Berlin Court of Appeals held, however, that in so far as the order prohibited the charging of the higher price it was justified under section 22(4) of the Act against Restraints of Competition, but that, on the other hand, the order to reduce this price to the lower level could not be based on this provision since the powers thereunder were limited to prohibiting the abusive conduct or declaring contracts to be of no effect.[1] In the Meto case the tie-in clause in question was declared to be of no effect and the supplier was prohibited from imposing similar clauses for longer than 6 months from the date of supply of the labelling machines.

363. In the Sporting Goods Fair case the respondent was ordered not to make the admission of exhibitors dependent on whether they supply exclusively to specialized retailers and to admit three particular exhibitors to the next fair. Leaving open the question whether section 22(4) only gives the power to prohibit abuses or whether it also authorizes the enforcement authorities to request specific conduct to be performed, the Berlin Court of Appeals reversed the second part of the order on the grounds that it did not sufficiently specify the details of the contract terms to be offered to the excluded exhibitors.[2] Finally, in the Petrol Prices case no order was made after the companies had lowered their prices voluntarily.

364. In Germany there is thus a problem of statutory remedy in cases where requests for particular positive conduct are to be made, a problem which still awaits final settlement by the Federal Supreme Court. A further problem arose in connection with taking preliminary action in order to achieve an immediate effect. Again the Court of Appeals has been very hesitant to affirm such actions.[3] The Federal Cartel Office has also followed a policy of informal settlements. The results obtained by such settlements include: admission of small petrol stations to distribution on motorways,[4] termination of the

---

1. Decision of 12th July 1966, WuW/E OLG 807 at 810.
2. Decision of 22nd July 1968, Kart 2/68 WuW/E OLG 907.
3. A preliminary order made in the Sporting Goods Fair case was reversed on the grounds that the appeal of the defendant against the decision of the Federal Cartel Office might be successful in view of the difficult legal issues and because the existence of the excluded enterprises was not seriously affected. Decision of 23rd February 1968, Kart 3/68.
4. Activity Report 1961, p. 13.

grant of preferential rebates in case of the purchase of other products,[1] cancellation of a 500% increase in the minimum purchase quantity[2] and lowering of electricity prices.[3]

365. In the *Netherlands*, if the Government is of the opinion that a dominant position exists whose consequences conflict with the public interest, it may publish data on the position or issue orders prohibiting unfair business practices, imposing obligations to supply, and regulating prices or terms of delivery (section 24 Economic Competition Act). Disobedience constitutes an indictable offence, when committed wilfully, otherwise a summary offence (sections 26 and 41 Economic Competition Act).

366. Of the cases decided on the basis of section 24(2) involved collective boycotts by market dominating groups of suppliers. In both cases the boycotting enterprises were ordered by the Minister to supply to the boycotted firms on the usual business terms.[4] Apart from these formal actions, a number of cases were settled informally.

367. In the *ECSC*, the High Authority is empowered to issue recommendations against public or private enterprises which have or acquire a dominant position, to prevent the use of such a position for purposes contrary to those of the ECSC Treaty [article 66(7)]. If these recommendations are not carried out satisfactorily, the High Authority may fix prices and conditions of sale to be applied by the enterprise in question, or draw up production or delivery programmes. In the case of the Oberrheinische Kohlenunion AG the dominant enterprise directed a recommendation to the defendant to terminate its policy of excluding wholesalers from supplying certain large customers.[5]

368. In *Belgium*, if an abuse of economic power has been found, the Minister proposes to the enterprises concerned recommendations for the termination of the abuse. If these proposals are not accepted, the Minister may issue a formal recommendation which, in the case of non-compliance, may be followed by a reasoned Royal Decree confirming the existence of the abuse and prescribing measures to terminate it (article 14(5) Act on Protection against the Abuse of Economic Power). Infringements are punishable by imprisonment or fines (article 18). No cases have yet been dealt with.

Application of Powers against Restrictive Business Practices in General

369. While the legislations just analysed provide for special control powers to deal specifically with detrimental effects of market dom-

1. Activity Report 1963, p. 60 (Dairy products).
2. Activity Report 1964, p. 32/33 (matches).
3. Activity Report 1964, p. 50 and 1965, p. 61.
4. Sipkes Case, (1961) N.S. No. 118; Lijmar Case, (1961) N.S. No. 151.
5. Recommendation of 11th July 1953; *Official Journal* 1953, p. 154. In another case (Rheinische Braunkohlenbrikett-Verkaufs GmbH) the High Authority found that a group of sellers had a market dominating position within the meaning of article 66, para. 7 and that measures thereunder might be taken. *Official Journal* 1960 p. 1,089.

inating positions, the laws of Denmark, Norway, and Switzerland do not contain special rules on the conduct of market dominating enterprises. Instead, the general rules against restrictive business practices apply, regardless of whether the practice involved is the result of a restrictive agreement or of a dominant position of a single enterprise or of a group of enterprises engaged in conscious parallel conduct. The same applies to Sweden and Ireland which do not use the concept of dominant enterprise or another similar concept in the texts of their laws.

370. In *Denmark*, the provisions of the Monopolies and Restrictive Practices Control Act apply generally to market situations in which competition is restricted in such a manner that the enterprises exert or may be able to exert a substantial influence on price, production, distribution or transport conditions (section 2). If such a situation results in unreasonable prices or business conditions, unreasonable restraint of the freedom of trade or unreasonable discrimination as to conditions of trading, the Monopolies Control Authority may, after negotiations to remedy such harmful effects, issue orders to that end (section 11 and 12). Such orders may cancel agreements, fix maximum prices and margins,[1] and direct suppliers to supply to specified buyers on usual business terms.[2] In practice, a number of cases have been settled informally.

371. In *Norway*, section 23 of the Act on Control of Prices, Profits and Restraints of Competition empowers the Price Council to prohibit refusals to deal which are detrimental to the public interest or would have an unreasonable effect on the other party. In a a number of cases the Price Council has intervened against unreasonable refusals to sell, some of these cases involving single enterprises dominating their market.[3]

372. In addition, dominant enterprises and restrictive business agreements supervised by the Price Directorate are subject to intervention by the Authorities under powers granted in section 42(3) of the Act on Control of Prices, Profits and Restraints of Competition. The criteria for intervention under this section concern restrictive practices which are deemed likely to have a harmful effect on production, distribution or other business activities in the realm, or are otherwise considered unreasonable or detrimental to the public interest. The reporting procedure for dominant enterprises will be dealt with later along with the other procedural questions.

373. In *Switzerland,* the Federal Economic Department may, after an inquiry by the Cartels Commission, institute proceedings before the Federal Court against a cartel or similar organisation which prevents competition or interferes with it appreciably in any one branch of the economy or occupation, in a manner that is incompatible with the public interest, especially one detrimental to

---

1. See e.g., Meddelser fra Monopoltilsynet (Report of the Monopolies Control Authority), 1964, p. 99.

2. See e.g., Meddelser fra Monopoltilsynet 1962, p. 267.

3. See e.g., Pristidende No. 5 of 1956, No. 18 of 1959 and No. 21 of 1959. For further cases see *Guide,* Norway, Sections 3 and 3.0.

consumers (section 22(1) Cartel Act). The Court in such proceedings may order the appropriate measures, in particular cancel or modify contract clauses and prohibit practices of the cartel or similar organisation in question. No use of these powers has been made so far.

374. In *Ireland*, the Fair Trade Commission can make recommendations for remedial action to the Minister for Industry and Commerce, who, at his discretion, may give effect to the recommendations by making an Order which becomes law if confirmed by an Act of the Legislature. In addition, the Fair Trade Commission may make, and has in fact made, a number of Fair Trading Rules relating to different commodities. While these Rules contain prohibitions on various restrictive business practices, they are only a code of conduct for particular trades, without the force of law.

375. . *Sweden* follows a system of negotiations laid down in the law to eliminate harmful effects of restraints of competition. The Freedom of Commerce Board which is entrusted with these negotiations can, as a general rule, not issue injunctions. In cases of refusal to sell the Board has, however, recently been given powers to take stronger measures as a last resort. A statute passed in 1966 empowers the Board to order an enterprise, on pain of a fine, to sell goods to certain buyers in cases where the Board has found the restraint of competition in question to have harmful effects and where it has not been possible to eliminate these effects through negotiation. A number of cases of refusal to sell have been settled by negotiation. [1]

c) *Conclusion*

376. The foregoing analysis has shown that under the "conduct" laws three different procedures for taking action against the detrimental conduct of powerful enterprises may be distinguished: (1) a direct prohibition of abuses, (2) intervention by application of special powers against powerful enterprises, and (3) intervention on the basis of general powers applying to restrictive business practices in general. It seems that all "conduct" law countries, regardless of which of these three procedures thay have adopted, are in a position to take compulsory action against "abuses". No law relies exclusively on control by publicity or "persuasion". Sweden, which followed till 1966 a system of negotiation, has meanwhile amended its legislation giving the Freedom of Commerce Board the power to order the enterprise concerned, on pain of a fine, to sell goods to certain buyers where the harmful effects of a refusal to sell cannot be eliminated by negotiation. Similarly, the United Kingdom has reinforced in 1965 its compulsory powers to act against violations of the public interest by monopolists. [2]

377. The availability of compulsory powers does not mean of course that all cases of "abuses" are settled by formal decision. Enforce-

---

1. See Guide, Sweden, Section 3., Cases No. 1, 2, 4 to 10, 11 to 13, 15, 18, 19 and 20.
2. See Section 3 of the Monopolies and Mergers Act of 1965.

ment practice, especially within the intervention system, shows many instances of informal settlements. This applies in particular to the United Kingdom where to date practically all cases have been settled by the enterprises concerned undertaking to follow the recommendations of the Monopolies Commission in so far as they were accepted by the Board of Trade. This practice amounts essentially to what is expressly specified in the Swedish law, namely to take formal action only if all attempts for an informal settlement have failed. As is illustrated by the new French rules under article 4 of the Ordinance No. 67-835 of 28th September, 1967, [1] such an informal procedure may also be applied under a prohibition system.

378. The practice of informal settlements may to some extent help to overcome the difficulties under some legislations of taking corrective action, i.e. action to force the dominant enterprise to conduct itself in a specific manner which is no longer abusive. These difficulties have in particular arisen in Germany where the Berlin Court of Appeals has interpreted the statutory power in section 22(4) to prohibit abuses as not covering orders to perform a positive action, e.g. to lower prices to a specified level or to admit an excluded applicant to a fair.

379. To what extent the absence of such express powers in the law operates as an impediment to achieve the result desired by the enforcement authority cannot be generally said. If there is only a single alternative to the "abusive" conduct (e.g., in a case of refusal to sell or discrimination) the prohibition of the conduct is normally sufficient to force the enterprise concerned to comply with the business behaviour envisaged by the enforcement authority. On the other hand, if there are several conduct alternatives (e.g., in the case of excessively high prices or excessively long term of restrictive agreements) a mere prohibition or invalidation of contracts may not suffice to achieve exactly the intended aim. Assuming for example, that it is found that a certain price is 20% too high, an order not to charge this price can be formally complied with by a reduction of 1% only. It is of course possible in this case to intervene against the reduced price as well, as long as it is not brought down to the 20% lower level originally envisaged, but in any case the effect on the entire action would be considerably delayed. For this reason it seems desirable that the law does not only provide for powers to prohibit, or intervene otherwise against abuses, but also makes available to the enforcement authorities reformative powers for the achievement of the envisaged market results.

2. *PROCEDURAL ASPECTS OF PUBLIC ENFORCEMENT*

380. An important procedural aspect – the distinction between the prohibition system and the intervention system – has already been

1. *Official Journal* of 29th September 1967.

dealt with. It has been pointed out that as far as public enforcement practice is concerned the difference between the two systems is only slight. In practice, both systems are primarily enforced informally; formal action in both systems is only taken in very few cases. In the following pages, two special aspects of public enforcement will be analysed: a) by whom the powers described in subsection 1 are exercised, b) the procedure of notification and registration in relation to market dominating enterprises.

a)   *Enforcement Competence*

381. This item includes a number of questions. First, a distinction can be made as to whether the statutory measures of control are to by taken by an administrative decision or by a decision of a court. This distinction is not necessarily identical with that between the intervention and the prohibition system as may be seen from the example of the EEC where the prohibition in article 86 of the Treaty is enforced by the administration and in Switzerland where enforcement requires a court order. Both in relation to administrative and to court enforcement a further distinction can be made as to whether the general authorities and courts are competent to deal with restrictive business practices cases or whether there is a special administrative authority or court for this purpose. Another important aspect is the question of both administrative and judicial review and the scope within which the reviewing agency or courts may review the initial decision. Finally, it will be shown to what extent separate expert commissions take part in public enforcement.

382. With the exception of France, Spain, and Switzerland, all countries dealt with in Part III, chapter I B (laws controlling the conduct of market dominating enterprises) provide for administrative enforcement. General administrative authorities are competent in Belgium,[1] United Kingdom,[2] the Netherlands,[3] in the EEC,[4] and in the ECSC.[5] A special enforcement agency is competent in Denmark,[6] Germany,[7]

1.   Under sections 14 and 15 of the Act on Protection against the Abuse of Economic Power the Government is competent to issue orders.

2.   The Board of Trade with the consent of Parliament; Section 3(11) Monopolies and Mergers Act 1965.

3.   The Minister of Economic Affairs together with the minister who is jointly concerned with the matter; Sections 1(1) and 24.

4.   The EEC Commission; Articles 3, 15 and 16 of Regulation No. 17, subsidiarily, the substantive provision of Article 86 EEC-Treaty may be applied by the authorities of the Member States "in accordance with their own provisions", cf. Article 9(3) of Regul. No. 17 and Art. 88 of the EEC-Treaty. This competence has never been used.

5.   The High Authority; Article 66(7) ECSC Treaty.

6.   The Monopolies Control Agency; Sections 11 and 12 of the Monopolies and Restrictive Practices Control Act.

7.   The Federal Cartel Office with the exception of regional cases where the State authorities are competent; Section 44(1) Nos. 1(d) and 3 of the Act against Restraints of Competition.

Norway[1] and Sweden.[2] As to the countries with court competence general courts are competent in France[3] and Switzerland,[4] while in Spain there exists a special court for restrictive business practice matters.[5]

383. In most legislations the decisions taken by the administration are subject to appeal, the exceptions being United Kingdom and Sweden where no appeal lies against the decisions of the Board of Trade and the Freedom of Commerce Board respectively. This is also true in Norway for Price Council decisions on refusal to sell; in other cases an appeal system exists. An appeal to a special appeal tribunal is allowed in Denmark subject to a further appeal to the ordinary courts.[6] In Belgium,[7] Germany,[8] the Netherlands,[9] the EEC,[10] and the ECSC[11] appeals go directly to the courts; in Belgium and the Netherlands to the administrative courts, in Germany to a special section of the appeal courts in civil matters, and in the EEC and the ECSC to the Communities' Court of Justice. Initial court decisions may be appealed against in France and Spain,[12] while in Switzerland the decision of the Federal Court is final. The scope of review of the appeal courts is apparently unlimited (including questions of fact and law) in Denmark, Germany,[13] Spain, and, in relation to decisions imposing a fine or a penalty, in the EEC.[14] It is limited to specific points of law in Belgium, the Netherlands and in the ECSC.[15]

384. In five legislations (Belgium, France, United Kingdom, the Netherlands and Switzerland), before decisions on measures against market dominating enterprises are made, an expert body must be asked for an investigation or for its opinion on the case. The findings and recommendations of these investigations and consultations are in most cases not legally binding on the administration.

1. The Price Council in cases under Section 23 of the Act on Control of Prices, Profits and Restraints of Competition. In cases under Section 32 the Price Directorate is competent.

2. Under the new amendment Act of 1966 the Freedom of Commerce Board has the power to issue orders against refusals to sell.

3. The criminal courts; Article 22 of Ordinance No. 45-1,484.

4. The Federal Court; Section 22(1) of the Cartel Act.

5. The Court for the Protection of Competition; Section 15 of the Act against Restraints of Competition.

6. Section 18 of the Monopolies and Restrictive Practices Control Act.

7. According to general principles of Belgium administrative law the ordinary courts and the Conseil d'Etat is competent to review Government orders.

8. Sections 62(1) and 73(1) of the Act against Restraints of Competition.

9. Section 33 of the Economic Competition Act. The appeal is decided by a special section for competition cases.

10. Article 173(2) of the EEC Treaty.

11. Article 33 of the ECSC Treaty.

12. The appeal goes to the plenary of the same court. Cf. Section 29 of the Act against Restraints of Competition.

13. Sections 62(21) and 70 of the Act against Restraints of Competition. The appeal from the Court of Appeal to the Supreme Court is limited to questions of law, Section 73 of the Act against Restraints of Competition.

14. Article 17 of Regulation No. 17.

15. Article 33 of the ECSC Treaty.

It does seem, however, whether expressly stated in the law or not, that the administration could not bring an action, if the expert body found that either no dominating position or no detrimental effects existed in a particular case.

385. In *Belgium*, after the Commissioner-Reporter, upon a complaint by an aggrieved person or upon the request of the Minister of Economic Affairs, has come to the conclusion that a dominant position is used in violation of the general interest, a request for an investigation is made to the Council for Economic Disputes.[1] If the Council finds that no abuse of economic power exists, the Minister is bound by this opinion. In the opposite case it is for the Minister to decide whether or not there are grounds for taking action. The opinions of the Council are not made public.

386. In *France*, the Technical Commission on Cartels and Dominant Position has to enquire into all offences against article 59 bis of Ordinance No. 45-1483, before the Ministry for Economic Affairs decides on the institution of a criminal prosecution.[2] Nothing is said in the law to what extent the opinions of the Commission are binding on the Ministry. Practice in cartel cases has shown so far that the Ministry will usually follow the judgment and recommendations of the Commission. In cases of urgency, repeated offences and of flagrant offences, the Commission does not have to be consulted. The opinions are made public in the activity reports of the Commission.

387. In the *United Kingdom*, the Monopolies Commission conducts an investigation after a case has been referred to it by the Board of Trade. The application of the powers against monopolistic practices depends on a finding of the Commission, in a report laid before Parliament, that things done by a "monopoly" operate or may be expected to operate against the public interest. The reports must be published after being presented to Parliament.

388. In the *Netherlands*, before action under section 24 of the Economic Competition Act against abusive practices of dominant positions may be taken, the matter has to be referred to the Economic Competition Committee.[3] The findings and recommendations of the Committee are not legally binding on the administration. The reports of the Committee are not published.

389. Finally, in *Switzerland*, the Cartel Commission is charged with investigations into practices of enterprises in market dominating positions. The Federal Economic Department may request the Commission to undertake special enquiries in order to establish whether cartel-like organisations have harmful economic or social effects (section 20(1) of the Act on Cartels). If the Commission finds this to be the case, it may recommend the parties concerned to abandon measures taken by cartel-like organisations. If the recommendations are not carried out, the Commission may ask the Federal Economic Department to institute proceedings in the Federal Court (section 22

---

1.   Section 7 of the Act on Protection Against the Abuse of Economic Power.
2.   Article 59 ter of Ordinance No. 45-1,483 of 30th June 1945.
3.   Section 25(1) of the Economic Competition Act.

of the Act on Cartels). The Commission's reports may only be published with the consent of the Federal Economic Department.

390. In conclusion to this survey of the various organisational aspects of public enforcement it may be said that the legislations covered by this study differ considerably from one another on this point. This must largely be explained by the fact that the decision of the legislator as to which institution enforcement of the law should be entrusted, as to whether and to what extent to allow appeals against the decisions of these institutions, and as to whether or not to include an independent expert body in the enforcement organisation, must be made on the basis of the general constitutional, legal and political structure of the particular country. For this reason, general conclusions on the appropriateness of one or the other national solution of the institutional and organisational problems will not be drawn in this study. This applies also to the question whether an expert body should be included in the law enforcement set-up. It may be said, however, that undoubtedly an opinion of the independent expert body may give greater authority to findings that dominant positions have detrimental effects which should be terminated. This may facilitate informal settlements of cases. It may also have more authority in the courts which may be more inclined to follow the administration's contentions if they are based on an opinion of an independent expert body. On the other hand, however, investigations by expert bodies may take too much time and thus delay immediate action. For example, France has taken this into account by prescribing a time limit of 6 months for such investigations and by permitting immediate action in urgent cases and in cases of flagrant or repeated offences.

b)   *Notification and Registration*

391. Three member states – Austria, Denmark and Norway – have introduced a system of compulsory notification and/or registration of market dominating enterprises. While in Austria no further control is provided for after a dominating enterprise has been registered, notification and registration in Denmark and Norway, where such a control exists, apparently serves not only the purpose of informing the enforcement authorities and the public about the existence of market dominating enterprises, but has also the purpose of facilitating the control of their conduct. In Norway, furthermore, dominant enterprises must submit each year an annual statement of accounts and a report on their activities to the Price Directorate (section 38 of the Act on Control of Prices, Profits and Restraints of Competition). Another system of notification, that under section 23 of the German Cartel Act, should be mentioned here. Although the primary purpose of this provision was to enable the authorities to observe more closely the development of mergers, the legislator apparently also intended to facilitate abuse control over dominant enterprises under section 22. This may be inferred from the fact that the cartel authority may, after being notified of a merger, summon the participants to a public hearing or invite them to submit a written statement, if it is to be

expected that as a result of the merger a market dominating position will be either attained or strengthened (section 24). The criteria for notification and registration in the 4 countries are the following.

392. In *Denmark*, the criterion for registration is the dominant position as such, expressed in terms of substantial influence on price, production, distribution or transport conditions (section 6(2) Monopolies and Restrictive Practices Control Act). About 200 individual dominant enterprises were registered in 1963. The enforcement of the registration requirement by the Monopolies Control Authority shows that no fixed criteria in terms of size, turnover or market share have been developed. [1]

393. In *Norway*, domestic enterprises which must be assumed to produce or distribute, individually or together with affiliates, at least one quarter of the total inland production or distribution of a commodity have to submit a report to the Price Directorate. [2] The same applies to persons who own or are responsible for the running of enterprises which are subsidiaries or subject to the controlling influence of: *a*) a foreign firm which may be assumed to have a substantial influence on prices in one or more countries or for one or more commodities or services, or which is associated with an association of firms, which, together, may be assumed to have such influence; *b*) an association of foreign firms or of Norwegian and foreign firms which may be assumed to have such influence as mentioned under (*a*). Finally, the Price Directorate may demand a report from enterprises not falling under the categories already mentioned, if their activities are of such importance for one or more trades in Norway that special supervision is considered necessary by the Directorate. The Norwegian system thus combines a fixed notification criterion (25% of the production or distribution of a commodity) with the more flexible criterion of market power (substantial influence on prices, important position in a trade).

394. In *Austria*, as in Denmark, the registration criterion is the market dominating position as such, but defined in the law in terms of fixed supply shares. An enterprise is considered market dominating, if its share of the supply on the domestic market of any goods or group of goods which appear in the customs tariff as a single tariff item or as a separate sub-item and which are not a by-product of the enterprise, exceeds according to the criteria customarily applied in the sector concerned when estimating production, the rate of 30% or, if the domestic market is supplied by more than three enterprises, the rate of 50% (section 36 (d) Cartel Act). It is important to note that the supply shares of 30 and 50% are calculated on the basis of the customs tariff which is not necessarily identical with the commodity concept applied in other legislations. A tariff item may cover several commodities for which separate markets exist and, on the other hand, several tariff items, because they are close substitutes, may constitute only a single commodity. The shares of

1. See e.g., *Guide*, Denmark, Section 3, Case No. 4.
2. Section 34 of the Act on Control of Prices, Profits and Restraints of Competition.

30 and 50% do, therefore, not necessarily reflect the market shares and thus the market influence of the suppliers concerned.

395. In *Germany,* finally, the criterion for notification is, alternatively, a fixed market share of 20%, or a certain size of the enterprises concerned (10,000 employees, 500 million DM turnover or 1 billion DM balance sheet total).[1] Germany is thus the only country with a notification criterion defined in terms of size. The legislator has introduced this criterion to supplement the market share requirement, because in many cases the enterprises considered to be subject to notification had claimed that it was impossible for them to ascertain their market share.[2]

396. The question which of the criteria for notification and registration just described is the most appropriate cannot be generally answered. Rather the answer seems to depend largely on the purpose of the notification and registration procedure. If this procedure primarily serves to supply more information to the enforcement authorities and to the general public about enterprises which may exert economic power, it may be more appropriate to establish fixed notification or registration criteria such as a certain market share (20% in Germany, 25% in Norway). Notification and registration based on such criteria leave it open to a later decision of the enforcement authority or the courts whether the notifying or registered enterprise has in fact a market dominating position. But even where the procedures have to fulfil only the described informative function, it is more appropriate to base notification and registration on the market concept, since the decision whether a market dominating position exists can only be made with regard to a market for a certain product or service, i.e. the relevant market. For this reason it may be doubtful whether notification determined by the share in the supply of a certain item of the customs tariff (Austria) or by the size of the enterprises involved (section 23(1) No. 2 of the German Act) is a proper means to ascertain the existence of actual market power.

397. If, on the other hand, the purpose of notification and registration is to establish, as a formal requirement for further action, that an enterprise or a group of enterprises is in fact market dominating, it is obvious that the criterion for notification and registration must be identical with that for the possession of market power as defined in the law. Where this definition is made in terms of a fixed market share, as for example in the United Kingdom (33 1/3%), a procedure of notification and registration will not raise greater practical difficulties than the "informative" notification systems just described. If market dominance, is, however, defined in terms of market influence (e.g., in Denmark) or of substantial competition (e.g., in Germany), it is clear that any notification or registration procedure which serves the purpose of establishing the existence of market power in the sense of the law will normally require a comprehensive market analysis before the notification or registration can be effected. But the

---

1. Section 23(1) No. 2 of the Act against Restraints of Competition.
2. Cf. Explanatory Memorandum to the Government Bill to Amend the Act against Restraints of Competition, Parliamentary Printing Matter IV/2564.

considerable expense of such a procedure may be justified, because in this case notification and registration establish at least a presumption that the registered enterprise or group of enterprises has a market dominating position. Under such a procedure, which is, for example, applied in Denmark, the enforcement authorities and the courts are relieved for all future cases of the difficult burden of establishing, every time action is taken, that the conditions for a market dominating position are still met. In addition, the registered enterprises are given definite notice of the fact that they are subject to control as market dominating enterprises.

398. It seems that this effect is the most important result which may be obtained by a notification and registration procedure. On the other hand, the importance of publicity and of the supply of additional information to the enforcement authorities as a result of notification and registration is more difficult to evaluate. This depends on whether notification and registration do in effect reveal facts of which the enforcement authorities and the public have not yet sufficient knowledge or which could not be obtained by applying the general investigatory powers. There is not sufficient information available on the basis of which a definite answer could be given.

3. *PRIVATE ENFORCEMENT*

399. Private enforcement, by one authority in the field once called "the strongest pillar of antitrust",[1] may also play an important role in the enforcement of the provisions concerning market power. This may be effected in two ways: *a*) private parties may be given a formal right to demand an intervention of the enforcement authority, or to participate as a party in its proceedings, and to appeal eventually to the courts, if the enforcement authority fails or refuses to intervene; *b*) where the prohibitions of the law or orders of the enforcement authority have been violated the aggrieved party may have a right to sue the violator directly for an injunction, damages or other appropriate relief. Further, agreements resulting from abusive practices of market dominating enterprises may be unenforceable.

400. In addition to these two aspects arising under the restrictive business practice laws a third aspect of private enforcement will be discussed. In a number of countries powerful enterprises are subject to certain restrictions and obligations in their dealings with others. Such rules were frequently developed by the courts on the basis of general law principles against unethical business conduct or against conduct in violation of good morals. Although they do not belong to restrictive business practice law in the strict sense, they will be briefly discussed in this study in view of the considerable practical importance which they still have.

---

1. Loevinger, Private Action – The Strongest Pillar of Antitrust, 3 *Antitrust Bulletin* 167 (1958).

a) Participation in public proceedings

401. A formal right to demand the intervention of the enforcement authority against specific practices of market dominating enterprises or groups, which can be enforced by a court action if the authority fails or refuses to intervene, is apparently not recognized in any of the legislations covered by this study. Germany and the two communities admit an appeal against the failure of the enforcement authorities to act, but the appeal is only admitted if the petitioner has in effect a formal right to demand their intervention. Such a right is, however, denied as far as the control of practices of market dominating enterprises is concerned. [1] A special procedure to enable private parties to participate in public proceedings is applied in Germany. Under Section 51(2) No. 4 of the Act against Restraints of Competition third parties may be admitted by the cartel authority to its proceedings if their interests will be substantially affected by the authority's decision. Admission gives the admitted party the right to appeal against the decision of the cartel authority. [2] No similar procedure is apparently found in the other legislations. [3]

b) *Private actions*

402. It seems that, in all legislations, agreements which violate a statutory prohibition of abusive practices of market dominating enterprises or an order of the enforcement authority or of a court to the same effect are unenforceable. Although this rule is not expressly stated in the restrictive business practice laws, it is well established on the basis of general law principles, regardless whether private actions for damages or injunctive relief are recognized or not. [4]

1. See Section 62(3) of the German Cartel Act and Articles 175 of the EEC Treaty and 35 of the ECSC Treaty. It does seem that some authors interpret article 3 of EEC Regulation No. 17 as giving the injured parties an enforceable right to demand the Commission's intervention. See Deringer, WuW/EWG-Wettbewerbsrecht, annotation 3 to Article 3 of Regulation No. 17; Steindorff, Das Antragsrecht im EWG-Kartellrecht und seine prozessuale Durchsetzung, AWD 1963 p. 357 seq. According to this view, persons suffering loss caused by practices which violate Article 86 of the EEC Treaty could ask the European Court to order the Commission to initiate proceedings, if the Commission failed to do so. See also: "Etudes de la CEE – la réparation des conséquences dommageables d'une violation des Articles 85 et 86 du traité instituant la CEE" by Professor Battifol, Brussels, 1966.

2. But even where an injured party was admitted to the proceedings, it could not appeal to the appellate court, if the authority refused to render a decision against a dominating enterprise since a right to demand such a decision is not recognized, see preceding footnote.

3. The question whether private parties may claim damages in public proceedings, e.g. in France by a "constitution de partie civile", will be discussed under (b).

4. In France, Spain and in the two Communities this principle is expressly stated in the restrictive business practice laws, but only with regard to agreements violating the prohibition of cartels. In Norway, private actions for damages are expressly provided for in cases of refusal to sell (Section 23(4) of the Act on Control of Prices, Profits and Restraints of Competition), otherwise not.

403. An express rule concerning private damage actions and injunctions in restrictive business practice cases is contained in the laws of Germany, Spain and Switzerland. Section 35(1) of the German Cartel Law provides for an action for damages in cases of wilful or negligent violations of "any provision of this Act or any order or the cartel authority or an appellate court issued under this Act, if such provision or order is intended to protect another person". In addition, section 35(2) indirectly refers to the German general legal principle that an action for an injunction may be instituted against any act which, if wilfully or negligently committed, would give the right to an action for damages. The right of action thus depends on whether the violated law provision or order has "protective character". This character has been recognized by the courts with respect to section 26(2) dealing, inter alia, with obstructive and discriminatory practices of market dominating enterprises as may be seen from a number of private suits decided by the courts.[1] As to orders under section 22(4), it seems that private actions could be based on such orders. In any case, the aggrieved party would have to await the issuance of an order by the cartel authority; a direct action could not be based on section 22(4).[2]

404. A direct private action without prior intervention of the enforcement authority may also be brought in Switzerland, if an enterprise is affected or threatened by an interference with competition which is declared unlawful under section 4 and 5 of the Cartel Act.[3] On the other hand, Spain allows private damage suits in the ordinary law courts only after the Court for the Protection of Competition has declared the restrictive business practice in question to be unlawful.[4] Apparently it is immaterial whether the provision on which the declaration of the Court is based has a "protective" character or not.

405. In the other legislations, the question whether private actions for damages or injunctions can be based on a violation of the statu-

---

1. See, e.g., Federal Supreme Court of 16th October 1962, WuW/E BGH 509 (private litigation between an automobile manufacturer and a wholesaler of automobile parts. Unfair hindrance of the wholesaler by the manufacturer requiring his authorized dealers to use only "original" parts denied); of 2nd April 1964, WuW/E BGH 613 (a dairy co-operative with a dominant position as buyer of milk was held to violate Sec. 26(2) because of less favourable payments to non-members); and of 20th November 1964, WuW/E BGH 647 (refusal of a cattle semen co-operative to supply to non-affiliated veterinary surgeons considered discriminatory treatment). Düsseldorf Court of Appeals of 19th May 1965, WuW/E OLG 725 (loyalty rebates granted to retailers by a dairy co-operative on the purchase of certain dairy products were not considered to be unfairly hindering dairy wholesalers because the co-operative did not have a dominant position with regard to the "tied" products).

2. The right of a direct action has recently been proposed by Mestmäcker, Das Verhältnis des Rechts der Wettbewerbsbeschränkungen zum Privatrecht, (1968) Der Betrieb 787, 836.

3. See e.g. judgments of the Federal Court in the Miniera S.A. case (ATF 90 II 501), in the case of Alex Martin S.A. v. the Swiss Association of Cigarette Manufacturers (ATF 91 II 25 and Guide Switzerland, 3.0 No. 1), in the case of Sessler and Co. S.A. v. The Swiss Association of Tobacco Manufacturers (ATF 91 II 313 and Guide, Switzerland, 3.0 No. 2), and in Walch v. Association of Swiss Spirits Merchants, 2 Publications de la Commission Suisse des Cartels 327 (1967).

4. Section 6 of the Act against Restraints of Competition.

tory provisions against abusive practices of market dominating enterprises or of enforcement orders prohibiting such practices has to be decided on the basis of general law principles. The answer apparently depends on whether the provisions and orders are considered to be solely measures of public policy for the public interest or whether they are, at the same time, intended to protect individual interests. Individual interests were not recognized by the French Cour de Cassation, for instance, when the court held that the provisions of Ordinance No. 45-1483 were enacted "in the general interest, to the benefit of the public and not to protect the individual interest of any user or consumer".[1] It has not been possible to ascertain to what extent the same view prevails in the other legislations and whether it precludes private damage actions and injunctions.[2]

c)   *Control under General Private Law*

406. In most of the countries covered by this study the courts have developed certain rules restraining powerful enterprises in their dealings with others. Three aspects are dealt with: *a*) protection of customers of a "monopoly" against unfavourable contract terms, e.g. against disclaimers of liability, *b*) protection against refusal to supply goods and services of vital importance for the consumer, *c*) protection of competitors against the use of "monopoly" power employed to eliminate them from the market.

407. As to the first category, the courts have imposed a number of limitations on the freedom of contract of "monopolists". Thus, under German private law, a "monopolist" cannot disclaim his liability for damages caused by a negligent or wilful violation of his contract obligations to the other party.[3] Apparently, similar rules have been developed in the other countries, too.

1.   Judgment of 19th November 1959, *Recueil Dalloz* 1960, 463. For this reason the Court denied the possibility of private damage claims in criminal proceedings (constitution de partie civile) and of private prosecutions (citation directe). It does seem, however, that separate actions for damages or injunction are nevertheless admissible. This has been held with respect to the general principle of freedom of competition established by the Decree of 2/17 March 1791. Cf. Cour de Cassation of 13th March 1963, *Recueil Dalloz* 1963, 367. In a private lawsuit between the Fédération Nationale des Cinémas Français and Radiodiffusion Française, the question whether the injured party in a case of violation of Article 59 bis, para. 4, of the Ordinance No. 45-1483 has a right to sue for damages was left open, because the court did not consider this povision as violated in this case. Cf. Tribunal de Commerce de la Seine of 8th March 1965, *Revue trimestrielle de droit européen* 1965, 286.

2.   In the case of the two Communities which have no special provisions on this point the question must be decided in each member State on the basis of national law. See Deringer, WuW/EWG – Wettbewerbsrecht, annotations 53 to 59 to Article 86. Deringer maintains that Article 86 has primarily a public law character thus excluding, in most cases, actions by private parties. See also "Etudes de la CEE – La réparation des conséquences dommageables d'une violation des articles 85 et 86 du traité instituant la CEE" by Professor Battifol, Brussels, 1966.

3.   German Supreme Court (Reichsgericht) of 8th January 1906, RGZ 62, 266.

408. As to the second category, the courts in Germany have imposed on "monopolists" an obligation to supply, if the products or services concerned are "vital" and if the other party depends on the supply of these products or services and has no recourse to other suppliers.[1]

409. Finally, a general private law rule has developed that "monopolists" may not abuse their position by "obstructive competition". Thus, the German Supreme Court held that a "monopolist" may not use a predatory pricing policy in order to eliminate outsiders.[2]

410. In many respects these private law rules have been superseded by the provisions of the restrictive business practice laws. Thus, as has been shown before, discriminatory and coercive practices of "monopolists" and refusals to supply are in most legislations controlled under the restrictive business practice laws. In some cases, however, the private law rules may still be of considerable practical importance, either because the particular practice in question is not covered by the restrictive business practice law provisions (this may be the case because the injured party is not an enterprise), or because no proceedings under these laws are instituted in the particular case by the enforcement authority.

---

1. See, e.g., decisions of the German Supreme Court, RGZ 132, 274; 143, 31 and 148, 334, mostly concerning public utilities (gas, water, electricity).

2. See Judgment of 18th December 1931, RGZ 134, 342 (predatory price war against an independent petrol retailer).

OTHER FACTORS INFLUENCING THE FORMATION OR CONDUCT OF POWERFUL ENTERPRISES

411. The control of market power under the restrictive business practices laws was examined in chapter I A of Part III. This chapter will deal with some of the other factors (laws, policies, structural factors) which may influence, favourably or unfavourably, the formation or conduct of powerful enterprises. It is evident that the situation regarding such enterprises cannot be properly evaluated simply by analysing the extent to which their formation or conduct may be and is controlled under the restrictive business practice laws. There may be other factors bringing about more or less the same results, by acting against the formation or maintenance of positions of market power or by limiting the practical scope within which such positions may be abused. Thus a governmental open market policy favouring the access of domestic and foreign competitors to the market may in many cases prevent market dominating enterprises from becoming a serious practical problem. Further, the possibilities for abusing an existing market dominating position may be limited by public price regulation for the product concerned or by even more direct government control (e.g., government ownership) or by countervailing private power.

412. On the other hand, there are factors which favour the formation and maintenance of market power. Patent law is perhaps the most striking example: its very purpose is to give the patentee a legal monopoly of the production and distribution of the patented article and to guarantee the maintenance of this position for a certain period of time. Trademarks may have the same effect, if the trademarked product has a strong market position by virtue of special consumer preference.

413. Finally, tax law has to be mentioned. In some countries tax advantages may be achieved if several economic activities are concentrated in the same enterprise. The best known example is a system of turnover tax where each transaction from one enterprise to another is taxed separately while the same transactions, when occurring within the same enterprise, remain taxfree. Such a system of taxation favours concentration and thereby the formation of large enterprises. However, as was pointed out in the previous chapters,

the problem of market power is not necessarily one of bigness or of economic concentration since the existence of market power is normally not dependent on a certain size or on the market share of the enterprises involved, even though the latter is a strong indication of actual market power and may be the only statutory criterion to determine market power within the meaning of the law (e.g., in the United Kingdom). For this reason, the phenomenon of bigness or concentration and the factors favouring this phenomenon are not further analysed in this study.

A. MARKET ACCESS

414. The access of outside competitors to the market involves two elements: a) the access of new domestic enterprises, b) the admission of foreign competition (imports, subsidiaries of foreign enterprises etc.). Only in the first respect may it be said that normally there exist, at present, no serious public law obstacles in the countries covered by this study.

415. The principle of free admission to trade and commerce is apparently well established in all legislations. With a few minor exceptions it seems that anyone who has the necessary professional qualifications is free to enter the market.

416. In many countries free access of domestic outsiders to the market is actively supported by financial aids to small and medium-sized enterprises. It is difficult to determine to what extent such aids are an instrument of social policy employed to maintain, for social reasons, a certain economic structure, or whether they are given with the particular intention of fostering or maintaining outsiders in competition with large powerful enterprises. It is not possible therefore to state exactly whether aids to small business may be an effective means of control of market power.

417. Competition by foreign suppliers is an essential factor in determining whether domestic suppliers have a dominant position in their home territory. Even if a domestic enterprise is the only supplier in its home market, competition from imported products may be strong enough to exclude the danger of market domination. For this reason, as was pointed out in Part I, competition from imports is taken into account when the decision is made whether a single domestic enterprise or a group of domestic enterprises has a dominant position on the home market.

418. This shows the great importance of free access of foreign suppliers to the home market, especially in smaller countries where frequently only one or very few domestic suppliers exist. Undoubtedly trade liberalisation between OECD Member countries has made great progress during the last 15 years. On the other hand there are still considerable trade barriers particularly between countries not belonging to the same economic group (EEC, EFTA, Sterling Block). Customs tariffs are in many cases still high enough to prevent foreign competition from being an effective check and balance to domestic

suppliers. The difficult problem in many, especially in the small countries, is to find a compromise between the national interest in the protection of domestic suppliers against too much competition from powerful foreign enterprises and the danger that this protection leads to market dominating positions which may be abused in relation to domestic buyers.

419. Tariff policy with the special intention of increasing foreign competition with powerful domestic suppliers has apparently only been applied in Canada. Under section 29 of the Canadian Combines Investigation Act the Government may abolish or reduce the import duties on a product, if a monopoly " ... promotes unduly the advantage of manufacturers or dealers at the expense of the public ". Since 1947 there have been nine reports under the Combines Investigation Act in which recommendations were made for reduction or removal of tariffs.[1] Of these nine cases, three were the subject of tariff concessions prior to the Kennedy Round of tariff negotiations, and the other six were the subjects of concessions during those negotiations. However, many factors enter into tariff decisions, and it is impossible to isolate the influence of the recommendations made under section 29 of the Combines Investigation Act. In the United Kingdom the Monopolies Commission recommended the abolition of import duties on colour film[2] and a reduction of import duties on cellulosic fibres.[3] No action was taken in this respect in the case of colour film: in the latter case the President of the Board of Trade instituted an immediate review of the duties on cellulosic fibres before coming to a conclusion on the Commission's recommendations on the level of the tariff. The results of this review have not yet been announced.

420. The great difficulties which have to be overcome before foreign suppliers are on an equal competitive footing with domestic enterprises can be observed within the framework of the EEC which, in spite of the fact that a great number of trade barriers for enterprises of other member states have already been removed, is still far from being a single, fully integrated market.

B. PRICE REGULATION AND OTHER FORMS OF GOVERNMENT CONTROL

421. In most countries prices for certain, or for all, products may be regulated by public authorities. Such price regulating powers exist for instance in the three Scandinavian countries. In Denmark, the prices and margins for goods and services supplied by cartels or

---

1. See, e.g., Report Concerning the Manufacture, Distribution and Sale of Ammunition, Ottawa 1959; Report of the Director of Investigation and Research 1959/1960, p. 14.
2. Report on Colour Film, *op. cit.*, para. 292.
3. Report on Cellulosic Fibres, *op. cit.*, para. 217.

market dominating enterprises cannot be increased as a rule without prior approval of the Monopolies Control authority.[1] In Norway, the Government has general powers to regulate prices.[2] In Sweden, the Government has general powers to regulate prices only under emergency conditions, i.e. if the country is at war or in danger of having war or if, for other reasons, there is a considerable risk of a substantial rise in the general price level in the country. A special power to regulate a price is given the Government in section 21 of the Restrictive Practices Act. According to this section, if the harmful effect of a restraint of competition is manifested by a particular price being obviously too high and the negotiations before the Freedom of Commerce Board have failed to eliminate this effect, the Government may, if the matter is found to be of public importance, specify a certain maximum price which may not be exceeded.

422. It is not intended to give a complete survey of all price regulation systems in Member countries. The few examples given may suffice to show that public price regulation may be a means to cope with abusive prices of market dominating enterprises. The fact that during recent years the scope of price regulation has been reduced indicates, however, that price control by competition is preferred to price control by administrative decision. If, under this view, price control is conceived as a means of market control where competition is not effective enough to perform this role, it seems preferable to place this control within the larger context of competition policy rather than to consider it as a separate branch of economic policy, possibly enforced by separate authorities. It seems that broad powers against abuses of market dominating enterprises including specific powers with respect to prices could provide sufficient price control in all cases where competition is not effective enough to guarantee competitive prices.

423. The great practical difficulties of controlling monopolistic prices within the framework of restrictive business practice legislation have already been discussed.

424. Rather than merely regulating prices, government control of dominating enterprises may go further and include entire management and, as a last step, state-ownership. Thus, in a number of countries monopolies and dominant enterprises are state-owned, in some cases even enjoying the status of a legal monopoly (e.g., for tobacco, alcohol, matches).

425. It is difficult to judge to what extent state-ownership of dominant enterprises and state monopolies are the result of considerations of competition policy or of other causes, e.g. fiscal reasons. It seems, however, that competition policy considerations have, if at all, only been involved in very few exceptional cases. As a general rule it may be said that state-ownership and state monopolies are considered to be an exception from the principle of free enterprise to which all OECD Member countries have subscribed and are, therefore, applied

---

1. Section 24 of the Monopolies Control Act. Under an amendment of 1960 exemptions from this rule may be granted.

2. Section 24 of the Act on Control of Prices, Profits and Restraints of Competition.

172

as a means of monopoly control only if all other means have failed to prevent actual serious dangers for the public.

426. No case is known where a government has established a state-owned enterprise for the particular purpose of creating competition with a dominant private enterprise or group.

C. COUNTERVAILING POWER

427. The term countervailing power is usually understood in a very wide sense and includes the actual or potential appearance of outsiders or of substitute products. In a more limited sense countervailing power refers to the individual or collective market power used by the opposite side of the market in defence against the use of economic power by the other market partner. In many countries such countervailing market power is formed by buying organisations of smaller enterprises, particularly by voluntary chains or co-operatives of wholesalers and retailers, but also by single large retailing enterprises such as chainstores and multiples. It seems that the formation of purchasing organisations of independent buyers is not subject to major restrictions under the restrictive business practice laws.[1]

428. Undoubtedly the existence of individual or collective countervailing market power has in many instances prevented powerful sellers from using their market power in the same manner as might have been the case had they faced only a large number of independent small buyers.[2] But to what extent exactly this has been so is difficult to prove. Some economists argue that the formation of countervailing power may effectively cope with the dangers presented by market dominating positions and should for this reason, be encouraged and supported by public authorities.[3] It is doubtful, however, whether reliance on countervailing power can be a satisfactory solution to the problems presented by dominant enterprises.

D. INDUSTRIAL PROPERTY LAW

429. A patent may give the patentee a dominant position on the market to the extent that there are no competing products. Such a monopolistic position is however rare. Technological progress is such

---

1. See, e.g., Decision of the Commission of the European Communities of 17th July 1968, *Official Journal* Nr. L 201/4 of 12th August 1968. (SOCEMAS).

2. In the case of the merger between GKN and Birfield, two leading manufacturers of certain automotive parts, which supplied mostly to large automobile manufacturers, the British Monopolies Commission said: "We are satisfied that the bargaining power of the buyers in this case is sufficient to ensure that the merged company will always be under the strongest pressure to keep its costs and its profit margins as low as possible". Guest, Keen, Nettlefolds and Birfield, A Report on the Merger, *loc. cit.*, at para. 131. Another example is the decision of the Japanese Fair Trade Commission concerning the merger between Nippon-Kana-ami Co. and Kyoto Kana-ami Co. (see para. 166).

3. See in particular Galbraith, *American Capitalism*, 1952, Chapter 9.

that at the present time the majority of patents relate only to improvements to existing products or processes, which are generally not sufficient to forestall completely the efforts of competitors. Apart from the fact that rapid growth of technology reduces the useful life of many inventions to a few years only, the significance of a dominant position conferred by a patent depends on:

   i) the period of the patent's validity,

   ii) restrictions on the working of the patent; for example the obligation to grant licences on reasonable conditions,

   iii) restrictions on the use of the patent right when it is used abusively and when it constitutes an abuse of a dominant position within the meaning of legislation on restrictive business practices.

430. The last two limitations raise the general question of the relationship between industrial property law and restrictive business practice law. The main issue here is whether individual or concerted practices and agreements which are lawful under industrial property law may be attacked under restrictive business practice law. In practice the problem has mainly been discussed in connection with patent licensing agreements, and several legislations have established the principle that such agreements violate restrictive business practice law in so far as they extend the rights of the patentee beyond the scope of industrial property law. [1]

431. On the other hand, the position of patent ownership as such and the use of the patent by the patent owner himself have apparently been attacked under restrictive business practice law only in the United States [2] where, as will be shown later, patent owners in a number of cases were ordered to grant compulsory licences or to refrain from enforcing the patent against infringers, or even to dedicate it to the public.

432. The following paragraphs will briefly deal with the duration of patents, with compulsory licences under patent law and with the restrictions on the use of patents under restrictive business practice legislation. Although the latter question belongs logically to chapter I of Part III, it will be discussed here along with industrial property law in general. Finally, an examination will be made of the extent to which trademarks may be used as a means of establishing a monopoly in the distribution of the trademarked product on a certain territory.

1. DURATION OF PATENTS

433. The duration of a patent in the countries covered by this study varies from 15 to 20 years. It is 15 years in Italy and Japan, [3] 16

---

1. See e.g., Section 20 of the German Act against Restraints of Competition; Report of the Attorney General's National Committee to Study the Antitrust Laws 1955 pp. 231–259; Buxbaum, *Restrictions Inherent in the Patent Monopoly:* A Comparative Critique, 113 Univ. Pa. L.R. 633 (1965).

2. See para. 437 with respect to Canada.

3. Section 4 Italian Patent Act, Section 67, Japanese Patent Act.

years in the United Kingdom,* 17 years in Canada,[2] Denmark,[3] Norway,[4] Sweden,[5] and in the United States,[6] 18 years in Austria,[7] Germany[8] and Switzerland,[9] and 20 years in Belgium,[10] France,[11] Luxembourg,[12] Netherlands[13] and Spain.[14] An extension is usually not possible.

2. COMPULSORY PATENT LICENCES AND LICENCES OF RIGHT UNDER PATENT LAW

434. Compulsory patent licences on reasonable terms may be a means of limiting the market power of the patent owner resulting from his monopoly position. It does not seem, however, that many of the patent laws of the OECD Member countries provide a sufficient basis for its use as an instrument of competition policy.

435. The most elaborate regulation on compulsory patent licences exists in the United Kingdom. Under section 37(2) of the Patent Act a compulsory licence may be granted for the following reasons:

> *i*) that the patented invention, being capable of being commercially worked in the United Kingdom, is not being commercially worked therein or is not being so worked to the fullest extent that is reasonably practicable;

> *ii*) that a demand for the patented article in the United Kingdom is not being met on reasonable terms, or is being met to a substantial extent by importation;

> *iii*) that the commercial working of the invention in the United Kingdom is being prevented or hindered by the importation of the patented article;

> *iv*) that by reason of the refusal of the patentee to grant a licence or licences on reasonable terms:

> > *a*) a market for the export of the patented article manufactured in the United Kingdom is not being supplied; or

> > *b*) the working or efficient working in the United Kingdom of any other patented invention which makes a sub-

1. Section 22, Patent Act.
2. Section 49, Patent Act.
3. Section 4, Patent Act.
4. Section 40, Patent Act.
5. Section 40, Patent Act.
6. Section 154, Patent Act.
7. Section 14, Patent Act.
8. Section 10, Patent Act.
9. Section 14, Patent Act.
10. Section 3, Patent Act.
11. Section 4, Patent Act.
12. Section 7, Patent Act.
13. Section 47, Patent Act.
14. Section 66, Patent Act.

stantial contribution to the art is prevented or hindered; or

c) the establishment or development of commercial or industrial activities in the United Kingdom is unfairly prejudiced;

v) that by reason of conditions imposed by the patentee upon the grant of licences under the patent, or upon the purchase, hire or use of the patented article or process, the manufacture, use or sale of materials not protected by the patent or the establishment or development of commercial or industrial activities in the United Kingdom is unfairly prejudiced.

436. Further, section 41 concerning foodstuffs, medicines, surgical instruments and curative devices requires a special form of compulsory licence intended to make such products available for the community "at the lowest price consistent with the patentees' deriving a reasonable advantage from their patent rights".

437. A similar regulation dealing with the economic effects of the patent monopoly exists in Canada. According to sections 67 and 68 of the Patent Act, compulsory licences may be granted after three years from the grant of the patent, if the patent owner has abused his monopoly position. An abuse is presumed to exist if: a) the invention was not exploited; b) production is made impossible by imports; c) the demand is not supplied; or d) there are disadvantages for trade. Also, section 30 of the Combines Investigation Act gives the Exchequer Court wide powers to deal with the use of patents or trade marks unduly to limit competition or to restrain or injure trade.

438. In other countries compulsory licences may be granted judicially and administratively, if this is in the public interest.[1] But apparently very little use, if any at all, has been made of this instrument to limit detrimental economic effects of market power derived from patents.[2]

439. In conclusion it may be said that although the duration of patents is limited in time and although compulsory licences may be granted in most countries, the market position obtained by virtue of a patent may still be an important factor of market power. The grant of compulsory licences on reasonable terms to any interested party seems to be an appropriate means of control against abuses of such power. For this purpose the statutory criteria for the grant of compulsory licences should be made sufficiently broad to enable the competent authorities to deal effectively with the whole range of detrimental economic effects of market power obtained through patents.

---

1. E.g., Germany (Sections 15 and 41 Patent Act), Netherlands (Section 34 Patent Act).

2. The practice as regards the granting of compulsory licences in Austria, Denmark, United Kingdom, Norway, Sweden, Switzerland is analysed by Neumeyer: Les restrictions à la concurrence et leur réglementation dans les droits des Etats de l'AELE relatif à la propriété industrielle, 1964, pp. 32-101.

3. CONTROL OF PATENTS
UNDER RESTRICTIVE BUSINESS PRACTICE LEGISLATION

440. The grant of a patent may give the patent owner a dominant position on the market for the patented product. The question therefore arises whether a patent which gives its owner such a dominant position and is abused by him may be controlled under restrictive business practice law, e.g., by requiring the patent owner to grant compulsory licences to other producers. This question has to be distinguished from another relevant question in this context, namely whether in cases of dominant market power based on patent ownership the control measures which are normally available to act against abuses may still be applied. If it is found, for example, that the owner of a patent which gives him a dominant position on his market charges excessively high prices for his product or discriminates between buyers, may his price policy be attacked or may he be ordered to refrain from further discrimination? Such measures would leave the patent situation unaffected. This question, to which the answer seems to be in the affirmative in the absence of a special statutory exemption in the restrictive business practices laws,* will therefore not be further examined in the present study.

441. Direct control of patents under restrictive business practices legislation is at present apparently exercised only in the United States.[2] While it is recognized as a "sound rule that monopoly power individually acquired solely through a basic patent, or aggregation of patent grants, should not by itself constitute monopolization in violation of section 2",[3] the use of patents is open to antitrust attack, if the patent was obtained by fraud from the Patent Office[4] or where it was used for monopolization purposes.

442. In such cases courts have granted a wide variety of relief all resulting in partial, temporary, or complete loss of the exclusionary power of the patent owner in order to end his market dominating position. The measures range from compulsory licensing on a royalty-free basis and injunctions against the enforcement of patents against infringers of the patent to the far-reaching order to dedicate the patent to the public.[5] Thus in the Shoe Machinery case the defendant, because of a violation of section 2 of the Sherman Act, was

1. See, e.g., the Judgment of the European Court of Justice of 25th February 1968, Case No. 24/67, where it was held that the applicability of article 86 was not *per se* excluded for the sole reason that the dominant position in question was based on a patent.

2. In Canada a first case involving a use of patents has been brought before the courts. See information in the Exchequer Court of Canada between Her Majesty the Queen and Union Carbide Canada Limited, 12th October 1967. The powers of the Court to make orders in such types of cases, e.g., to declare the patent void, are specified in Section 30 of the Combines Investigation Act.

3. Report of the Attorney General's National Committee to Study the Antitrust Laws, 1955, p. 226. The section cited refers to the Sherman Act.

4. Walker Process Equip. Inc. v. Food Mach. and Chem. Corp., 382 U.S. 172, 1965 Trade Cases, Para. 71,625.

5. These and other types of relief in patent antitrust cases are discussed by Hollabough and Rigler, *Antitrust Bulletin* 1967, pp. 327 sequ.

ordered to license the production, use, and sale of his machines at a reasonable royalty to interested persons.[1] In another civil proceeding the only significant producer of electric lamps in the United States who had been found to have abused his patents relating to lamps in violation of sections 1 and 2 of the Sherman Act was ordered to dedicate all his patents on lamps to the public.[2] Licensees of the manufacturer also were subjected to the dedication requirement because they had received benefits from the illegal practices. In addition, the manufacturer was ordered to licence other patents on a reasonable royalty basis within a period of five years from the date of the judgment. The court pointed out that these orders were necessary to dissolve the dominant position of the defendant achieved and maintained in great measure by its extension of patent control.[3] As is illustrated by the recent case American Cyanamid Co. v. Federal Trade Commission,[4] the Federal Trade Commission, too, has the power to require, as an antitrust remedy, the compulsory licensing of patents on a reasonable royalty basis.

443. A further limitation of patent power under the restrictive business practices laws results from the fact that the courts have recognized the right of persons sued for infringement to challenge the validity of the patent on the grounds that its acquisition or use violates the antitrust laws.[5]

4. *TRADE-MARKS*

444. A trade-mark right does not confer on its holder a dominant position on the market in question unless the products covered by a particular trade-mark are not in effective competition with other trade-marks or with other substitute products. Under trade-mark law the trade-mark owner has the exclusive right to use the mark in commerce. This right is, however, subject to the principle of territoriality. By granting licences for a certain territory or by registration of the trade-mark either in his own name or in the name of a foreign subsidiary or distributor in other countries, the trade-mark owner may restrict the distribution of his product so as to give either himself, his subsidiary, or a distributor an exclusive right to distribute the product in a particular territory. This may be done with respect to the home market and – the more frequent case in practice – with respect to the exportation of the product to other countries.

1. U.S. v. United Shoe Machinery Corp. 110 F.Supp. 295, 1952–1953 Trade Cases, para. 67,436.
2. U.S. v. General Electric Co., 115 F.Supp. 835, 1952–1953, Trade Cases para. 67,576.
3. Examples of consent decrees ordering compulsory licensing are U.S. v. General Motors Corp., 1965 Trade Cases, para. 71,624; U.S. v. American Cyanamid Corp., 1964 Trade Cases, para. 71,166; U.S. v. Radio Corp. of America, 1958 Trade Cases, para. 69,164.
4. 1966 Trade Cases, para. 71,807.
5. See e.g., Precision Instrument Mfg. Co. v. Automative Maintenance Machinery Co., 324 U.S. 806 (1945).

445. To what extent trade-mark law admits import restrictions will now be examined. Three situations can be distinguished with regard to registration of the trade-mark in the country of importation:

  i) the trade-mark is registered in the name of the foreign manufacturer himself,
  ii) the trade-mark is registered in the name of a domestic subsidiary,
  iii) the trade-mark is registered in the name of an independent domestic distributor.

In all these cases the question arises whether the registrant can prevent, under trade-mark law, the importation by third parties of the original product. [1]

446. As to the first situation, the Supreme Courts of Germany,[2] Italy,[3] the Netherlands[4] and of Sweden[5] have denied a right of the manufacturer to prevent parallel imports. The contrary has been held by the Austrian Supreme Court.[6] The situation in Canada is substantially the same.[7]

447. As to the second situation, the Swiss Supreme Court[8] held that the domestic subsidiaries of a foreign manufacturer could not prevent parallel imports of the original product unless buyers risked being deceived. The Court of Appeals of Düsseldorf, Germany,[9] also held that a domestic subsidiary of a foreign manufacturer could not prevent such parallel imports. No decision to the contrary is known, but it is clear that on the basis of the Austrian Supreme Court's view parallel imports could also be prevented by a domestic subsidiary of a foreign manufacturer.

448. Finally, as to the third situation, the courts seem to be inclined to permit the domestic trade-mark owner or licensee to prevent parallel imports.[10] but the question is apparently not yet finally settled in most countries.[11]

---

1. This means that the product comes from the same manufacturer and is physically identical.

2. Judgment of 22nd January 1964, BGHZ 41 p. 84 (Maja).

3. Judgment of 20th October 1956, Foro Italiano 1957 I 1021.

4. Judgment of 14th December 1956, Nederlandse Jurisprudentie 1962, No. 242 (Grundig).

5. Judgment of 17th October 1967, No. B 25 (Polycolor and Polylock).

6. Judgment of 4th September 1957, Grur Ausl. 1961 p. 520

6. Jugment of 4th September 1957, GRUR Ausl. 1961 p. 520 (Brunswick).

7. (1960) 32 C.P.R. 99 (Remington). See also Harold G. Fox, Q.C., Recent Canadian Decisions, *Canadian Patent Reporter,* Vol. 37, pp. 192-193, Toronto 1962.

8. Judgment of 4th October 1960, GRUR Ausl. 1961 p. 294 (Philips).

9. Judgment of 14th July 1964, GRUR Ausl., 1965, p. 204 (Revlon).

10. E.g., Dutch Supreme Court, judgment of 19th April 1965 (Grunding).

11. In the EEC arrangements to use trade-mark rights in order to prevent parallel imports may violate article 85(1) of the EEC Treaty. See Judgment of the European High Court of July 1966 (Grundig/Consten). See also Schumacher, Das Territorialitätsprinzip im Warenzeichenrecht und der Gemeinsame Markt, GRUR Ausl. 1966 p. 305-312. In Sweden, a trademark licensee was denied the right to prevent parallel imports. See Supreme Court judgment of 17th October 1967, *supra.*

449. To the extent that parallel imports of the trade-marked product in all the three situations just described may be prohibited under trade-mark law, the enterprise entitled to trade-mark protection in a certain country has a monopoly in the distribution of the trade-marked product. Whether this leads to a position of economic power depends on the availability of sufficient other similar or substitute products. The admission of parallel imports is normally an effective means to ensure that such power, if no sufficient competition from other products exists, may not arise or be abused. Parallel imports should therefore, be admitted to the extent that there is no danger of confusion as to the identification of the manufacturer and the quality of the product. This may be assumed to be the case where the product is "original", i.e. coming from the same manufacturer and identical in quality and packaging.

E. TAXATION

450. As has been noted in the introductory remarks, the influences of tax law have to be distinguished according to whether large enterprises, or concentration processes, or market dominating positions are favoured. While examples of tax laws favouring large enterprises and concentration processes can be found in a number of countries covered by this study, no case can be ascertained where tax law favours market dominating enterprises as such. By favouring large enterprises and concentration processes tax law may, however, in some cases promote indirectly the formation of market dominating positions. Under this aspect tax advantages for large enterprises and for concentration will be briefly discussed.

451. Tax advantages for large enterprises as such mainly result from the fact that certain tax benefits, although they are theoretically available to all enterprises, can in many cases, for practical reasons, only be taken advantage of by large enterprises. As an example the rules on special reserve funds (for investments or pensions) or on depreciation funds can be cited. Small enterprises frequently have difficulties in taking advantage of the tax benefits for such funds, because their financial resources are insufficient for their establishment. By favouring large enterprises, tax law favours at the same time concentration which enables small enterprises to obtain the tax advantages of large enterprises.

452. Concentration may further be promoted by tax law in two respects. First, tax advantages relating to turnover tax may be obtained by concentrating several economic stages in the same enterprise or group of affiliated enterprises, if transactions within the same enterprise or between affiliated enterprises are tax-free or tax-reduced. This effect existed, for example, in Germany, where, under the old turnover tax system applied until the end of 1967, each transaction from one enterprise to another was taxed separately, while equivalent transactions within the same enterprise or group of affiliated enterprises were free of turnover tax. Thus, a manufacturer

of finished products could avoid turnover tax on the purchase of raw materials by merging with his supplier. The same effect could be achieved by vertical integration of distribution.

453. Finally, tax advantages from concentration may be obtained where several enterprises belonging to the same group of affiliated enterprises have on balance to pay less tax than if they were unaffiliated. This is frequently the case as regards income and company tax, because the profits of subsidiaries are not taxed separately.[1]

454. To facilitate concentration as an aim of economic policy a number of countries have introduced tax privileges for mergers. The most important of these privileges is that hidden reserves and liquidation proceeds resulting from a merger are taxed at a reduced rate.[2]

455. It is not possible in this study to establish more clearly the exact degree of influence of tax law on the size of enterprises and on concentration, nor to what extent such influences, if any, favour market dominating enterprises. From the point of view of competition policy, a tax system which neither favours nor discourages large size and concentration of enterprises, in other words which is "neutral" in relation to competition, seems to be the most appropriate.

1. For a more detailed analysis of this aspect see Bühler, Die steuerliche Beeinflussung der Unternehmenskonzentration im Ausland (Frankreich, Niederlande, Italien, Belgien, Osterreich, Schweiz, Grossbritannien und USA), in: Die Konzentration in der Wirtschaft (1960), vol. 2, pp. 1167 seq.

2. This problem is analysed in the Memorandum of the EEC Commission on Concentration in the Common Market of 1st December 1965, SEC (65)3500, under II B.

Part Four

SUMMARY AND CONCLUSIONS

SUMMARY AND CONCLUSIONS

456. This study has analysed the laws of OECD Member countries, of the EEC and the ECSC in so far as they deal explicitly with market power. It has been found that there are three basic approaches to the problem of controlling market power: a structural approach essentially directed against anti-competitive mergers and monopolization, a conduct approach centering on individual acts of the business conduct of powerful enterprises, and a combination of both approaches. While the majority of laws rely exclusively on a conduct approach, there is no example of an exclusively structural approach. Even the United States system, which has by far the most developed structural control system, includes some elements of conduct control in respect of market power. [1] A combined structural/conduct approach, though with much less emphasis on the structural element, is further found in Canada, Japan, the United Kingdom and the ECSC. Some other countries and the EEC follow a system of conduct control, sometimes accompanied by slight structural elements in the form of a registration of significant mergers (Germany and Spain) or of restrictions on structure in extreme cases of abuses of market dominating power (Belgium, EEC). [2]

457. The application of laws dealing with market power ordinarily requires a definition of the relevant market in each particular case, both with respect to the product or service involved (product market) and the territory (geographic market). The study has attempted to analyse the relevant market concept in the light of actual cases that have arisen under the various laws.

458. With regard to the product market it has been found that there is no uniform method based on objective criteria by which markets can be defined for all future cases. Since a particular demand can often be satisfied by several physically different products or services, the extent to which substitute products or services are

---

1. This leaves aside, of course, other elements of conduct control which do not require the existence of market power, such as concerted conduct (horizontal and vertical agreements in restraint of trade), discrimination as prohibited by special antidiscrimination laws, etc.

2. See Section 15 of the Belgian Act on Protection Against the Abuse of Economic Power. In the EEC the applicability of Article 86 of the Treaty to mergers with a monopolistic effect is still a theory of the Commission not yet confirmed by the Court of Justice.

taken into account in defining the relevant product market is often the determining factor. A number of formulae or tests, such as "functional interchangeability", "cross-elasticity of demand" and "peculiar characteristics" have been applied by courts and administrative authorities to distinguish close substitutes from the less close; but the cases show that these formulae are merely some of the relevant factors taken into account in a policy decision which has ultimately to be made in the light of the statutory purpose of the particular law to be applied.

459. The attention paid to substitutes is the first indication that the definition of the relevant market is closely connected with the competition issue. For, whether a substitute product constitutes an economic alternative to particular consumers or users does not merely depend on its physical characteristics but also on the market conditions for its supply, especially its price. The question whether physically different products or services constitute a single product market resolves itself essentially into one of whether these products are significantly competitive in relation to one other. This has been very clearly expressed in some United States cases which have defined the market as the " area of effective competition ".[1] The close interrelation between the definition of the relevant market and the competition issue becomes further apparent from the fact that the narrower the product is defined (the extreme case would be to limit the market to the product of a particular supplier of a branded article), the smaller will be the number of suppliers of the particular product and the more likely the finding that one or a group of them has a predominant share on the market.

460. The definitions of geographical markets in the cases studied present a similar picture. Again no fixed rules have been developed which would allow a prediction to be made without great difficulty of the outcome of each particular case. Furthermore, these definitions confirm the close interrelation between the relevant market and competition issues, as is perhaps best illustrated when the geographical market was characterized as the "area of competitive overlap ".[2] In practice, the geographic market issue has been important only in so far as it has subdivided national or community territory into regional and local markets. One of the reasons for its relative unimportance has been the existence of economic barriers (e.g., transportation difficulties, consumer preferences) to supplies from outside regional or local markets to customers located there. Generally, it may be said that the problem of defining distinct regional and local markets will normally come up when it is found that a substantial share of sellers do not sell in all parts of the country

1. See also the following definition in the Merger Guidelines of the Department of Justice: "A market is any grouping of sales (or other commercial transactions) in which each of the firms whose sales are included enjoys some advantage in competing with those firms whose sales are not included. The advantage need not be great, for so long as it is significant it defines an *area of effective competition* among the included sellers in which the competition of the excluded sellers is, *ex hypothesi*, less effective ", *op. cit.* No. 3 (emphasis added).

2. United States v. Philadelphia National Bank, 374 U.S. 321, 357 (1963).

(community) and thus do not "competitively overlap" with other sellers. Whether such a "regionalization" of business relations is strong enough to call for a definition of distinct regional and local markets can only be determined in the light of the particular circumstances of the individual case.

461. On the other hand, no cases have been found in which the geographic market issue has been of importance in the opposite way – that of extending markets beyond the area in which the respective law applies, i.e. national or community territory. Even in those countries which belong to the EEC, and, generally, in small countries with a relatively high share of foreign trade in national product, the relevant geographic market in cases decided under national law has not been defined to include the territory of other countries or of the EEC as a whole. Although the majority of the laws studied have expressly limited the relevant geographic market to their area of applicability, the fact that others did not, indicates that an extension of markets beyond national or community territory is not excluded for purely legal reasons, e.g., for reasons of public international law. It has, however, been demonstrated in this study that there is no need for such an extension as long as foreign product alternatives (imports) are taken into account when the question of market power is decided upon. No case has been found in which such product alternatives, as long as they were of some significance, have been disregarded.

462. It is clear from the foregoing that lists of relevant markets applicable to all laws and to all future cases cannot be given. The market being essentially the "area of effective competition" and "the area of competitive overlap", it is not even possible to give such a list for each particular law. For, since the competitive situation is ordinarily subject to a constant evolution, the markets defined may have to be modified in the course of time. This is what is meant when it is sometimes said that the market has also to be defined in terms of the time dimension.

463. Theoretically, the definition of the relevant product market may be simplified by basing it on essentially physical or technical characteristics only. This has been done, for example, though purely for registration purposes, in Austria, and the market definitions under some other laws, e.g. in the United Kingdom,[1] seem to indicate some tendency in this direction. Since, however, the influence of substitute products will then have to be considered as part of the appraisal of the competition situation in the particular case, the question is merely shifted from the issue of market definition to that of competition.

464. The application of the laws dealing with market power ordinarily requires, in addition to the definition of the relevant market, an appraisal of the competitive situation on the market in order to determine whether the degree of market power or lack of substantial

---

1. See Section 3(1)(a) of the Monopolies and Restrictive Practices (Inquiry and Control) Act 1948 and Section 2 of the Monopolies and Mergers Act 1965: " ... goods (services) *of any description* ... " (emphasis added).

competition specified by the law for taking action (actionable market power) has been or is likely to be attained. With respect to the relevant market issue it was shown that the great majority of countries follow by and large the same basic rules. It is felt that in the individual case the statutory purpose of the particular law applied has to be taken into account. However, the criteria for actionable market power differ substantially not only between the various legislations but also within the same legislation. To bring out these differences more clearly, the division throughout this study between merger and monopolization laws and laws dealing with "abusive" conduct of powerful enterprises has been observed.

465. As regards the merger laws, a clear distinction can be made between the law of the United States and the other laws, both as concerns the method to determine actionable market power and the extent to which the various aspects of mergers (horizontal, vertical, conglomerate and joint ventures) have been examined in actual cases. In recent United States practice a strong tendency may be observed, which is borne out by the Merger Guidelines of the Department of Justice, towards the determination of market power in terms of market structure (mainly market shares and concentration ratios). This is especially true with respect to horizontal mergers. The other laws have so far not developed similar fixed structural criteria, and the market share and concentration ratios which they have considered as "critical" have in all cases been substantially higher than in the United States. Further, the United States has gone much further in taking into account the potential competition aspect. In fact, this aspect has been in some cases the only one on which actions against mergers have been based.[1]

466. These features reflect the strong emphasis of the entire United States market power law on the maintenance of market structures which do not give the individual firms any significant degree of market power. This distinguishes it basically from the other merger laws which, even when they do not accept as justification economic or other beneficial effects the merger has produced or is expected to produce, permit mergers which may increase the market power of the combined firm substantially as long as competition on the market may still be expected to be reasonably workable. Where justifications other than in terms of competition are acceptable, as in the United Kingdom, this may go so far that in exceptional cases the combined firm is permitted to acquire a 100% share in the supply of a particular product. One of the reasons for this policy is the belief that other factors, including conduct control under the conduct laws, may be sufficiently effective to prevent abuses of the acquired market power, a belief which also underlies those legislations which do not have any structure control at all.

467. As to monopolization, the analysis in this study has shown that no legislation provides for action against the mere possession of monopoly power by individual firms or groups following a long term

1. See, e.g., United States v. The Gillette Co., Civil Aviation No. 68-141 (D. Mass. 1968).

policy of parallel business behaviour. Of the three countries that have provisions on monopolization – Canada, Japan and the United States – the United States comes closest to such a *per se* rule against monopoly power by prohibiting "the wilful acquisition or maintenance of (monopoly) power as distinguished from growth or development as a consequence of a superior product, business acumen, or historic accident".[1] Monopoly power, generally described as "the power to control prices or exclude competition"[2] is essentially determined (as in merger cases) by the market share of the firm concerned, but with a "critical" market share of around 80% established by the cases decided so far, the threshold for taking action is far higher than in merger cases.

468. While, in the United States, the law against monopolization is, under the conditions just described, primarily directed against the existence of monopoly power, with some elements of conduct control involved, the Canadian and Japanese monopolization provisions have, in practice, been used only as an instrument of conduct control. In any case, no "monopolies" have been split up under these provisions as was done in the United States in most section 2, Sherman Act cases. Under these circumstances the monopolization provisions, at least in the case of Japan, may be considered as performing the function which the laws against abuses of dominant market power have in other countries.

469. Market power under the laws using a conduct approach is determined by two different methods. In a few countries, of which the United Kingdom is the most important example, actionable market power is determined on the basis of the formal criterion of a certain share in the supply of the product concerned. In the case of the United Kingdom, single enterprises or groups of enterprises which prevent or restrict competition between them with respect to the product concerned and which have a supply share of 33 1/3% are considered to be "monopolies" and are subject to monopoly supervision. This formal concept of market power under the law parallels in this respect the formalization of the market power determination in merger and monopolization cases in the United States.

470. In the other "conduct" laws market power is defined in terms of actual influence on the market. It is here that the legal concept of "market dominating enterprise" or "dominant position" is used. Although only some of the legal texts have expressly defined this concept, it may be generally said for all laws that the essential element is that an enterprise or a group of enterprises with no significant competition between them is not exposed to substantial or effective competition on the market. Such a finding requires an appraisal of the competitive situation on the market on the basis of the particular circumstances of each individual case.

471. Even though not many cases have yet been decided, practical experience with the second method has already made apparent the

1. United States v. Grinnell Co., 384, U.S. 563, 570-571 (1966).
2. United States v. E.I. Du Pont de Nemours and Co., 351 U.S. 371, 391 (1962).

difficulties of complying with the requirement that a comprehensive market analysis should be undertaken in each case. These difficulties are particularly great where a group of enterprises supposedly engaging in parallel market behaviour (oligopoly situation) is involved. Several laws permit this situation to be brought within the concept of "market domination". For this reason this study has pointed to the possible advantages of a formal method to determine market power as is applied, for example, in the United Kingdom, whilst fully recognizing that a formal criterion, such as a certain market share, may bring within the law enterprises which have in reality no dominant market power, or may exclude others which, though not reaching the required market share, are in fact market dominating. A combination of a formal and substantive market power criterion, as applies in Norway, could possibly avoid these disadvantages. In any case, to make the law operational a certain degree of formalization may become necessary and the recent development in the antimerger law of the United States underlines this necessity. So far the still very limited practice under the "conduct" laws reveals no similar tendency in law enforcement to develop formal standards in terms of market shares and concentration ratios as expressed in the Merger Guidelines of the Department of Justice.

472. A further method to facilitate the determination of market power in the absence of a formal legal standard is to conclude the existence of market power upon a finding of certain abusive practices. Such a conclusion, which has been made in some German cases, requires that it can be said, on the basis of past experience, that the abuses found could only be practised by enterprises possessing market power. Insufficient experience is available as yet to indicate whether such a conclusion is generally possible and whether specific practices could be considered as "indicators" of market power and, if so, under what circumstances.

473. The concept of market domination being defined in terms of absence of substantial competition on the market, it is obvious that abstract lists of dominant enterprises for each particular market cannot be given for all future cases, in view of constantly changing conditions. This parallels the finding with respect to market definitions made earlier in this study. The share in the supply of a certain product may indicate whether a single enterprise has market power under a law using the formal criterion of a certain supply share (e.g., in the United Kingdom), but even under such a law the question whether a group of enterprises has actionable market power requires an examination of the actual competitive situation on the market. It may, therefore, be generally said that without such detailed market studies in each particular case an account of the actual existence of market power cannot be given.

474. The analysis of the cases both under the "structure" and the "conduct" laws has shown clearly that foreign product alternatives (imports) are taken into account in the determination of market power. This may have two different consequences: (1) the presence of sufficient foreign product alternatives may maintain effective competition on the market even though domestic enterprises have a pre-

dominant share of domestic sales (in the extreme case there may only be a single domestic enterprise selling on the market); (2) the disappearance of competitive foreign product alternatives as a result of mergers between domestic and foreign enterprises may lead to actionable market power on the domestic markets of the respective countries or community. Examples of both types of cases have been given in this study.

475. It may therefore be said that the development of foreign trade has an influence on the existence of market power. The more important foreign trade is for a particular country or community, which may be expressed as the percentage of exports and imports in relation to national product (a percentage which is usually higher in smaller countries than in larger ones) and which depends largely on the level of national and international trade barriers, the less likely will it be that domestic enterprises have a dominant position on their home market. This underscores the great importance of any removal of public trade barriers to international trade. The considerable progress which has already been made in this respect does, however, not mean that with the increasing opening-up of national markets in recent years, the issue of market power has lost its importance at the national level. The numerous cases analysed in this study show that it is still of importance and it is not likely that the complete removal of public trade barriers will relegate the problem of dominant national enterprises to insignificance. Other economic and political factors, e.g. governments' concern with balance of payments or unemployment considerations, may lead to some products of a dominant national enterprise enjoying a privileged position on the national market and hence to the need for some kind of control.

476. The finding of actionable market power has different legal consequences according to whether "structural" or "conduct" laws are to be applied. Under the "structural" laws (antimerger laws and to some extent, monopolization laws) the existence or expected formation of market power is ordinarily the undesirable element to be counteracted. Consequently, it is normally the position of market power as such, its prevention or dissolution, which the law envisages. The issue of market power and the detrimental effects to be dealt with by the law are therefore largely identical. The "conduct" laws, on the other hand, are ordinarily not directed against the position of market power as such, but against specific "abusive" acts of the business conduct of powerful enterprises. Only in exceptional cases, e.g., in Belgium[1] and in the United Kingdom,[2] do these laws provide for action against the continuation of positions of market power. The main issue under the "conduct" laws is to identify those practices of powerful enterprises which are considered as "abusive", "in violation of the public interest", etc.

1. See section 15 of the Act on Protection against the Abuse of Economic Power authorising the Government as a measure of last resort to prohibit acquisitions by a dominant firm.

2. See section 3(5) and (6) of the Monopolies and Mergers Act 1965 authorizing the Board of Trade to prohibit further acquisitions by a dominant firm or to require the division of such firm.

477. The analysis of cases in this study shows that a wide variety of practices have been considered "abusive" in the broad sense of covering all criteria used by the various laws, including refusal to deal and differential treatment, restrictions on distribution, "abusive" prices and business terms, "abusive" use of financial interests in other enterprises, import restrictions, and "abusive" advertising expenditures. Refusal to sell and differential treatment are the most frequent practices, as regards number of cases and number of countries in which they have arisen. These practices present apparently the least difficulties of proof of the existence of an "abuse".

478. It is not possible to bring all these cases into a single general formula. Apparently only one country, Germany, has attempted to establish a general rule when holding that "every practice of a market dominating enterprise is abusive which produces market results which could definitely not have been obtained under effective competition".[1] The essence of this formula is to impose on dominant enterprises the obligation to behave as if they were exposed to effective competition on the market, the standard being the market conduct and performance of enterprises on a comparable real market or, where such a market does not exist, as may frequently be the case, a comparison is made with a hypothetical competitive situation on the market concerned. It is obvious that ordinarily only when a comparable real market exists can specific indications of the standard of competition be obtained. In other cases of supposedly "abusive" prices, additional data are normally needed such as costs and profits calculations before definite conclusions on the abusiveness of a particular practice can be made. The development of a general formula covering all "conduct" laws is further burdened by the fact that some laws, especially that of the United Kingdom, go beyond a mere correction of specifically identified harmful effects on certain competitors or customers and aim at a more detailed regulation of markets.[2] This may explain why in the United Kingdom such practices as financial interests in other firms and excessive advertising expenditures were dealt with under the aspect of "abusive" practices of powerful enterprises.

479. The examination in this study of the corrective ways the various laws deal with adverse effects of market power has shown that the laws normally make available the necessary instruments to remedy the detrimental situations as defined by them. Difficulties have arisen where the law permits only criminal actions against anti-competitive mergers, which – for reasons of constitutional law – is the case in Canada, and where "abusive" conduct of powerful enterprises may only be prohibited without the possibility of giving to the enterprises concerned specific directions as to their future business conduct (e.g., to order resumption of supplies in the case of an abusive refusal to sell). It has been found that from the public enforcement point of view it does not make any difference whether "abuses"

---

1. Federal Cartel Office, decision of 2nd October 1967, WuW/E BKartA 1189, 1193 (Meto case).

2. The standard of "violation of the public interest" is thus broader than the abuse concept.

of powerful enterprises are directly prohibited by law or are merely subject to public intervention in individual cases. One of the reasons is that the law is often enforced in an informal manner with a view to obtaining voluntary compliance rather than applying compulsory powers by formal decisions.

480. The procedures applied by the various legislations to enforce the laws dealing with market power show a great variety of solutions on such questions as judicial or administrative procedure, judicial review of administrative decisions, the use of consultative expert bodies, the use of a registration and notification procedure and the role of private enforcement. These solutions have to be seen against the general constitutional, legal and political background of each individual country or community.

481. This study has examined the existing laws in so far as they deal with the particular aspect of market power. It has shown the basic approaches to the problem, how they have to be seen in relation to one another, what the standards are for determining market power and its detrimental effects and how these standards have been applied in practice, and, finally, what methods are available to cope with such effects. This has left open the question whether the basic element of all the laws studied − the concept of market power − is adequate to assure the ultimate aims of these laws, which consist in maintaining, as far as is considered desirable within the general economic policy goals of the individual country, effective competition and protecting competition from the disturbing influences of private business power. In other words, the question whether the law is consistent from an economic point of view has not been dealt with. The second question left open in the foregoing analysis is that of comparing critically the existing approaches in Member countries with one another, stating their pros and cons and possibly giving recommendations as to future policy, for example, in the detailed form of a model law on market power or in some other way. Both questions are important enough to deserve mention at the end of the present study.

482. The adequacy of the traditional market power concept to deal effectively with the more modern forms of business power has recently been questioned in an article by the American antitrust economist, Professor Corwin D. Edwards, "The Changing Dimensions of Business Power"[1] which related to the situation in the United States. Edwards maintains that three developments in the modern United States business pattern have made the traditional concept of market power obsolescent. This concept relates to a single powerful firm which (a) controls so much of the supply of a product or service that buyers have no adequate alternatives and (b) is protected, by barriers to market entry, from new suppliers who might substantially impair its control of supply. Edwards states (i) that the typical form of big business is no longer that of a single firm controlling most of a market or industry and encountering as competitors only

---

1. Article appearing in: Das Unternehmen in der Rechtsordnung, Festgabe für Heinrich Kronstein, (The business enterprise and the law: dedicated to Heinrich Kronstein, Karlsruhe (Germany) 1968, pp. 237-260.

firms much smaller than itself, but one in which several big enterprises, more or less comparable in size, occupy most of a field of
activity. In other words, oligopoly ("combinations of bigness and
fewness") not monopoly is the typical modern business structure and
the great diversity of oligopoly patterns makes it much more difficult
than under the traditional monopoly concept to predict and identify
the effects on competition and to develop specific standards which
would allow these effects to be effectively coped with. (*ii*) the traditional concept of sharply defined markets has become largely obso-
lete because of the continuous overlap of buyers and sellers relations,
both as regards the territory ("The interaction of suppliers fills the
sales territory not in well-defined and segregated markets, each like
a fenced field, but in the way a fog fills a landscape – as a continuum of varying density, here thicker, here thinner, without clear
boundaries") and the product, in view of constant technological
development extending the range of substitution. This change has
created the need to give more importance to potential competition,
a factor which, in Edwards' view, "is to strengthen the case for the
view that competitive interaction is a continuum that cannot be ade-
quately conceived within the context of a particular market". (*iii*) the
ever-increasing diversification of many modern enterprises is changing
traditional patterns of business decision and competitive interaction,
especially where large diversified firms with many products compete
with specialized single-product firms. Diversified firms, as Edwards
states, have the ability "to rechannel funds and spread risks, sub-
sidize one activity from the proceeds of another, enjoy the benefits of
joint revenue, spread large lump-sum costs over multiple products,
undertake vertical integration, get bargaining advantages from threats
to do so, and resort to reciprocity". This gives them an advantage
over their specialist competitors, thereby changing the traditional
pattern of competition. Where they compete with similarly diversified
firms, competition with them is likely to move away from price competition to non-price forms (e.g., sales promotion, innovation) due to
availability of large financial funds to retaliate against competitive
price cuts. Size and financial power of firms, factors to which the
traditional concept of market power pays no attention, become thus of
primary significance.

483. Edwards concludes that because of these developments

"the concept of monopoly is inadequate to cover the phenomena
of business power and the concept of oligopoly is inadequate to
replace it. Different kinds of power can be derived from (*a*)
control of a preponderant share of a single segregable market;
(*b*) position as one of a few competing firms; (*c*) possession of
a large aggregate of resources in comparison with one's competitors; and (*d*) diversity of activities across fields of operation.
The first is properly called monopoly (though effects partly due
to the third are sometimes attributed to it). The second is
properly called oligopoly. The third can be called bigness, and
the fourth diversification. Business power structures today contain blends of all of these, and hence are hard to describe,
analyse, or appraise on the basis of a single one of these con-

cepts. Discussion of such power structures gives monopoly an emphasis that it no longer deserves; attributes to oligopoly a significance greater than it probably has; and makes little serious effort to cope with bigness and diversification. Yet these are the forms in which business power is growing most rapidly, is subject to least legal curb, and is hardest to appraise as to the elements of good and bad ".

484. As was said earlier, Edwards' article has dealt with the situation in the United States, but there can be no doubt that the same problem, though perhaps not yet to the same extent, is present in all modern industrialized countries. In his discussion of the oligopoly problem which, as noted in Part II, has not yet been attacked under section 2 of the Sherman Act, Edwards has pointed out that oligopolies are covered by the market power laws of several European countries. The analysis of these laws in the present study has shown that it must be considered as a still open question whether they can effectively cope with oligopoly. The few cases of typical oligopoly situations, which have been tried so far, such as the German Petrol case, do not yet give enough indication that these laws provide the proper remedy.

485. The definition of the market may not be of equal practical importance, because it will often be possible to find a reasonable compromise. But it must be recognized that some degree of over-simplification and formalization and the risk of long litigations over the appropriate market definition will remain.

486. Finally, although no detailed data on business diversification outside the United States are available, it can be observed that the trend to more diversification is universal. If Edwards' analysis of the effects of this trend on competition is right, they will have to be faced in the other industrialized countries as well.

487. It would exceed the scope of a legal study to go further into the problem raised by Professor Edwards' article. For the purposes of the present study it is sufficient to note in conclusion that the basic question whether the present legal concepts of market power are adequate to cover all, especially the modern, forms of business power, is still open and needs further consideration.

488. The second question – how the various approaches to the problem of market power that have been found should be evaluated and what recommendations as to future policy should be made – requires not only a detailed analysis of the reasons why particular legislations have adopted one or the other approach or have not yet dealt with the problem at all, but also a minimum of knowledge of the actual economic results of the application of each approach. The latter, even if there were a generally accepted method to assess the economic effects of restrictive business practices law in general and of market power law in particular, is essentially a matter of economic analysis and would thus have exceeded the scope of a legal study.

489. The precise reasons why a particular country adopts a structural or conduct approach or some combination of both, are in most cases not clearly ascertainable and can only be inferred from the legal

texts. A basically structural approach may reflect the belief that the maintenance of effective competition should be given priority over other economic policy objectives and that this can be done only if market structures encouraging the competitive conduct of firms are preserved or created. The general philosophy underlying a conduct approach is that an interference with structural changes, especially mergers, is unnecessary. It is felt that, on the one hand, adverse effects of market power, if they arise, can be sufficiently corrected by other factors such as conduct control and free market access encouraging potential competition. On the other, structural interference may prevent the achievement of other economic policy objectives to which priority is given, such as the promotion of concentration to accomplish economies of scale and other economic advantages or to strengthen domestic firms in competition with foreign rivals. These basic assumptions of the consequences of market power and the decisions on the priorities to be given to the different economic policy goals have to be seen in the context of the general economic and political environment of each particular country and community and cannot be measures by purely legal standards.

490. Two conclusions *de lege ferenda* seem however possible on the basis of the analysis of existing market power laws:

1. A purely structural approach is not sufficient to cope with all aspects of market power. As has been shown in this study, the laws against mergers and monopolization cannot prevent all forms of market power, especially not market power resulting from normal business growth, and there may be positions of market power, with their origin, in most cases, in a period before mergers were controlled effectively, and where structural measures, such as dissolution or divestiture, are for various reasons not feasible. The main example are oligopolies where, as illustrated by the situation in the United States, it is uncertain whether they are covered by the anti-monopolization laws and whether a further division of the individual oligopolists would change their pattern of business behaviour. It seems therefore that even where there are rigorously enforced provisions against anti-competitive mergers and against monopolization, there is still a case for a system of conduct control along the lines described in this study.

2. On the other hand, a purely conduct approach cannot always be regarded as a sufficient safeguard for the maintenance of effective competition. For, whatever the strength of the factors working against market power, if mergers and monopolization practices lead to monopolistic market conditions, destroying even the minimum amount of effective competition, it seems doubtful in the long run that an abuse control can guarantee the economic benefits expected from competition. It appears therefore that the law should normally provide at least some basis for intervention against extreme changes in market structures, which in the long run seriously endanger the maintenance of minimum competition on important markets.

491. Thus, a combination of elements of structural and conduct control seems generally to be the appropriate solution. But how these elements should be combined, whether more importance should be given to one or the other, is ultimately a policy decision that has to be made in the general context of each particular country and community, taking into account especially such factors as the scope of restrictive business practices law in general,[1] the role of competition in economic policy, the existing structure of business and the priority given to structural changes in the interests of economic rationalization. The present study, by stating the legal background to the problem of market power, may facilitate this difficult decision.

1. As has been noted on several occasions in this study, general restrictive business practice law, e.g., provisions against restrictive agreements or discrimination, may cover particular aspects of market power and thus reduce the need to provide for special relief under market power law.

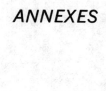

ANNEXES

Annex I

INTERPRETATION OF CERTAIN TECHNICAL TERMS
REFERRED TO IN ARTICLE 15(1)(b) OF THE EFTA CONVENTION

(See paragraph 243)

The second Working Party within the EFTA Organisation on restrictive business practices, which has been working during 1966-1968, had the task, i.a., to agree upon the clarification of certain technical terms referred to in Article 15. As to the provision on enterprises with a dominant position the Working Party agreed on the following interpretations, which thereafter have been endorsed by the EFTA Council:

i) the words of that paragraph «*actions by which* [...] *take unfair advantage*» mean that the dominant position must be abused. The establishment or holding of a dominant position is not in itself contrary to paragraph 1(b) of Article 15;

ii) the words of that paragraph «*one or more enterprises*» mean that the dominant position may be held either by one enterprise (monopoly) or by several enterprises (oligopoly);

iii) the existence of a *dominant position* must be ascertained in the light of the relevant market including the relevant area, the range of goods involved and possibly of the period of time in that particular case;

iv) as to the *relevant area*, paragraph 1(b) of Article 15 specifies that there must be a dominant position «*within the Area of the Association or a substantial part of it.*» Whether the territory of a single Member State can be considered to constitute a substantial part of the Area of the Association will depend on whether the firm or firms holding the dominant position will be able to exert a dominant influence on the flow of intra-EFTA trade at issue in the particular case;

v) the range of goods involved must be determined in each particular case. Account should be taken of the possibility of substituting one product for another.

Annex II

CASES AND REPORTS CITED

(The numbers refer to paragraphs in the present publication)

GERMANY

Sporting Goods Fair, 74, 96, 113, 235-6, 291, 363-4
Automobile Industry, 42-4
Melitta, 300
Meto, 73-4, 96, 113, 116, 233-4, 238, 293, 304, 362, 478
Petrol Price, 97-101, 110, 113-4, 116, 227, 237, 296, 363
ZementKontor Unterelbe, 231-2, 235, 296, 304, 362

CANADA

Food Distribution, 171
Eddy Match Co. Ltd. *et al.* v. Regina, 66, 219-222, 338
Electric Signs, 170
Regina v. British Columbia Sugar Refining Co. Ltd., 41, 168-9, 324
Regina v. Canadian Breweries Ltd., 41, 167, 169, 324
Rex v. Canadian Import Co., 324
Regina v. Union Carbide Canada Ltd., 441
Rex v. Staples, 324
Report on the Manufacture, Distribution and Sales of Matches in Canada, 219
Report concerning the Manufacture, Distribution and Sale of Ammunition in Canada, 419
Report on the Monopoly in the Distribution of Propane in British Columbia, 67

ECSC

August-Thyssen Hütte AG and Phœnix-Rheinrohr AG, 192-3, 202, 204
German Steel Syndicates, 195-8, 204
Hoesch-Dortmund-Hörder and Hütten Union Hoogovens, 194, 204
Rheinische Braunkohlenbrikett-Verkaufs GmbH, 103, 113, 367
Sacillor, 51
Sidmar, 50
Oberrheinische Kohlenunion AG, 288, 291, 367

EEC

Grundig and Consten, 72, 448
Parke, Davis and Co., 242, 440
Socemas, 427

DENMARK

Radio and T.V. Sets, 283-4
Gas and Electric Kitchen Ranges, 282, 291
Electrical Household Equipment, 104, 113, 117
Omega and Tissot Watches, 70, 117

SPAIN

Carbonell y Cia S.A., 105, 240, 348
La Seda and Perlofil S.A., 53

UNITED STATES

American Tobacco Co. v. United States, 212, 216
Crown Zellerbach Corp. v. Federal Trade Commission, 37
Erie Sand and Gravel Co. v. Federal Trade Commission, 25, 37
United States v. Aluminium Co. of America (Alcoa), 32-3, 115, 134, 212-3, 228, 335
United States v. Aluminium Co. of America and Cupples Products Corp., 31
United States v. Anheuser-Busch Inc., 315
United States v. American Cyanamid Co., 336, 442
United States v. American Smelting and Refining Co., 315
United States v. Bethlehem Steel Co., 25, 37
United States v. Brown Shoe Co., 2, 24-30, 34, 56, 127-30, 132, 145-6, 202, 203
United States v. Columbia Pictures Corp., 25
United States v. Continental Can Co., 34, 39, 134
United States v. E.I. Du Pont de Nemours and Co., 24, 25, 56-9, 64, 72, 122 144, 212, 330, 467
United States v. El Paso Natural Gas Co., 121
United States v. Ford Motor Co., 147
United States v. General Electric Co., 442
United States v. General Motors Corp., 442
United States v. General Shoe Corp., 315
United States v. Gillette Co., 203, 208, 465
United States v. Grinnell Corp., 55, 60-64, 211, 212, 213, 215, 335, 467
United States v. Jos. Schlitz Brewing Co., 38, 86, 208
United States v. Kennecott Copper Corp., 31
United States v. Kimberly-Clark Corp., 315
United States v. Lever Bros., 31
United States v. Maryland and Virginia Milk Producers Assn., 25
United States v. Mobay Chemical Co., 160, 208
United States v. National Steel Corp., 31
United States v. Pabst Brewing Co., 39, 134, 136-7, 203
United States v. Paramount Pictures, 216
United States v. Penn-Olin Chemical Co., 159-60
United States v. Philadelphia National Bank, 36, 37, 40, 62, 64, 127, 131-3, 135, 138, 460

OECD SALES AGENTS
DÉPOSITAIRES DES PUBLICATIONS DE L'OCDE

ARGENTINE - ARGENTINE
Editorial Sudamericana S.A.,
Humberto 1º 545, BUENOS AIRES.

AUSTRALIA - AUSTRALIE
B.C.N. Agencies Pty, Ltd.,
178 Collins Street, MELBOURNE, 3000.

AUSTRIA - AUTRICHE
Gerold & Co., Graben 31, WIEN 1.
Sub-Agent : GRAZ : Buchhandlung Jos. A. Kien-
reich, Sackstrasse 6.

BELGIUM - BELGIQUE
Librairie des Sciences
76-78, Coudenberg, BRUXELLES 1.
Standaard Wetenschappelijke Uitgeverij
Belgiëlei 147, ANVERS.

CANADA
Queen's Printer - L'Imprimeur de la Reine.
OTTAWA.

DENMARK - DANEMARK
Munksgaard Boghandel, Ltd., Nörregade 6
KOBENHAVN K.

FINLAND - FINLANDE
Akateeminen Kirjakauppa, Keskuskatu 2,
HELSINKI.

FORMOSA - FORMOSE
Books and Scientific Supplies Services, Ltd.
P.O.B. 83, TAIPEI,
TAIWAN.

FRANCE
Bureau des Publications de l'OCDE
2 rue André-Pascal, 75 PARIS 16e
Principaux sous-dépositaires :
PARIS : Presses Universitaires de France,
49 bd Saint-Michel, 5e
Sciences Politiques (Lib.). 30 rue Saint-Guillaume, 7e
13 AIX-EN-PROVENCE : Librairie de l'Université.
38 GRENOBLE : Arthaud
67 STRASBOURG : Berger-Levrault.

GERMANY - ALLEMAGNE
Deutscher Bundes-Verlag G.m.b.H.
Postfach 9380, 53 BONN.
Sub-Agents : BERLIN 62 : Elwert & Meurer.
HAMBURG : Reuter-Klöckner : und in den
massgebenden Buchhandlungen Deutschlands.

GREECE - GRECE
Librairie Kauffmann, 28, rue du Stade,
ATHÈNES-132.
Librairie Internationale Jean Mihalopoulos
33, rue Sainte-Sophie, THESSALONIKI.

ICELAND - ISLANDE
Snæbjörn Jónsson & Co., h.f., Hafnarstræti 9,
P.O. Box 1131, REYKJAVIK.

INDIA - INDE
Oxford Book and Stationery Co. :
NEW DELHI, Scindia House.
CALCUTTA, 17 Park Street.

IRELAND - IRLANDE
Eason & Son, 40-41 Lower O'Connell Street,
P.O.B. 42 DUBLIN 1.

ISRAEL
Emanuel Brown,
35 Allenby Road, and 48 Nahlath Benjamin St.,
TEL-AVIV.

ITALY - ITALIE
Libreria Commissionaria Sansoni
Via Lamarmora 45, 50 121 FIRENZE.
Via P. Mercuri 19/B, 00 193 ROMA.
Sous-dépositaires :
Libreria Hoepli, Via Hoepli 5, 20 121 MILANO.
Libreria Lattes, Via Garibaldi 3, 10 122 TORINO.
*La diffusione delle edizioni OCDE è inoltre assicu-
rata dalle migliori librerie nelle città più importanti.*

JAPAN - JAPON
Maruzen Company Ltd.,
6 Tori-Nichome Nihonbashi, TOKYO 103.
P.O.B. 5050, Tokyo International 100-31.

LEBANON - LIBAN
Redico
Immeuble Edison, Rue Bliss, B.P. 5641
BEYROUTH.

LUXEMBOURG
Librairie Paul Bruck, 22, Grand'Rue,
LUXEMBOURG.

MALTA - MALTE
Labour Book Shop, Workers' Memorial Building,
Old Bakery Street, VALLETTA.

THE NETHERLANDS - PAYS-BAS
W.P. Van Stockum
Buitenhof 36, DEN HAAG.
Sub-Agents : AMSTERDAM C : Scheltema &
Holkema, N.V., Rokin 74-76. ROTTERDAM :
De Wester Boekhandel, Nieuwe Binnenweg 331.

NEW ZEALAND - NOUVELLE-ZELANDE
Government Printing Office,
Mulgrave Street (Private Bag), WELLINGTON
and Government Bookshops at
AUCKLAND (P.O.B. 5344)
CHRISTCHURCH (P.O.B. 1721)
HAMILTON (P.O.B. 857)
DUNEDIN (P.O.B. 1104).

NORWAY - NORVEGE
A/S Bokhjörnet, Akersgt. 41, OSLO 1.

PAKISTAN
Mirza Book Agency, 65, Shahrah Quaid-E-Azam,
LAHORE 3.

PORTUGAL
Livraria Portugal, Rua do Carmo 70, LISBOA.

SPAIN - ESPAGNE
Mundi Prensa, Castelló 37, MADRID 1.
Libreria Bastinos de José Bosch, Pelayo 52,
BARCELONA 1.

SWEDEN - SUEDE
Fritzes, Kungl. Hovbokhandel,
Fredsgatan 2, STOCKHOLM 16.

SWITZERLAND - SUISSE
Librairie Payot, 6, rue Grenus, 1211 GENÈVE, 11
et à LAUSANNE, NEUCHATEL, VEVEY,
MONTREUX, BERNE, BALE, ZURICH.

TURKEY - TURQUIE
Librairie Hachette, 469 Istiklal Caddesi, Beyoglu,
ISTANBUL et 12 Ziya Gökalp Caddesi, ANKARA.

UNITED KINGDOM - ROYAUME-UNI
H.M. Stationery Office, P.O. Box 569, LONDON
S.E.1.
Branches at : EDINBURGH, BIRMINGHAM,
BRISTOL, MANCHESTER, CARDIFF,
BELFAST.

UNITED STATES OF AMERICA
OECD Publications Center, Suite 1305,
1750 Pennsylvania Ave, N. W.
WASHINGTON, D.C. 20006. Tel : (202) 298-8755.

VENEZUELA
Libreria del Este, Avda. F. Miranda, 52,
Edificio Galipan, CARACAS. '

YUGOSLAVIA - YOUGOSLAVIE
Jugoslovenska Knjiga, Terazije 27, P.O.B. 36,
BEOGRAD.

Les commandes provenant de pays où l'OCDE n'a pas encore désigné de dépositaire
peuvent être adressées à :
OCDE, Bureau des Publications, 2 rue André-Pascal, 75 Paris 16e.
Orders and inquiries from countries where sales agents have not yet been appointed may be sent to
OECD, Publications Office, 2 rue André-Pascal, 75 Paris 16e

O.E.C.D. PUBLICATIONS, 2, rue André-Pascal, Paris-16e - No. 26.025-1970
PRINTED IN FRANCE